BALANCE OF NATURE

Book 3 of the *Savage Land* Trilogy

By Jacqui Murray

From the *Man vs. Nature* Series

978-1-942101-68-0 (print)
978-1-942101-69-7 (digital)

Other Books by Jacqui Murray

Dawn of Humanity Trilogy

Born in a Treacherous Time (Book 1)
Laws of Nature (Book 2)
Natural Selection (Book 3)

Crossroads Trilogy

Survival of the Fittest (Book 1)
The Quest for Home (Book 2)
Against All Odds (Book 3)

Savage Land Trilogy

Endangered Species (Book 1)
Badlands (Book 2)
Balance of Nature (This book)

Savage Land sequel

Planned

Rowe-Delamagente Series

To Hunt a Sub
Twenty-four Days

Nonfiction

Building a Midshipman: How to Crack the USNA Application

Praise for *Man vs. Nature*

The stakes are high, danger is ever present and struggle for survival is real. Yu'ung is a character that is easy to love. Her intentions and desires are honorable with the safety of her tribe first and foremost in her thoughts. She's strong and capable. But most of all, the powerful, compelling story itself drew me in and didn't let go. If you are up for an adventure that will have you holding your breath at times, this book is for you! –Amazon Reader

Once again, author and master of prehistoric fiction Jacqui Murray took me on a thrilling journey back in time with her recent book, Endangered Species. Murray transports readers to 75,000 years ago, where Neanderthals (the People) and Homo Sapiens (the Tall Ones) face constant threats and survival challenges. –Amazon Reader

Move over Jean Auel (author of Clan of the Cave Bear*) for Jacqui Murray. I went to bed right after dinner last night because I had to finish this book and would have stayed up all night to do it. What a fabulous read. –Amazon* Reader

I've traveled back through time with Murray's prehistoric fiction, starting 1.8 million years ago with her Dawn of Humanity trilogy, and then advancing to 850,000 years ago with her Crossroads trilogy. This book is the first in The Savage Land trilogy, bumping readers up to modern times, well almost modern—75,000 years ago! Murray's extensive research into the lives of the Neanderthals is evident in this book, which lays the groundwork for the rest of the trilogy. The research is fascinating, and something that I highly appreciate. The attention given to the daily lives of the People, including their challenges and ever-present dangers, does make this story a slow burn until near the end when the main plot literally "explodes" in the form of a volcano, forcing the People and Tall Ones to begin a perilous migration that, I expect, is the focus of the next two books. –Amazon Reader

What a treat to read a fiction work that goes so far back into prehistory. I enjoy reading prehistoric fiction in general, but this is a rare gem. The author successfully combines facts with imagination to create a believable story about our ancient ancestors. We peek into a distant mirror at a people who reflect our own hopes, emotions, and fears. –Amazon Reader

Born in a Treacherous Time *is a brilliantly researched book with an interesting and realistic story-line. I have read all Jean Auel's books and enjoyed them but I found the first book,* Clan of the Cave Bear, *to be the best by far. Why you ask? Because it was realistic. I appreciate that in a historical book of this nature. I loved this about* Born in a Treacherous Time. *The story and interaction between the various group members rang true to me. –Amazon* Reader

Thanks to Murray's book Born in a Treacherous Time, *I view the world and the creatures within it (including humans) with new eyes. –Amazon* Reader

I loved this book even more than the first in Jacqui Murray's Dawn of Humanity *trilogy. This new chapter in the story of Lucy and her eclectic little tribe picks up straight after the first left off and the reader is swept back to the prehistoric past where life is an ongoing set of challenges to be faced in the search for food and water, shelter, and safety. –Amazon* Reader

I have always been fascinated by what it was like to live in bygone eras. This book so satisfies this, as well as telling a good story. –Amazon Reader

I've waited I think a year for this book! I loved it so much and look forward to more of Lucy's adventures. –Amazon Reader

I'm always looking for books about primitive man. Loved the way she had the different species living together and interacting And of course, I fell in love with most of the characters. She writes very descriptively but has done her research. If you are interested in early man, this book is for you. Can't wait for book 3 ——Amazon Reader

Murray's novels are always filled with a plethora of facts about prehistoric man. What they ate. How they hunted, communicated, and survived. I can't begin to fathom the amount of time that goes into researching the worlds she creates. What strikes me the most about her stories is how people—and animals —from different cultures learn to live together. Come together. And form a pack. It's a wonderful lesson in today's tempestuous times. –Amazon Reader

Table of Contents

Characters

The People—Neanderthals

Aynoh—Yu'ung's mother
B'o—Yu'ung's hunt partner
Ese—B'o's pairmate
Jhat—female tribe member
Jvelk—mixed Tall One and People
Laak
Ruk—Jhat's child
Shanadar—proto-Shaman
Wik
Xad
Yu'ung—the People's Alpha

The Clan—Neanderthals

Ant
Krekk and Jad—Ant's parents
Flint
Kazeb; aka Liis—co-Alpha with his brother Turk
Turk—co-Alpha with his brother Kazeb

The Tall Ones (Chosen)—*Homo sapiens*

Bhidid
Braanroorv
Eknilk
Fierce—Leader
Grub
Seer—a spiritual guide for the Chosen, a proto-shaman

The Ones—Mix of *Homo sapiens* and Neanderthals

Asvulk—Kruutud's pairmate; Neanderthal
Gevol, a Tall One
Kruutud—Leader, a Tall One

The Canis Pack

Blaze
Ocha
Ragged Ear
Spirit
Ump
White Streak

Glossary of Terms

Alpha	*Leader of the Neanderthal tribe*
Angry Mountain	*any volcanic eruption; in this case, Mt. Toba*
Backtrail	*path traveled to return to wherever the tribe or member started*
Big Rock	*what we call the Rock of Gibraltar*
Cudgel	*a short, heavy stick; what the Tall Ones call a club*
Dominant side	*the right side; since many were right-handed, this was the strong side*
Endless Sea	*what we call the Atlantic Ocean*
Extreme sight	*when images and landmarks that are blurred to others appear clear to some*
Haft	*glue a stone tip to a shaft to create a spear*
Homebase	*main Upright camp where they sleep and eat*
Kith	*what Primitives call their tribes*
Kin	*what Primitives call their tribe members*
Lead Warrior	*a Tall One term for primary male skilled to defend the tribe*
Leader	*Alpha of a Tall One band*
Mate	*coupling; a casual activity, not a permanent relationship*
Nest	*where they sleep at night*
Pack	*the Canis*
Pairmate	*lifelong partner*
Predult	*younger than a subadult*
Primitive	*physiologically inferior to other Upright species; often refers to* Homo erectus *in this trilogy*
Sky fire	*lightning*
Shoreless sea	*the Mediterranean*
Spirits	*precursor to gods, God; supernatural entities*
Strong side	*the right side; since many were right-handed, this was the dominant side*

Tall Ones	Homo sapiens; *Fierce's band called themselves the Chosen*
Upright	*any animal who walks on two legs. This included Primitives (*Homo erectus*), Neanderthals, Chosen (*Homo sapiens*).*
Weak side	*not the dominant side (they had no terms for "right" or "left")*

Author's Nonfiction Introduction

Savage Land delves into a time when man approached extinction as a species. Scientists disagree why, but DNA confirms if not for equal measures of luck and inexplicable circumstances, Nature would have beaten us. Drama, intrigue, mystery, heroes, and in no small measure, miracles saved us. We conquered fire, sewed clothes, applied chemistry to create glue and preserve food, and invented advanced weaponry. Evidence exists of our ancestors' reverence for the dead, belief in superior beings, appreciation for art, music, and self-adornment.

Savage Land details how Neanderthals endured the world's physical challenges. It is as exciting as the most riveting thrillers, as informative as biographies, and fact-filled in the way of the best creative nonfiction. The three books in the trilogy provide limitless teachable moments similar to those in popular survival stories. Our forebears' brilliance lives on in our genes where thirty percent of the Neanderthal genome continues, proof that they could do anything they set their minds to, the ancient traits suitable to Nature's primary imperative—survival—even today. They reigned as the planet's apex predators until the era of *Homo sapiens.*

Enjoy this fictionalized account of your ancestors' existence. The characters are built from Neanderthal relics and artifacts unearthed from many of their habitats that have helped researchers extrapolate what their lives were like. The proto-wolves Ump, White Streak, Ocha, and Ragged Ear are indeed spirits meant to introduce the seeds of spirituality. Such details are not preserved, but speculation abounds regarding when man began our relationship with supernatural beings. If interested, the Canis' stories are revealed in earlier trilogies.

The *Savage Land* trilogy is based on facts. In the absence of pure evidence, conclusions are deduced from accepted scientific opinions from those who studied Neanderthals. Check the *Bibliography* for names.

Each book can be a stand-alone though they build on prior events.

- *Endangered Species (Book 1)*—the worst volcanic eruption man ever lived through forced the People to abandon their homes.
- *Badlands (Book 2)*—the People and the Chosen leave the Altai Mountains to migrate beyond what we call the Mediterranean Sea.
- *Balance of Nature (Book 3)*—a tribe haunted by the past. Lies that threaten a new beginning. A reason to find the truth.

Introduction

They tore deep into Nature's flesh with their digging sticks. In the past, Nature released devastating floods, explosive volcanic eruptions, and deadly droughts to control the bad behavior of the life forms that claimed her surface as home. She destroyed those who paid no attention, threatened those who demanded respect without giving it, and forced all who didn't bend to her will to suffer the consequences. Nature felt no pity. Unforgettable lessons worked.

But not with these creatures. They obeyed intuition over instinct. They eschewed knowledge that roots, stems, bark, rocks, animals, insects, all life—the air they breathed—belonged to a collective whole, not Nature itself. Little mattered to those who walked upright except for their desires. The more who survived, the more toxic they became to everything she valued. By the time Nature realized the depth of their travesties, she was no longer sure she could stop them.

They must own the consequences.

Part 1

The Tall Ones Meet the Clan

Chapter 1

75,000 years ago
The area we now call Gibraltar

Shouts woke the brothers from their sleep.

"A boat—on the Endless Sea! Headed toward us!"

At night? How is that possible? But Kazeb didn't ask because it didn't matter. What mattered was that it was there.

He and Turk had waited long for this news, Kazeb with excitement, Turk with dread. Without discussion, they raced across the grassland, leapt over crevices, the width familiar even in the dark, and then scrambled up Big Rock's knobby flank, grabbing tiny ledges with their fingers and toes with a speed mountain goats would envy. The behemoth's height dwarfed all hills on the peninsula save the distant, towering range that separated it from others.

The brothers summited the crest and crouched behind a thick patch of scrub at the cliff's edge. The brisk breeze atop the promontory whipped Kazeb's hair around. He clenched his fists, gritted his teeth so tightly he should have broken a tooth, and waited for the vague elongated shadow on the water's inky surface to reveal its intentions.

Is it them? He glanced at his brother's square face. *Turk thinks it is.*

Sun's steady arrival slowly erased the dark, made the sea shimmer in shades of blue as waves crashed against the coastline. Just below the surface, under the foam, were sharp shoals. Any boat must tediously avoid these, better yet, continue down the shore where there was no risk, unless they knew of the sole safe mooring used by natives and those they shared the location with, like they did with the Tall Ones from long ago.

Turk hissed, "It's them, Liis."

The Clan called him Liis, but he preferred "Kazeb," the name awarded him when he agreed to guide the Tall One Fierce to the sea's end. That was far beyond anywhere he had ever traveled, but Fierce claimed Kazeb's knowledge of the area was invaluable.

"We can't tell who is onboard, Turk," he said, though who else knew of the hidden cove?

Kazeb rose and scanned a full circle, hoping whoever came on that craft wasn't looking up here.

"What are you doing, Liis?"

"I need to see if they're alone, or do more come from other directions."

Flat grassland bordered one flank of the promontory, water the rest. Sun's earliest rays colored the sky in pinks and blues. Birds plummeted into the crystalline water. Fish with no desire to be food dove. Farther away, pigs rooted through the stubble and a herd of deer feasted on ever-abundant fresh young shoots, protected by the range of mountains from unexpected predators.

When we finish, that's where we will go.

He turned back to the shoreless sea. Visible on clear days, a faint brown outline shadowed the horizon, what the Tall One Fierce had called home.

Turk said, "They knew enough to stay in the calm waters when darkness arrived, to avoid the underwater shoals."

Sun broke above the horizon, telling the boat it was safe to continue. The craft nimbly skirted the shoals, aiming for the spot a similar vessel had beached long ago. Kazeb gripped his spear tighter. Fierce had promised to return once his exploration was completed. Kazeb trusted his word, but the more time passed, the more he wondered if he had been lied to.

"Liis!" Turk interrupted his reverie. "There is another boat, behind the first!"

Now Kazeb saw it. Both prows plowed through the water, their shapes clear in the sunlight. Shivers ran through Kazeb.

These aren't like Fierce's craft … but we have seen no one from that direction either by sea or foot.

Kazeb studied the gaggle of Uprights, their bold stripes, the confident stance of the slender male in the bow of the front boat. All fit his recollections of the Tall One band. His gaze drifted to the back boat, a shorter stockier figure at the prow.

Is he Fierce's guide? My replacement? But why would he be behind Fierce?

Legs wide for balance, sunlight glinting off flame-red hair, the sturdy figure scanned the Big Rock. To Kazeb's surprise, his gaze paused at the clump of brush where the brothers hid. He couldn't see them, of course. Both had mudded their skin and squinted to keep Sun's glare off their eyes. Still, the figure shouted to One-who-might-be-Fierce and pointed.

Turk gurgled, "Are they looking for us? But why come back here, considering what they did?"

"We don't know for sure—"

"Who else would it be?" Turk's voice a strangled yelp.

They argued this question often. The Clan Healer originally thought the deadly illness had been caused by insects or a toxin in the air, but before he died, he admitted an individual could have poisoned the members' food and water. Who could say?

Kazeb didn't bother to reply, busy admiring the vessel's sleek profile, so unlike the Clan's flatter, smaller ones. The sailors effortlessly beached it at the base of the monstrous rock where the brothers hid.

Voice fiery, Turk hissed, "Our destiny has arrived, why we survive and the rest died."

Chapter 2

2 years earlier

Liis and Turk represented the most talented among the Clan. Besides broad muscular shoulders, brawny limbs, and beefy chests, their quick minds connected events in ways others couldn't. The brothers had already led in emergencies, made decisions all wholeheartedly agreed with, so when relentless cold and starvation forced the tribe to abandon their ancestral home, Liis and Turk were unanimously selected as co-Alphas.

While prevailing opinion suggested they migrate away from the mountains, along a path used by other tribes, intuition drove the brothers the opposite way, through the untamed, uninhabited wildness of the range's soaring heights on hazardous trails everyone declared impossible. Stories abounded of those who climbed the treacherous flanks and were never seen again. No one judged it a serious option which was why the brothers picked it.

"What lies beyond must be virgin territory rich with herds and plant food and few competitors, but we won't climb *up* the mountains. We will go *around* them," and they set out.

The route was a narrow corridor few even knew existed, edged on one side by the shoreless sea, the other by boulders, rock walls, and soaring foothills. There was limited food and less water, the shoreless sea undrinkable, poisoned by salt. The brothers hoped if they traveled far enough down the shore, the water would purify. It didn't, so instead, they survived on morning dew, water vines, and the blood of animals they could catch. Birds, ground fowl, and rabbits were easily taken with throwing stones, not in great quantities, but sufficient that no one starved.

"Challenging, but doable" became their motto, often chanted with a sneer, rarely without some doubt, but it always energized the group.

When they finally circumnavigated the sprawling foothills and arrived at the range's opposite side, lavish fields greeted them as well as fruit trees, bushes stuffed with plump berries, and a sprinkling of woods, but no herds.

"With all this grassland, they must be somewhere," Liis reminded everyone and marched onward.

Since the sea's water even here remained toxic, the Clan headed away from it, across the rolling hills in search of prints or trace to guide them to the local waterholes. By day's end, a smattering of ponds and lakes had been located, but still no herds. They did see nominal amounts of pigs, boars, squirrels, goats, bears, and rabbits, enough the Clan wouldn't starve, but neither would it thrive.

One night, around a meager meal of toads, lizards, and a snake, augmented with roots and stems, the Clan Elders shared stories of what they had done in the starving times of their youth.

"We, too, were adjacent to the largest body of water any of us had ever seen, and like the shoreless sea, it was poisonous. Though we couldn't drink its liquid, we ate the animals that lived in it."

"How did you catch them?"

The Elders shrugged as one. "We were too young to be involved, not even predults. The meat showed up at the hearth fires. We ate it."

Liis turned to Turk. "Surely the shoreless sea also includes edible fish. We just need to figure out how to catch them."

Hunting from rafts proved tricky. Many hunters lost their balance, couldn't hold onto the slippery fish, or those they caught slid off the rocking platform. But the receding tide left shallow pools ashore and in them, a plethora of stranded fish. Some could be eaten raw. Others—experimentation devised satisfactory cooking methods for them. The Clan, with the encouragement of the Elders, adjusted to the changed diet.

By the time Moon came and went, they had established reliable sources of food and water. That left only one task.

In the past, the Clan migrated when they exhausted local resources, which made temporary camps sufficient. Here, on this peninsula, abundance made migration unnecessary. The question became whether to live in enclosed spaces as in the past or open-air homebases, favored if caves couldn't be found. The brothers argued.

Liis: "The thick walls protect us against enemies and predators…."

Turk: "We have few of either here."

Liis: "An inside hearth warms us better."

Turk: "Days and nights are comfortable enough without a fire—"

Liis: "When daylight fades, fires allow us to continue our work."

Turk: "That is true outside, also, and hearths vent better in open air."

Liis: "Even if what you say is true, we have no hides for the enclosure."

In open-air sites, animal pelts were strung between tree trunks pounded into the ground to block the cold, wind, and unwanted predators.

Liis: "We have seen mammoth and bison skeletons. A cave could provide protection until we track down the herds."

Turk: "Or we live in the open, among trees, while we locate them."

Liis gave in. He was tired of arguing and didn't think it mattered anyway.

"Then we station sentries on the Big Rock to alert us of intruders."

Turk guffawed. "There aren't any! They won't come from the mountains. Our former Clan must think us dead—proof of the naysayers' wisdom—and who can build rafts sturdy enough to cross the vast swath of sea? No, we are safe here, brother—"

"But we are foolish not to keep watch."

Turk bobbed his head. "Agreed."

Overwatch scouts, often with the brothers, studied the bodies of water that surrounded most sides of Big Rock.

"Strangers won't come down the middle of the shoreless sea. They'll follow the coast, end up on the route we took, and reveal themselves in plenty of time for us to prepare. No, intruders that should concern us would come from that brown mirage across the sea."

"Scouts have studied the strait off the tip of Big Rock, the shortest route between that land and us. It is unpredictable, calm one breath, churning into perilous waves the next. The rafts we use on lakes and rivers wouldn't survive. Crossing requires a kind of water craft that probably doesn't exist."

Nevertheless, the brothers talked often about how to prepare for what they didn't know.

Moon came and went, over and over. No one emerged from the water or the foothills, so the Clan settled into a predictable lifestyle. With the means of surviving and continuing their lifestyle in place, the time had come to return decision-making to the tribe.

That's when a Clan subadult raced in with news. "A boat approaches!"

Liis and Turk sprinted up Big Rock's craggy slopes with nary a misstep. They did this often, even at night without Moon's light. Once they crested the peak, they concealed themselves in the copious brush and scanned the dark sea. If not for the moonlight sparkling off the ripples, they would have missed it, shaped like a hollow trunk rather than tied-together logs.

Dawn finally lightened the sky enough for Liis to pick out the Uprights aboard. They were taller, skulls larger, foreheads higher, visages flatter than the Clan, without the brow ridges that kept rain and sun from Liis' eyes. Colors striped their dark skin like those on

Badger or a young Boar. One male stood spread-legged in the front, unaffected by the swaying deck, hands on his hips, eyes on Big Rock.

Our rafts go where the surf takes us. Why doesn't this log-boat?

Turk gulped. "The boat flies."

Big Rock's sheer face appeared unscalable. If Liis and Turk emerged in front of it on the shore, it would be as though from the air itself.

Liis mouthed, "You and I confront them. The scouts hide until a time of our choosing. The intruders won't know how large our group is."

Turk nodded and they started downhill, crouching low enough to be hidden by the scraggly grass and scrub. This side of Big Rock was steeper and slicker than the back side, so by the time Liis reached the bottom, his calves burned and his knees pulsed. The fight for balance and to move as gracefully as possible sent spasms through his back. While he squatted, breathed the pain out of his body, the scouts arrived, lances and cudgels low to the ground. By pre-arranged plan, they hid among the boulders that dotted Big Rock's shore.

By the time the brothers and scouts were in place, the boat had moored and the Uprights disembarked. Liis had no doubt the Clan members had arrived unseen, the strangers' attention on finding the safest place to land, but to be sure, the brothers diverted any attention to themselves, strode upright with no effort to conceal their presence. They were spotted immediately, studied briefly, and then the intruders searched behind and around for more tribe members. As expected, they missed those hiding. The brothers said nothing, unmoving, eyes hooded, waiting. A mosquito whined by Liis' ear, but he ignored it.

They are taller and slimmer than they appeared at first and walk awkwardly, as though they've been on the water for a long time.

Turk murmured, lips barely moving, head forward, "They are suspicious we aren't alone, but can't find the others. Most importantly, they don't know if we are friend or foe."

Liis possessed enormous physical strength from thrusting heavy wood pikes into the skin of herd animals and his muscular body showed it. He wondered how these scraggly outsiders with their fragile lances hunted, though they seemed well fed. Did the colored stripes help?

With such slight bodies and scraggly spears, they wouldn't be difficult to defeat.

Turk whispered over his shoulder to the scouts, "When you reveal yourselves, intimidate without threat, lances in hand though these strangers may not be hostile."

Liis, the friendlier brother, said, "I will talk to Tall-One-who-must-be-Alpha," and stepped toward the male who had stood in the boat's bow.

Turk did the same, but frowned. "Tall One?"

"Well, they are. What would you call them?"

Turk blinked. His eyes flickered, and he rubbed his neck. "Tall One fits."

Tall-One-who-must-be-Alpha strode toward them, followed by the rest of his entourage. He gargled incomprehensibly, but his hand actions and pleasant smile promised no harm—if they were to be believed.

Liis motioned toward the craft. "What is that?"

Tall-One-Alpha jabbered rapidly with a strange, low cadence unlike anything Liis had ever heard. At first, the utterances tumbled over each other, as though desperate to leave the Tall One's mouth. The sounds lurched, some drawn out or emphasized for unknown reasons.

I think they're discussing what to do now that we've appeared.

All the Tall Ones kept their weapons at their sides, but their eyes remained a predator's, prepared for trouble. To lower the tension, and knowing his scouts had spears cocked, Liis stowed his lance in his shoulder sack and slapped his trunk.

"I am Liis. This is Turk," his said while his hand movements conveying the message to these strangers who babbled so bizarrely. "We are Alphas."

He was about to rephrase, but Tall-One-Alpha touched his torso. "Fierce. Leader for my band."

At least, that's what Liis thought he prattled.

Turk must have agreed because he mumbled, "Is Leader like Alpha?" But didn't expect a response. How would Liis know?

Sun was still low in the sky, barely over the promontory's crest, but already blazing. A sheen of perspiration coated Liis' forehead and sweat trickled down his back.

They are not even sweating. Where do they live that Sun's heat doesn't cause sweat?

Without a word, Turk turned and took off at a trot for Big Rock, motioning to the scouts. The Tall Ones showed no reaction at the appearance of the scouts. Did they know they were there?

With a flourish, Liis said, "Turk invites you to our camp," hoping his grin and Turk's movements made the meaning clear.

Fierce craned his neck up to Big Rock's precipice. He gibbered to a stocky beast as towering and thick as a boulder and then motioned to Liis, "Grub thinks you want us to climb this rock face."

Liis grinned and tramped after Turk. The crunch behind him through the brittle scree announced their decision to follow. Silent walking, critical for Clan members, didn't seem important with these outsiders. Did their home terrain have no risks? Even large herds would have plenty of time to flee.

Liis heard the sound of sliding. He turned, saw a Tall One flailing, but he regained his balance.

They are agile.

Liis turned back, wrinkled his nose, and hoped whoever carried the rotting carcass would dispose of it before reaching the Clan's camp.

He began to create a series of questions he must ask the strangers, starting with how they picked the one section of beach where their craft could safely moor. Had they seen the shoals, been experienced enough they didn't present a problem? And why not avoid the risk, sail farther down the coast where they could see fields and woods rather than a soaring rock bluff?

Scrabbling sounded behind him and a bevy of rats almost knocked him over.

He steadied himself and called back, "They want the spoiled meat you carry," and made no effort to obscure his disdain.

Fierce scrunched his brow. Relying on a combination of words and motions, he said, "Our mistake. Our homebase is far away. This is our first visit here. The sea islands had no meat so we couldn't replenish our stores and settled on the rats. They seem … abundant. If you are short on meat, we are happy to share."

"Your rat companions may eat your leftovers. We have as much food as we need."

A line cut Fierce's brow as he jabbered to his tribe. They smiled, clearly eager to abandon the fetid meat.

"Be careful here, Fierce."

They'd arrived at a cutoff that would shorten the trip over Big Rock, but test the Tall One's mountaineering abilities.

Liis stopped at the entrance to a passage, removed his foot covers to provide him better grip, and said, "Water collects in a hollow, but it is pebbled which helps prevent some of the slippage. The farther in you progress, the drier."

He wasn't sure how much Alpha-Leader Fierce understood, so motioned he follow, then strode forward, pointing and nodding as he picked his steps cautiously in places he knew to be safe.

The slope steepened with several mulch-laden sections that often collapsed from excessive weight. He turned to warn Fierce just as the hillside gave way. Fierce's feet slid out from beneath him. The colossus named Grub snatched for his Leader's windmilling arms which caused him to also plunge downhill. Liis flung himself after them, slid on the scree, and bounced on a moss-covered rock. He lunged for a bush that had held his weight in the past, but catapulted past. At the last moment, a hand snatched his wrap and pitched him into a patch of coarse underbrush.

To his surprise, Fierce and One-called-Grub stood close by, barely breathing hard, eyes fixed on him.

"You injured? Did Grub toss you too roughly?" Fierce rubbed his hands over his torso, neck, and head while scrunching his face. Liis couldn't miss his concern despite the garbled words.

Liis scrambled to his feet and gaped at the male mountain. "He snared me while I flew by as though I were a piece of straw."

Fierce chortled. "I've seen him lift an entire mammoth calf alone. If you are his friend and in trouble, a stampeding herd couldn't stop him from coming to your aid. That's why he's our Lead Warrior."

Warrior?

Liis grunted his appreciation and felt a tingle of respect. Fierce paid no attention to the battering he'd received, as though these were usual occurrences.

They are sturdier than I judged.

Liis wobbled, and Fierce said, "This is the path to your camp?" and strode into the lead, his confidence surprising Liis.

Has he been here prior to us? If so, why return?

Liis called, "There is one more tricky passage I'll have to show you." As he passed Fierce, he saw a wide abrasion on his shoulder. "A Clan member can salve that at the camp."

Liis reacquired the lead just in time to bump the group into a bleak tunnel. "This will save a lot of time."

Most paused, cautious of a trap. A few words from Fierce, Liis assumed to remind them they shouldn't be intimidated by squat hirsute males in battered wraps, and they marched into the dim, dank tunnel.

Liis said, "Those who don't want to come this way can climb to Big Rock's crest and descend the opposite side, or wait on the shore."

Chapter 3

2 years ago (cont'd)

Liis laughed to himself as he strode into a tight tunnel. He was sure the constricted opening filled with the stench of rot, thick webs left by Spider's industry, and the scattered husks of long-dead animals would discourage many from following. It might have, if not for Fierce. The Tall One Leader howled some babble to the column, then strode in steps behind Liis as did Fierce's band, stooping where needed under a canopy too low for their great height. They grumbled, bumped into the prickly sides, roared good-natured complaints to each other, and pounded onward.

I wouldn't have thought them so brave.

Liis sped up, stomach growling. This was the fastest route to the opposite side and he was hungry. He exited the tunnel, climbed a short rocky path, and stopped under a vertical hole.

Wait till they see this.

Fierce huffed up to his side. "What are we waiting for?"

"Next, we squeeze up that chimney."

Fierce tipped his head up. "There's no light."

"There is, the splotch at the top. That is where we go. You can't get lost. Do as I do."

Without another word, Liis climbed. Within a breath, maybe one more, all he felt beneath him was air. He pressed his back to one side of the chimney, feet to the other, levered his way up from one handhold to another he couldn't see but knew to be there. Using the opposing faces for traction, he ascended one hand's distance and another, feet scraping rock, until the chimney narrowed. There, he wedged himself and rested, his aching muscles appreciating the respite. He was drenched in sweat, muscles flagging with fatigue, but quitting never entered his thoughts. He glanced back to be sure Fierce saw this good place to pause, if needed, and then continued.

One last stretch….

He tapped around, found a minuscule toe ledge he'd long ago etched into the chimney, pushed off as he pulled up, hard, braced front and back, and flung himself over the lip with muscular arms accustomed to throwing heavy rocks and carrying carcasses that weighed more than he did. Then, he lay flat, soaking in the victory.

The range that cut the Clan off from the rest of the world soared ahead, cloaked in white. There was no easy way across the snowy ridgeline, every step imbued with a deep fear of storms, predator attacks, and missteps, and no possibility of a hearth fire for warmth after a punishing day. None knew this munificent peninsula lay on the other side of their misery. Most died. Some turned back before that happened. Liis hoped their stories would keep the Clan safe.

Scrabbling sounds came quicker than Liis expected. He rolled out of the way just as Fierce popped out. Behind him, Grub, and another of the Tall Ones—Crevkukk?—dangled from the Male-Mountain's fist.

Grub's muscles quivered, but a grin spread over his face. "That was fun!"

As soon as all the strangers had exited the chimney, Liis pushed to his feet and ploughed forward, drawn by the scent of cooked flesh. By the time he and his entourage reached the Clan's hearth, Liis was drooling. Turk, the scouts, and many of the Clan were already eating and regarded the new arrivals with curiosity. Liis settled by his pairmate, Bhota. The Tall One males squeezed in among the Clan wherever there was room. Liis guessed hunger outweighed reticence. Each placed their thin lances to the side but within reach. They were somewhat like Clan spears, a pointed stone affixed to an overly straight shaft without the heft.

Turk glowered, a mix of impatience and worry. "I don't trust the huge male, the one whose mother must be an old tree, his father a boulder—"

"Grub. He plucked me up on a tumble downhill as though a blade of grass. He might have saved a tribe mate—Crevkukk?—in the chimney."

Turk grumbled. Liis poked the flames with a forced laugh. He understood his brother's mistrust. The few Tall Ones they ran into before now disrespected the earth, often killed more in a herd than they could eat, took the best parts, and left the rest. The Clan wasted nothing, preserved uneaten flesh or distributed it among neighbors. Innards, meat, fat, tendons, skin, and organs all served a purpose. In the past, they coexisted with these big-headed, slender-bodied interlopers with their squanderous habits by avoiding them. Now, they were sharing a meal.

Turk huffed. "The words are strange."

"I have already decoded most of them. There are only so many."

Deciphering sounds was something Liis found easy whether animals, birds, or Uprights. The Tall Ones, like the Clan, repeated sounds in different orders, cadences, and speeds. Liis simply fit them in amongst the rest, figured out the patterns, and eventually, what was said gained meaning. The hand and facial gestures helped.

Fierce and Grub motioned, pointing next to Liis.

He waved, "Eat. We have plenty," and winced as pain shot through his shoulder. "The gourds have stew and water."

The Tall Ones didn't need further encouragement. They plopped down, loaded bark platters with the variety on the hearth, and dug in.

If they came from as far away as One-called-Fierce claimed, they likely expected to eat food caught in the shoreless sea, but the plan must have failed because they ate with a vengeance.

Liis' pairmate Bhota poked his bruised shoulder and abrasions. He didn't react so she said, "If they hurt later, I'll wrap them."

As everyone ate, the females snuck glances at the new males. Both sides grinned when caught.

Fierce asked with a mix of words and awkward motions, "Who do I talk to, Liis, you, or Turk? Or both?"

Liis didn't understand what the question meant. Instead, he rubbed the exposed skin on his lower arm and tugged a rope of his longish straightish hair, then asked, "Why is your hair and skin dark like Raven's, and curly?"

Fierce chortled. "We wondered the same about you. Isn't so much hair hot?" communicated with similar touching of his skin and hair and then waving a hand in front of his panting mouth.

The brothers shrugged, Liis with the start of a grin, Turk the opposite.

I wonder if it's hotter where they come from.

Turk wiped drips of stew off his mouth with his wrap. "You live far from here?"

Grub washed roots and shreds of meat down with water. "Across the shoreless sea."

Liis stared into the open water. "That is like saying we live along it."

Fierce said, "I can be more precise. When the Moon shrinks to a crescent, draw a line between the horns. Extend it beyond the horizon. Where it intersects the brown strip is our homebase."

Liis blinked, stunned by the sense in that. "How did that log bring you so far? The water you crossed is too rough for our rafts, but not your vessel? And the trip—it must have taken more than all of day's light."

Fierce chortled. "That was part of the excitement. We have never traveled so far from our homebase. Others of our kind have, most never returned, which made the prospect even more exciting. We wanted to see what defeated them."

"You didn't fear you too would disappear?"

"Never. Nor did the Elders who sent us. We are the apex of our band. We assured the Elders that the footsteps of those who failed would provide the answers to whether this land is a future homebase or a deadly trap."

"We have questions about that, but first, how does one sail as far as you did? You can't see where you go at night."

Fierce grinned. "At night, we steer by Moon and its stars, winds and clouds, the changes in the sea's swells, and the activity of sea creatures. These tell us the water's depth which tells us how far away land is and impending storms."

Fierce saw Liis' shock, but misunderstood. "We aren't here to cause trouble, Liis, even if others of our kind have in the past."

Turk asked, "Then why are you here?"

Grub peered from under hooded eyes, gaze roving through the gathering. "To meet you, of course."

His body and facial expressions all matched his words. *He tells the truth. The question becomes, why?*

Fierce punched Grub and added, "Our home changes. Herds have become smaller. Many that migrate during the hot air time don't return. Why, we can't figure out. The plants also change—dying, drying out, and thinning. We must go farther to find cat-tails, grass, tubers, berries, sprouts, and nuts—foods we rely on in the absence of meat. That often means crossing into the territory of another band. It is customary to fight others for resources."

"You would kill over stems and flowers?"

"Would and have, but that only works with sufficient foodstuff to fight over. Our Elder, Seer, envisioned a better way. He noticed the herds often migrate here—not to this promontory but the shoreless sea's coast. He sent groups of explorers to find out if this was a practical new homeland. Some followed the herd routes toward Sun's waking place. We instead sailed across the sea so we can start at Sun's sleeping place."

Turk caught Liis' eye and said, "I can't imagine fighting over food. We would simply find more."

Fierce narrowed his gaze. "What if you and another both want the same herd or the same fruit?"

Liis said, "We would hunt together, then share the largess. If it's fruit or nuts, we move on," and then added, "Truth, that rarely happens. We didn't run into a lot of our kind or yours where we formerly lived, and seldom here. You'll see if you remain with us for a while."

Liis burned this lesson into memory. He'd been wrong about them being weak because their bodies were. Their real power wasn't physical. It was truth-telling. They were hiding nothing from the Alphas. The trick was to hear what they were saying.

Turk popped to his feet, jammed the blunt end of his shaft into the ground. It stood brawny and proud, then gestured toward the slender limb beside Fierce.

"That fragile weapon couldn't feed your tribe even if you found herds."

Fierce remained relaxed and responded with open hands, "We will demonstrate if you allow us to stay here during our exploration."

Stay with us?

All eyes turned to Liis and he concentrated on the fragrant flesh harvested from the sea, chewing while scanning the mixed group of Tall Ones and Clan.

He wiped his forearm across his mouth. "We have few herds, but much flesh in the Endless Sea. Can those weak pikes you seem so proud of kill meat that swims?"

Fierce laughed. "As effectively as on land." He nibbled at a piece of white meat, glanced around, and said, "You mentioned someone could treat injuries."

A young female with burnished hair that shone under Sun's waning light stepped toward them.

"I can."

Liis motioned as he bit open a shell and extracted the soft meat within. "She is our Healer since the Elder died. Show her which of your males need treating."

Fierce pointed to one and another. "Eknilk was bitten by a huge fish while trying to catch a fish from alongside our vessel, and Braanroorv was stabbed accidentally with a harpoon."

"What about you?" She touched the scrapes Fierce had acquired while crawling through the shortcut.

"These are fresh. If they get worse, I will seek your assistance," he said.

She left with the injured in tow.

Fierce asked Liis, "How many tribes—Clans—live with you?"

Liis shrugged. "Most reside beyond the range you see in the far distance. Only a few of us made our way here."

Grub left to release his water. When he returned, the females without pairmates scooted aside to make room for him. They giggled at his jabbering though likely misinterpreted the words. He wriggled until his hips touched his neighbors which made them giggle more, and his lips split into a grin.

"I am Grub." His dark gaze landed on one after another. "With me are Bhidid, Eknilk, Braanroorv, Crevkukk, and Qad. We appreciate the food and respect your hospitality."

A few chuckled which elicited another beam from Grub. Crevkukk, the youngest, waddled in amongst them, laughed at all the right times, let them run stubby fingers through his curly hair, rub his dusky sable skin—so much darker than any of the Clan—and squeal over its smoothness. Then, he did the same, stunned by their sleek hair and tawny-colored skin. That his utterances were incomprehensible babble seemed inconsequential. By night's end, everyone communicated what was necessary.

A Tall One again called himself a warrior and Liis asked Fierce to explain.

"Warriors defend against enemies with weapons. Where are yours?"

"Nowhere and everywhere. Males and females, adults and subadults, hunters and scouts—all safeguard all. What enemies are here that we should be prepared for?"

Lines formed over Fierce's eyes. "Others of my kind came here. Few reported back. We didn't know if it was because of hostile natives, inclement conditions, or they chose to stay." He shrugged. "We prepared for all possibilities."

Liis licked his fingers. "My kind are called Clan. You, we call Tall Ones because of your height. Other Tall Ones did traverse our previous home, but didn't make contact with us. You do. Why?"

Fierce slurped the last of the stew on his bark platter. "First, we are the Chosen, called that because—"

Grub stopped him, whispered quickly, "Fierce. If you reveal how dominant we are in our homeland, they may deem it a challenge."

Liis pretended to be distracted by Turk, but understood every word. Fierce glanced at Liis, noted his hand wrap tightly around the lance.

He leaned closer to Grub and whispered, "He knows what you said. He is smart. We would make a mistake underestimating him," and then pulled back, offered Liis a conciliatory grin.

Liis' eyes were now slits, the wan smile on his lips faded. "Do you expect me to trust you just because One-called-Grub arrested my fall? I have survived worse."

Fierce changed his tone. "Our intent is not to anger you. You are stronger than most of our kind and, based on how fast you unraveled our communications, smarter!"

Liis might forgive, but Turk's eyes flattened and his voice, though mild, silenced those inclined to befriend the new arrivals.

"Chosen? What kind of a name is that?"

He motioned the megalith Grub to his feet. At full height, Grub would make a hillock proud. Turk cricked his neck upward, glanced sideways at Liis, and grinned.

"It means nothing to us. We call you Tall Ones because you are."

Grub slapped Turk on the shoulder and bellowed, a laugh echoed immediately by Liis and then Fierce. Soon, everyone was chortling about the silliness of names.

Liis wiped his mouth on his sleeve, settled to his haunches, and said, "Tell us of your journey."

Fierce described his home, the huge size of their Clan—or "band" as he called it—and how this promontory was a stopping point, not a final destination. He and Grub each interspersed comments in the dialogue. Occasional nods and grunts of agreement accented the conversation.

Without a word or reason, Liis and Turk scrambled to their feet and marched up an overwatch. From here was a view across the shoreless sea to the band of brown on the horizon.

When Fierce caught up, Liis asked, "If you've never been here, how did you know the way?"

"Changes in the color and consistency of clouds inform you about wind direction and speed. That is true also with water. Variation in hue indicates an increase and decrease in depth and temperature."

He cupped his palm behind his ear, listening to the call of a white full-chested bird common on the peninsula. "That bird lives on our side also. It flies far out over the water, but never so far it can't return to its nest. Shortly after we set out, one dove, grabbed a fish, and flew *this* way, not back to our shores. That told us you were close enough."

Turk leaned in to Liis. "They are not as foolish as they appear."

The Clan had no experience crossing vast bodies of water. The waterholes in their former homeland and this one were either crossed with flat rafts or avoided. Liis enjoyed comparing strategies with one who had sailed across swaths of water on a vessel that wasn't logs tied together with vines.

Why didn't we think of glue?

He cocked his head. "You navigate the seas as we navigate land, but instead of moss, prints, and scat, you rely on stars, Moon, and Sun."

Fierce directed intelligent eyes at Liis that seemed to understand what he meant.

"Our home looms there, on your horizon, as yours does on ours. We came here knowing it would take a long time, but exploring is what we do. Distance means nothing. It is about opportunity."

"How about a trip that outlasts daylight?"

"When Sun sleeps, we establish a skymark—a star we keep in the same position as we aim toward our destination. If a cloud blocks it, we switch to another. Sailing is easier than it sounds, harder than it appears."

The chorus of crickets grew louder, accompanied by frogs to announce night's arrival.

Liis asked, "How long will you be here?"

"How long would it take to wander the entirety of this peninsula and the surrounding areas?"

Liis chuckled. "Most of the peninsula is bordered by seas, one side by snow-tipped peaks. No need to go beyond those. It is too cold and why we left." He didn't bother with the alternate route his Clan had taken. "What you see between the seas and the spires is rich with food, temperate air, and few enemies. You will enjoy those excursions."

"You say there are few predators or enemies?"

Turk answered. "The peninsula is hard to reach and those here are too satisfied to risk being driven away." He dropped his arms. "But no one would call it expansive as you describe your home. If you leave and choose to return, don't bring your bands. You will overwhelm us."

The males went on to discuss why Clan shafts were heavier and Tall One's lengthier, what glue was used to attach the tips, and how far a well-wielded lance could penetrate a hide. Conversation flagged.

Fierce popped to his feet. "Let's see your terrain from that perspective," and proceeded to a high ridgeline.

From the crest, they peered at the wrinkled patchwork below of arid grasses, craggy hills, and well-worn canyons. Past these were desiccated creek beds that twisted through the earth. Sun was completing its slow descent behind jagged bluffs, shadows lengthening and darkening as dusk became night. The quiet was broken by the songs of nocturnal insects, Owl's haunting hoot, and the occasional screech as prey lost to predator. Liis cherished this environs for its mystery and wonder. When the Clan settled here, he had felt peace, purpose, or something he couldn't yet label. Whatever it would grow into, he could no longer imagine life without it.

"Let's return."

They descended the cliff, headed for the glow of the fire, a bright marker in the deepening dark. Food had been consumed, but some Clan members remained around the hearth, sharpening spear tips and repairing wraps. Fierce rested elbows on thighs and tented his hands.

"There is one reason besides to explore why we come here. Our healer, Seer, asked us to contact a female called Aynoh and a male called Shanadar. Are either of these here?"

Liis snapped an airborne insect from the air, crushed it between his fingers, and shrugged. "Those are unusual names. Are they Primitives? Or your kind?"

"Yours."

"Before we came here, in a neighboring tribe, there was a subadult named Jun who changed his name to something like Shanad—maybe Shanadar—and then left on a long journey. No one ever saw him again."

"Do you know where he went?"

"He said toward Sun's waking place because of a vision. That's all I know."

Turk gestured agreement and asked, "Why do you seek them?"

Fierce widened his hands, palms up, fingers apart. "Seer did not explain why or where to locate either. We decided to travel until the sea ends and ask the tribes we meet. If no one knows, rather than stay along the coast until we reach our home, we will explore inland. Seer is sure someone knows them. He is never wrong."

Liis said, "We haven't circled the sea or ventured inland. Turk—what do you think?"

But his brother was too busy scowling to answer. Pairmates had retired as had females willing to share their nests with the newcomers. Only a few remained. Liis followed Turk's line of sight and poked his chin toward one of the newcomers.

"Fierce. Who is that one?"

"Bhidid? I think he's considering mating. Is it a problem?"

"You should ask her pairmate, but he will not return until tomorrow."

"Bhidid wouldn't–" but instead of finishing, shouted, "Bhidid!" The surprised male jolted to his feet. "Overwatch tonight!"

Liis beckoned one of the Clan scouts. "Show One-called-Bhidid the lookout."

Bhidid asked no questions, dashed away, and soon was silhouetted against the Moon-lit sky.

Liis popped a chunk of white meat into his mouth. Between chews, he said, "You asked earlier about the meaning of Alpha. He is the tribe member selected to guide the Clan through unusual circumstances."

"Comparable to me as our Leader."

"Mmm…." Was that true?

Liis's equivocation didn't bother Fierce. "And you both share the position?"

"We do, which is unusual. Our Clans are small, typically no more than you can tick off on the fingers of both hands. All are generalists, expected to perform any function—cook, sew, knap, scout, track, or treat simple injuries. Only Alphas are specialized. To commit more than one individual to this job, to take him away from general duties to serve the Clan, is never done except in our Clan. Turk and I fulfill both generalist and specialist roles. Neither is demanding to us because we enjoy solving problems, unearthing unknown solutions."

He glanced at Fierce. "Is that also why you lead, to improve the lives of your band?"

Fierce rubbed the nob under his mouth—what he called a chin—something Liis had noticed he did if he was thinking or to signal confusion.

He said, "In a sense. Decisions have the support of Seer, the Elders, and the Leads. The band never disputes them and all abide by them."

"How do you know it's the right one?"

He rubbed his chin again. "Well. Most follow established routines and pronouncements of Seer and the Elders, but this one—to explore a new area, to seek out individuals Seer saw in his visions—was more like your description of solving problems. Leaders have discretion in decisions that move a band forward. That is what Seer expects of me—of this group—as we explore."

Now it was Liis' turn to be confused. He tried brushing his chin, thinking maybe it helped solutions pop up, but without a nob, he had to settle for tugging his lip. That only postponed responses and distracted listeners.

Is that its purpose for Fierce, too, to delay more than advise?

Deciding it a waste of energy, Liis pulled a spear from his satchel with a loosened tip. Someone had heated glue in a gourd.

As he slathered the sticky bark-sap mixture on the juncture of stone and shaft, he asked, "Who decides on a Leader?"

"Any can compete for the status of Leader as well as Lead."

"Lead?"

"The primary among the warriors, trackers, hunters, and scouts. Leads and Leaders prove they are the best through challenges. Anyone can dispute my position as Leader or Grub as Lead. The test takes place in the roughest country around our homebase, without water, with endless hills and broad sandy patches of gravel, where life goes to die. The survivor wins."

Liis was appalled. "How does that prove leadership?"

"A Lead must pay attention to all senses better than Coyote, Eagle, or Bear. Nothing must beat him, not geography, heat, fanged-and-hooved critters, predators, or competitors. He must always win. When that is no longer true, another Lead takes over."

Liis grabbed a handful of sand and smoothed the tip, preparing it to be fused. "It sounds stressful. I don't envy you that life."

Fierce grinned. "You enjoy problems. I live for solutions."

Liis checked the connection between shaft and stone, satisfied he'd applied sufficient glue, and set the weapon aside. It would be hard by morning.

Fierce stifled a yawn. "You and I, we must continue our talks when daylight returns."

Chapter 4

2 years ago (cont'd)

The next days, Turk fulfilled Clan Alpha duties while Liis traipsed with the outsiders from the shoreless sea to the Endless Sea. They trotted through valleys of flowers, beneath skies that exploded with stars, and feasted on soft white flesh from the water. He and Fierce spoke of the past, the future, what would—or should—never be. Liis felt a camaraderie rare with any but Turk.

"Come." Liis beckoned Fierce and his band up yet another wretched trail as they scaled the sheer, barren cliffs on the back side of Big Rock, broken occasionally with spotty greenery and thirsty shrubs. Liis thought the Tall One's scrawny legs would cause them to fall behind, but they kept up. The climb was worth it. At the crest, they were treated to an unrivaled panorama of the isthmus, the rugged flank descending to the shore, and the mesmerizing visitors' homebase clinging to the horizon.

"On clear days like now, the view stretches across the strait to your home. Other times, the air is thicker than morning fog, impossible to see through. I feel as though I am floating."

Fierce spun slowly and then stopped. "Liis. The ridges that separate us from your former home, do they ever spew smoke or flames, or send fire rivers across the terrain?"

Liis shook his head. "Why would they?"

Fierce sucked in a breath. "One more question before I answer yours. Does the ground around the mountains ever shake? Or crack open and swallow everything?"

Liis had no idea what Fierce was asking. What he speculated was impossible.

"How does fire spurt out of a mountain? And how—why?—would the earth we stand on split?"

"I ask because that happens where we live. Mountains spit a fiery stream of liquid rock and cinder out of their gullet high into the air, almost touching Sun. When the molten clumps drop, they burn all life they touch. We don't know if they're angry or sick or something else. It just happens with no way to prevent or stop it."

Liis was appalled. "Do you think ours will do that?"

"No. A mountain announces its intention to vent with a growl and wisps of smoke drifting from the peak. Then, our healer, Seer, climbs to the summit. If the throat is dark, it means the anger has released some other way, the rumbles no more than the grumble of an upset stomach. But if the gullet is filled with sizzling bubbles, as our throats do when we retch, Seer orders us away. We don't return until the crown no longer smokes. That often takes long and is why we seek a homebase without such disruption."

Liis' mouth dropped open. "I have never seen or heard anything like that from either side of the range. The greatest peril on the opposite side was the cold. Here, it is the channel between the shoreless and Endless Sea. Often, choppy waves pummel the surface and strong winds whip the water into frothy white caps. Below the surface is worse. Turbulent currents rush in all directions. If we launch our rafts, they don't survive. Even on days when the surface is calm, it changes without notice. Because of that, we avoid the channel and harvest our food in other areas."

"Have you tried to reach Endless Sea's end?"

"No. Elders told stories of those who left to find where Sun slept or at least, what lay over the horizon. They never returned."

Over the next days, the newcomers demonstrated how they stalked water prey using a fragile lance with a barb hafted to the tip in place of a stone. Fierce stood spread-legged in the tidepools and skewered the creatures. The tool—which he called a harpoon—worked on shelled and scaled fish, even those that squirmed like snakes. The shallow pools must have seemed safe until the water critters realized they were trapped, at the mercy of a harpoon-wielding predator. Liis' pairmate Bhota impaled one bigger than herself and hauled the monster in alone. The flesh fed everyone for days. Even Clan subadults returned with armloads of flesh. Uneaten food was preserved. Children guarded it against scavengers as it dried. All hunters learned to take only what could be eaten as with herd animals. No one knew how many fish lived in the sea and they didn't want to run out.

One day, scouts brought exciting news of a close-by herd. Liis invited the visitors to participate in the hunt.

Turk spat out, "You can show why your fragile spikes are superior," with the irritated tone he reserved for those he deemed dull-witted.

Despite Fierce's patience and Grub's affability, Turk didn't warm to the outsiders as Liis did. Turk expected them to turn on the Clan and wanted to be prepared. Liis wondered when he would erupt, like the mountain Fierce talked about in his home, the only sign a touch of steam off his head or ears.

Nevertheless, Fierce grinned as always. "The first reason is that we throw from afar while you thrust from up close. That puts you within range of the deadly horns, heads, claws, and fangs."

Fierce extended his lance to Turk and Liis. "Feel this. It is lightweight, which makes it easy to throw, and the shaft is flat so moves on a line through the air." He tapped the point. "The tip is like yours, able to pierce the toughest hides."

Fierce ran a hand down the wood. "We fashion spears over many nights, and we practice. A lot."

Liis said, "I see your band in a field with their spears as you and I depart, to explore. They often aren't back by the time we are."

"Aim, throw, kill. Repeat. Repeat. Repeat. Without practice, we can't hit quarry from a distance. With it, we never miss."

Turk gestured at a toppled hardwood tree a handful of strides away. "Can you hit that?" His tone said they couldn't.

"Watch."

Fierce stood, feet separated, one foot in front. He raised his spear to shoulder height, level with the ground, hand in the middle behind his ear. He took one stutter step forward, another, and launched the lance. It flew through the air and plunged into the wood.

"No…. That can't be…." Turk muttered and trotted toward the target, the spear wobbling but holding.

When he reached the stump, he made eye contact with Liis as he yanked the spike out.

Liis couldn't hold back a grin. "Many are killed on hunts or too injured to continue. We talk of a better way, but never thought of this."

He was already practicing in his mind, imagining Fierce's grip on the lance, how he threw with his entire body.

Turk trotted up. "A stump doesn't move. Animals do."

"We'll show you with this herd your scout found. If you like what you see, we will teach you to use them and make your own."

Turk's jaw muscles bunched. Liis, too, gritted his teeth. What favor did the newcomer expect in return for help?

The combined group traveled the next day at a ground-eating pace, over flat sun-bleached grass and broken boulders ranging in size from a melon to an overgrown bush. The Sun at its hottest, they stopped at a bed of rocks heaped in a mound taller than Liis. A subterranean spring bubbled at its base. While the rest rehydrated, Liis clambered up a snaking trail to the top of a hillock. A family of mountain goats made their way amid a cluster of rolling mounds, and a few nervous hares sprinted for burrows before a circling Eagle could catch them.

Just beyond were the Giant Red Deer.

Liis beckoned Fierce and Turk and murmured, "We aim for spots that kill quickly. Is that your strategy, Fierce?"

"Yes, but—"

Liis interrupted with a sage smile. "Watch us. We are skilled at approaching quietly, downwind, picking the most vulnerable in a herd. They don't even know we're there until we're too close."

Fierce seized his arm. "Liis. We will set up across the field. Wait until we're in place. Then, charge, but don't attack. Stampede them toward us. We will stop them."

"If you fail—"

"Then we turn the herd into your spears. They will be exactly where you want them."

The brothers nodded together, Turk reluctantly, and the Tall Ones darted across the field. As promised, the Clan drove the herd to Fierce and his hunters attacked. One throw, one kill. No one missed. All hits in vital spots so the animal died quickly. By the time the Clan hunters caught up to the killing field, as many carcasses as the tribe could carry littered the field, their fur-covered bodies sprouting shafts.

Liis waved his hunters off. "No reason to chase the survivors. We can come again tomorrow."

The group gutted the carcasses, dumped the offal far enough away that scavengers would not sniff out the backtrail, shouldered their bounty, and headed back to their homebase. The meat was cooked alongside roots and leaves. The adults cut and hung what wasn't eaten and youngsters guarded it from predators. The Tall Ones showed the Clan how to create the throwing spears with thinner tree limbs, the straightest of branches taken from the hardest of trees. Practice would come later.

The next day, the mixed tribe tracked the herd survivors and followed the same procedure. As Sun prepared to sleep, the hunters again dragged in, weighed down by both meat and success, exhausted but jabbering happily. Meat consumed and processed, newcomers mated with willing Clan, their goal relaxation, the females to add children to the Clan. Experience taught them that the offspring of couplings between related parents often were sickly or died young. If an opportunity presented itself to mate with non-family, all took advantage. Almost all infants of these matings were healthy. Without new scouts and hunters, they would become extinct.

Turk disagreed with the liaisons. To him, children with the Tall Ones' weak physiques would be crushed by daily physical demands. The Clan would become increasingly vulnerable as the frail new members replaced existing robust adults. Liis argued that their cleverness—like inventing the throwing spears—would offset inferior physicality and result in a more resilient adult and dogged Clan.

In the end, the females decided. One after another, they fattened from mating.

Over the next days, Fierce and his explorers showed the Clan males where to harvest branches for throwing spears, how to smooth away bumps and curves, in preparation for practice. They were respectful, never gave cause for the Clan to feel endangered. All liked the Tall Ones except a sullen adult named Druyl. Druyl had tagged along on the Clan's migration because no one in the main tribe wanted him. On overwatch, he invariably slept. His tools were poorly maintained, and he never filled community stores of food, cordage, or stones. No one would mate with him so he didn't even contribute children. He disappeared often without explanation. Liis assumed it was to find a more receptive tribe, but he always returned. Why would any tribe welcome him? The only reason the Clan allowed him to continue with them was that Druyl had a knack for identifying illnesses and then harvesting the right herb for treatments. The Healer valued that. Liis dreaded the time the Healer would die and the Clan would be at Druyl's mercy.

Druyl told Liis and Turk that Fierce spoke of a plan to take over, something about poisoning the Clan before the Tall Ones left and then returning with more warriors. The brothers didn't believe him, but one Clan member—Mook—did. Mook agreed with whatever Druyl said and soon mimicked his mentor's animosity.

The time came for the Tall Ones to resume the search for Shanadar and Aynoh. Fierce asked Liis to guide them, and he immediately agreed.

I will learn to heal, bring those skills back to the Clan. Then, we can get rid of Druyl.

The night before the Tall Ones left, Fierce gave Liis the Tall One name, "Kazeb," which meant "Guide."

"I will paint you with Chosen shades. Any of my kind we run into on our travels will call you friend."

Liis-now-Kazeb touched the swaths of color on Fierce's cheeks. "How do I make these without your guidance?"

"Watch."

He heated red and yellow ochre separately, stirred in water—though urine would serve well in the absence of water—until it was the consistency of paste, and painted his cheeks and forehead. Kazeb hid the pain from the burn, focused on the significance.

The Clan shared a final meal amid laughter and promises. Even Druyl participated, heating the stews, serving Clan members so they could spend the remaining time with the departing Tall Ones. The brothers sat to the side, enjoying the rare levity, surprised by Druyl's atypical friendliness. Rarely did he help with chores. This night, he couldn't do enough.

Turk growled quietly. "He refuses to feed the visitors. He has never trusted them."

Kazeb stuffed a handful of softened leaves in his mouth. "He won't feed us, either. I suppose the stripes and the necklace—"

"And the name Fierce gave you."

Kazeb bobbed his head. "All makes me one of them, and you by association."

Turk grumbled his agreement.

Kazeb awoke to the sound of retching. Several Clan members including his pairmate had a malady unfamiliar to the healer.

"Fierce. I must stay until Bhota recovers. Our healer needs my help."

"We will leave markers. You will have no problem tracking us."

He slipped a thin cord from his neck strung with a collection of fangs, small bones, deer teeth, and shells he picked up on his trips intermixed with natural materials from his former home—bark, seeds, and colored pebbles. He always wore this necklace. Now, he gave it to Liis—Kazeb.

"Wear this. If you run into my kind, they will see you as Chosen. We are influential. No one will bother you."

Fierce left. Kazeb would join him when his Clan's health improved.

It didn't. Those who were sick became worse. They coughed constantly and bled from orifices for no reason the healer could determine. Soon, their muscles stiffened and they were forced to lie in bed, sightless eyes shut, bodies exhausted, but unable to sleep.

The healer scoured the countryside for anything to help while Druyl and Mook delivered the broths, mulches, and poultices to the sick. Kazeb was stunned. Never in the past did either put anyone ahead of themselves.

What changed?

Then the deaths began. First, females with babies died, followed by the sickest, then the brothers' pairmates and anyone else who exhibited symptoms. When the healer too died, the healthy fled. One departing member snarled that the brothers had failed, been duped by the strangers. Kazeb started to ask him to explain, but Druyl hustled the male away, reminding him he would be safe on a distant part of the peninsula.

Finally, only the brothers, Druyl, and Mook remained, as if somehow, they alone among the Clan were immune to the illness. Eventually, Mook too left, but Druyl refused to be driven out. Besides, he argued, where would he go? Kazeb didn't believe him. Druyl accepted the misery and death as though he expected it—welcomed it.

Kazeb asked what Turk thought, and he scoffed. "Don't turn your back on him. Something's wrong here that we can't see, but I will."

Chapter 5

Turk shook Kazeb awake from dreams of dying Clan members, voices accusing him of failing, and pleas falling on deaf ears.

"Liis. Let's go. I located a cave far from here with no evidence of habitation. There's a fissure in it where we can dump the bodies."

Kazeb scrabbled to his feet, emotions raw from kicking and turning all night. It had been many nights since he enjoyed a deep, uneventful sleep. That didn't seem an option anymore. Not now. Not after. His shoulders slumped under the weight of what they must do, but knowing his brother was with him, bearing the load, cheered him.

Turk offered a wan smile. "As soon as the stink and poison of bodies are gone, the dreams will end. We will start over. It will be fine, brother. You'll see." He turned away, then muttered over his shoulder, "Druyl offered to help."

That sent tingles down Kazeb's back. Druyl never helped which meant he had a reason.

Turk, Kazeb, and Druyl each shrugged a carcass onto their shoulders and strode out of the death camp. No one worried the disease could jump to them because it would have by now. It took a hand of Sun's overhead travel to reach the cave. Turk had already left torches in the back of the cavern, sticks topped with huge cones saturated with sap. All they required was fire.

"I'll lead." Turk lit one and trudged into the tunnel's stygian darkness.

Druyl whined, "We could get lost in this maze."

Kazeb looked sideways at the male who had been unreliable before the deaths and untrustworthy since. "One entrance, one exit. Don't leave the trail."

He glanced at Turk, could tell he had the same thought. *How does Druyl know there are other tunnels?*

A winding passage left everyone scraped and abraded, but ended at a gorge deep enough that no light reached the bottom. Each pitched their carcass over the edge, listened for the plop, then retrieved the last of the poisoned bodies from the homebase. Back at the cave, Turk lit a torch, but they didn't need it. A trail of rats led to the fissure. One after another, the furry long-toothed critters leapt in to feast on the fetid carrion.

Kazeb laughed. "They will soon join the corpses as food for scavengers dumb enough to follow."

The final torch sputtered out as the gruesome task was completed.

Turk said, "I have a spare torch in my shoulder sack. I'll get it."

Turk's steps hadn't disappeared longer than a breath when a sharp shove knocked Kazeb off-balance. He yelped, flung his arms out to grab for Druyl, but the Clan member shuffled out of range. Kazeb yelped again, lost his balance, and stumbled backwards into emptiness. His head smacked against the damp fissure as his fingers clawed for purchase. He snatched at a thin root, had just enough time to kick a shelf into the dirt his toes could grip before the mangled root pulled from its earthen bed. Turk's words caromed through his brain—*Don't turn your back on him*—but this wasn't the time to flagellate himself, not with his heart thudding against his ribs, the gnawing below loud in his ears.

Turk's offhand comment as they tossed carcasses over the fissure's lip popped to mind. *Keep away from that ledge sticking out so it doesn't snag the wrap!* He had drawn Kazeb's attention to a scanty shelf of infinitesimal width protruding from the face. Most would suppose it inconsequential, but Turk had recognized its potential as a problem. Now, it could be Kazeb's salvation.

His hands flailed in a crazed search for the sliver of dirt, almost brushed over it, but managed to clasp it as the hold supporting his toe—and therefore his body—gave way. He tightened his grip and clung. Kazeb was strong everywhere, including his fingers. As a youngster, he hung by the tips of his digits, pretending to be a mountain goat. If they could leap from one minute ridge to another, with nothing more than hard hooves, why couldn't Kazeb? In fact, he excelled at it in no small measure because he refused to lose.

"Liis?" Druyl's voice was soft but taunting. "You stumbled. Are you all right?"

If Druyl realized Kazeb clung just below the top of the fissure by his fingertips, he'd try to dislodge him so Kazeb tamped down his frenzied breathing and kept the scrabble of his toes rummaging for a hold as quiet as possible. The fissure cantilevered, hiding him somewhat under the lip's overhang. Without a torch, Druyl wouldn't see him.

But Kazeb saw Druyl, his eyes blinking as he searched for the Clan member he hoped to kill. Kazeb had gazed into a rattlesnake's eyes more than once. Druyl's had that same flat, dead look.

I have to hold on until Turk returns.

"Tell me where you are! I'll toss a vine!"

Druyl hadn't brought one, but tossed a hand-sized cobble down, hoping if Kazeb lived, he'd spontaneously reach out. It hit Kazeb, but he kept the shock inside his mouth.

That proves what I already knew.

Kazeb fumbled quietly with his toes to take the weight off his weakening fingers.

Kazeb heard muted pounding. *Turk!* Light splashed through the darkness.

"Druyl! Where is Liis?"

"He tripped! I tried to save him. I called …. I heard a thump."

Kazeb tilted his face up, but remained silent. It wouldn't do to provide a disturbance, an opportunity for Druyl to shove his brother before Turk figured out what happened. It didn't take much to uncover the lie in Druyl's words. If additional fresh meat lay in the crevasse, the noise of the rats chewing would increase. It didn't.

Turk's voice turned acerbic. "A mountain goat climbs with less skill than Kazeb."

A step away from the fissure. *Time for a diversion.*

"He pushed me!"

Turk howled, and then Kazeb heard a thump. Druyl fell backward, whirling his arms as he tumbled past his would-be victim. He caught Kazeb's eye, reached out, but was too far away to grab him. Turk had made sure of that. Druyl screeched as he crunched into the putrid bodies. His shrieks became frantic and then garbled as the rats bit into the fresh flesh starting with the soft face.

"Hang on, Liis! I'll get a vine," and Turk sprinted away.

Kazeb gripped tighter, ignored his cramped fingers, drew strength from the chomps below, dug toeholds into the wall and relaxed into them. His weight crumbled one shelf so he slammed his foot to create another, motivated by the wet tearing, the stinking body fluids, and the rodents' feeding frenzy. Beady eyes glanced upward and then skittered back to their ready supply of fresh flesh. Those who couldn't squirm through the packed mass of wriggling claws leapt, but not high enough.

Hurry, Turk!

The stench from below made him dizzy. His hold, despite the strength of his fingers, slipped with sweat and he wriggled, hanging by one hand at a time to dry the other.

Footfalls approached. "Turk! I'm here! Throw the vine!"

But nothing tumbled his way. He squinted up. "Mook?" *I am in trouble!* But he couldn't stop himself from begging, "Help me!"

"You killed Druyl."

The words were almost obfuscated by a distant shout. "Hang on, Liis!"

"Be careful! Mook is here and not as a friend!"

Mook scowled and slunk away. Turk skidded to a stop at the lip of the fissure and tossed the vine down. His eyes glistened, cheeks wet in the torchlight as Kazeb crawled out.

"Mook came after you killed Druyl and left me to die." He scanned cautiously and said through clenched teeth, "I think they intended to kill us, reunite those who remained by saying it was safe to return because we were dead, and claim Alpha leadership. Where does such evil come from?"

Turk glared into the tunnel's dark depths. "Was anyone with him?"

Kazeb hugged himself. "No."

"Let's finish before we get any other surprises."

Bodies disposed of, Kazeb wanted to flee the darkness that almost turned into his tomb, but refused to allow fear to overcome common sense. He let Turk lead, measured his breaths, and by the time they reached the cavern with its splash of sunlight, had calmed.

Turk said, "Shadows are long outside. We are almost out of time."

As they hurried toward the mouth, Kazeb picked up a feral scent and a subtle change in shadows over the cave's opening as though someone—Mook?—moved across it.

Not Mook. Something worse.

"Turk! Look out!"

A massive tawny cat, its lean muscular body built for stealth and speed, blended perfectly into the gray-brown of the boulders. Its usual strategy would be to drop onto its prey—Turk—dig in with claws as long as a finger while its canines ripped through the neck. It must have known this Upright was not alone, but expected the other—Kazeb—to flee in fear of his life.

The tip of Cat's whiskers came into view and it sprang, fluid and silent, raw instinct driving it, the feral power almost overwhelming. Saliva splashed Kazeb as the beast flew over his head, intent on Turk. Kazeb too reacted on instinct, yanked his cudgel from the pouch on his shoulder and swung, knowing his brother would duck. The fire-hardened wood slammed into Cat's cranium, a bite away from victory. Kazeb's body shuddered from the hit. The predator's howl morphed to a pained cry. Cat tumbled away in a heap of fur and paws, skull smashed.

Turk gawped. "How did you see it?"

"I smelled it."

Turk wobbled to his feet and said, "We each saved the other today," then set about chopping the carcass into portable pieces. They wrapped the pelt, enough for a shirt, to preserve later. No part of the beast who unexpectedly gave its worthy life to the brothers would be wasted. Then, they left, eager for the safety of rock walls and a hearth before daylight expired. They didn't get far when the earth under their feet shook. Boulders tumbled down the hillocks and sloshed water over the shores of a nearby pond.

When it ended, Kazeb said, "This must be what Fierce talked about—the earth shaking beneath his feet."

Turk turned back. "Let's ensure the shaking didn't expose the burial crevasse. The toxins might be lethal to others of our kind."

They needn't have worried. The mouth had collapsed and buried the bodies forever. Neither the poison nor their enemies would cause any more trouble.

The next day, they cleaned the stench of death from their skin and hair with dried berries from a particular bush kept for that purpose. Combined with water, it produced a lather that removed both dirt and odors.

Dead buried, Kazeb still didn't join Fierce. The brothers, as the only remaining Clan members, continued with meaningless but necessary duties, hoping that those who fled would return if they saw normalcy replace chaos. Even if no one rejoined them, they had each other.

Warm air made way for cold. Moon grew and shrank more times than Kazeb had digits. He no longer blamed the Tall Ones for the poison, but couldn't establish the cause.

Kazeb asked Turk if he suspected Druyl or Mook. "They gained from our loss. How did Fierce benefit?"

Turk clung to a fiery anger for the outsiders. "They talked proudly of those who kill for no reason and left the day before the disaster."

The brothers argued. Kazeb wanted to resolve the differences. Turk wanted revenge. Over time, their intractable bond frayed and Kazeb didn't know what to do about it.

"They will return," Kazeb promised. "And we'll ask."

Part 2

The People, the Chosen, the One—a New Homebase

Chapter 6

6 months before arrival at Big Rock

Thunderous rain drowned out any sound outside save the crashing channel breakers. Yu'ung drank deeply from the water gushing over the cave's mouth, then curled in a fetal position by the cave's mouth and stilled, senses alert. Her ears twitched to whispers around her, the shuffle of guards as they traded duties, the rattle of an elder's sleep. Fat drops bounced with noisy plops, collecting into puddles that would hydrate the group when the rain stopped. Shanadar slept with his Canis pack Ump, White Streak, Ragged Ear, and Ocha. Recently, that also included the child Xad. They all denned together, shared food, and talked in howls and barks, though Xad less than the others because he was still learning their communications. Xad's obligations included the People, though always behind Shanadar, the one who rescued him.

The One called Shanadar "odd." The People considered him a gift. He had saved Yu'ung's life, guided the People confidently while Yu'ung delivered the elder Old One to the Mountain People's homebase to die, and brought a Canis pack to help the People. Their contribution to the People's safety was impossible to measure.

Shanadar's assistance was not altruistic, though. Xhosa, the visionary female he and Yu'ung both talked to in dreams, insisted. She had promised that guiding the People during Yu'ung's absence would take him where he must go.

Laak woke Yu'ung with a shout as he left on patrol with the Chosen. She was Alpha, must always know where her scouts and trackers were. The rain had abated, leaving a damp world. Yu'ung sloshed through overflowing puddles to an area set aside for waste, equidistant from the One's camp. Kruutud, Gevol, and those who survived the One's failed attack on Fierce's warriors huddled far from the People, their offers to guard, hunt, and build a new vessel to carry them to their next homebase, continually rejected.

They destroyed Fierce's ship, slaughtered many, and threatened the Chosen and the People without remorse. I don't trust them either.

They called themselves the One because they were a blend of Tall Ones and the People. Fierce called them traitors to be abandoned on one of the shoreless sea islands without means of escape, in that way, neutralizing their potential for future harm.

Yu'ung cast back to a time when the People co-existed with the Mountain People, far away in the cold hills. The last time Mountain exploded in a murderous rage, it destroyed both homebases as well as the resources that supported the tribes. The Mountain People migrated deeper into their beloved hills while the People left to search out a new home. Joining them were the Chosen, sometimes called Tall Ones, now her mother's band, and the stranger Shanadar with his Canis pack.

Since then, Yu'ung had buried her mentor, been captured by and escaped slavers, suffered with the orphaned boy Jvelk, taken in waifs desperate for a new start, and found the future she had given up on. The demands of survival matured her. Under her direction, the People made a deal with the Chosen. They would help build a replacement for the craft destroyed by the One and the Chosen would take the People to what was called the Big Rock.

Did the One delay us to give reinforcements time to reach them? Or to persuade Fierce to teach them to build and sail the magnificent craft demolished in the storm?

She brushed the thoughts away. The reason no longer mattered.

A trill rang through the air.

Not a morning bird. Shanadar plays his bone flute, the song so beautiful, all life stops to listen.

Yu'ung breathed in, tasted the salty air, and welcomed the day. Sun broke through the dreary gray clouds to reveal a wet, sparkling terrain.

Aynoh, Yu'ung's mother and Fierce's pairmate, shouted, "We are harvesting fish."

Ruk, one of the People's youngest, raced around to distribute materials and messages, always cheerfully and without hesitation.

Yu'ung scaled the slippery cliff, Jvelk right behind. They'd spent a lot of time together before Yu'ung reunited with the People. Jvelk claimed Yu'ung and Laak were as close to friends as he had since his father's death. Yu'ung enjoyed the new adult. His life experiences had bestowed upon him wisdom that most didn't attain until much later.

In clear view, farther down the crest, stood the Chosen Bhidid and Braanroorv.

"Anything unusual?" she motioned to them.

No response meant no, so Yu'ung studied the environs. Shallow rivulets of water from last night's rain cut through the ground in a rush to the sea. Ese, B'o's pairmate, blocked the flow so she could collect it before it mixed with the salty sea.

Ruk padded down the spongy shoreline and asked of no one in particular, "Why collect water? The sea overflows with it."

His question, though innocent, set off alarms in her subconscious. She flew forward—

Fierce got there first, closely followed by B'o, and slapped the child's hand away.

"Because this is undrinkable."

The child's mouth formed a circle. "Why?"

Yu'ung stumbled up wheezing as she regained her balance, "Explain … to him."

"Let me do that with a story. My demesne is dotted with lakes. That water, as in your homeland, is fresh and pure. The first time we sailed on the shoreless sea, we assumed it was the same. Everyone sated their thirst with its water. When they grew nauseous, they blamed it on the part of the sea they were in—"

Ruk broke in to share his knowledge. "Like rotten fish or decayed meat we shouldn't eat."

He nodded. "Like that. They rowed to another part of the sea where they thought the water tasted better, but then vomited, and something behind their eyes drove spikes through their foreheads. Again, the sailors failed to connect the illness to the water and guzzled handfuls to settle queasy stomachs.

"The youngest passed out and all knew something was wrong. They hurried back to shore where the healer said the lake was tainted. They were lucky to be alive."

Fierce crunched a shell open and swallowed the meat inside.

"Ruk!" Jhat's voice stern. "Come!"

The boy waved his arms in imitation of his pack mates' exuberant tails and raced toward his mother.

As Ruk rejoined Jhat, B'o muttered to the tight group around him, "I am suspicious of Kruutud and Gevol. Gevol speaks only what Kruutud thinks."

Fierce growled, "The Canis don't trust them either."

Yu'ung dug her toes into the sand. "Why?"

B'o bit into a small shell the size of a snail and swallowed. "Their words say different from their bodies."

A stress crease appeared between Fierce's brows as he rose. *When did he last sleep?*

"We'll be here for a while to build the new boats. No one must become complacent."

"Boats?"

The stress crease grew. He rubbed his eyes, red from staring into the night's darkness. "We won't all fit in one," and left with no additional explanation.

Yu'ung warmed her hands over the fire, listening to the People as they ate. Laak and Jvelk, the newest adults, took a bag of heated stew to Eknilk and Bhidid on overwatch. Grub, dark scrutiny on the One, chewed through a shell to the soft meat inside, but didn't seem to taste it. Across the clearing, Gevol and Kruutud tilted together, lips moving in quiet murmurs. The lone female, Asvulk, placed a handful of roots on a rock to cook, then crouched by the fire as she repaired a hole in her wrap. The meal would be meager, taking no advantage of the inherent wealth that surrounded them, but no one offered more.

Grub spoke between chews. "They are too few to be a concern."

Fierce asked, "Have the scouts found any trace besides this tribe?"

"Nothing. No trails, no old sites. Kruutud threw his best at us. He has no choice but to behave until we reach his destination. The question is, will supporters there cause us problems?"

"If there are any."

Grub huffed. "If that."

Fierce grabbed a steaming piece of white flesh, strode adjacent to the One, and announced, "Anyone interested in the migration plans may follow me."

Chosen and People not on overwatch, with Ocha and her pack, scrambled after him. The Ones glared at the approaching crowd. Kruutud muttered quietly to Gevol, words that brought a smirk to the new Lead's lips.

Fierce tossed Asvulk the fragrant flesh. "Here. You didn't destroy our vessel or try to kill us."

Asvulk deftly snagged it out of the air, not bothering to cover her surprise. Every One tracked Fierce as he strode by, eyes haunted, biding their time until he passed out of sight.

Their motives were transparent.

Fierce barked without making eye contact with anyone, "No boat space will be provided for any who take her food," and trotted toward a bluff with a view of the demolished craft, the distant expanse of shore, and the endless length of the shoreless sea.

Kruutud shouted, "I should come with you, Leader, to provide the One's input."

"I will be sharing duties for the upcoming trip with those Chosen and People involved in preparations and sailing. None of them will include the One so your input is not necessary, nor is it welcome. You may listen, nothing more."

Fierce mounted the hill's steep sides, joined at the top by Yu'ung, B'o, and the rest of the People, the Chosen, and the pack. Kruutud staggered into position beside the Chosen Leader, wheezing from the steep climb. Fierce ignored him. Yu'ung felt something like pride rise within herself for this tall, determined male, formerly an enemy, now pairmate of her mother.

Gevol huffed to Kruutud's side equally winded, and crouched, arms over his knees, fingers picking at the stubbly grass. Churlish grimaces stretched over both their lips. As the balance of the One panted onto the clearing, sweating in the cool breeze, they saw what their Leader Kruutud undoubtedly planned, him beside Fierce as though united in their command.

Yu'ung ran a hand over her mouth. B'o didn't bother to hide his smile.

They failed to wrest control last night and expect to remedy that with new tricks. They don't know they play right into Fierce's hand.

Behind Yu'ung, Asvulk scurried to stand with Ese, B'o's pairmate. As a proven friend, the People made room for her.

Fierce wasted no time establishing dominance. "Suggestions for the fastest way to proceed."

Kruutud blurted out, "I think–" but Fierce stopped him.

"We don't care what you think. You have tried too often to kill us and couched excuses in lies. Listen. Quietly."

Kruutud slammed his mouth shut as Ump growled.

As Fierce described the necessary details, Laak spoke in muted tones to Yu'ung, "I suggested exiling the One—not Asvulk—but Fierce reminded me it is better to keep them where we can see them."

Since Laak's original poorly engineered attack on Fierce at the People's former homebase, Laak spent as much time as possible with the Chosen Leader. Fierce had spared the subadult's life because he saw in him a fearlessness that would serve the People. Events culminating in this migration meant their time as apex predators was past.

Kruutud squirmed and Gevol growled, but neither argued with Fierce.

B'o said, "We found no enemy sign directly outside, but they could be farther away."

Kruutud sputtered, "I can address that—"

"Without lies?" Fierce, B'o, and Yu'ung asked together. "I doubt it."

Shanadar's ears pinned back and his nostrils flared.

Like Ocha when she senses danger.

Fierce spoke directly to Kruutud, cutting off whatever stammered response he was about to make. "The Canis will collect your tribe's scent and then search the surroundings. Any hidden One will be dealt with, as will you for concealing them."

Shanadar, Ump, Ragged Ear, White Streak, and Ocha wandered through the disheveled scattering of Ones. Most stunk of desperation, their wan faces reflecting doubt for their ill-fated choice to aid Kruutud, but also an obstinacy that prevented them from admitting the mistake. Neither the People nor the Chosen offered sympathy or empathy. If anything, it was impatience that a group could be so foolhardy as to follow one so ill-advised.

It came to a head when Ragged Ear growled and Gevol growled back. The One warriors took that as a signal to rise in revolt. The Canis as a pack yowled and charged. Ragged Ear started with Gevol, smashed into him, sending him onto his back before he could get his arms up to defend. Gevol screeched, tried to kick, which made Ragged

Ear chew on his ankle. Ump bit through the arm of one, then knocked another down and slobbered over his face and throat. White Streak chased a shrieking male off the edge of the cliff. All Ocha had to do was raise her lips. Her victim fell, howling, and crab-walked backward through a nettle bush.

Gevol paled at the bedlam. Sweat prickled his hairline as he squeaked, "Stop them!"

Shanadar whistled and the pack returned to his side. He stared at Gevol, then Kruutud, until both cowered. "The stench of evil drenches your wraps, your skin and hair, as it does those around you."

He bent to the Canis, scratched between their ears, purring soothing assurances in Canis.

Fierce explained, "You threatened their pack. The only reason you live is because Shanadar stopped them, but he won't do it again, not if you work against us."

Shanadar added, "To be clear, the Canis make their own decisions. I don't control them."

Fierce addressed the traumatized One assemblage. "Where are the rest of the One?"

He got exaggerated headshakes, some with tears. Most trembled uncontrollably. Asvulk approached and was greeted by the Canis with flat ears and thumping tails.

She spoke quietly. "They're right, Fierce. The ones you seek are either dead or safely arrived at an island somewhere in the shoreless sea."

Fierce thanked her, but still, Yu'ung could tell something made him uncomfortable. When Shanadar headed out with his clawed-and-tailed team, Fierce joined him. Xad scampered after them, but Shanadar waved him away.

"Practice the flute, Xad. The time will come you'll be the one to play it."

Chapter 7

Everyone drifted to their respective hearths. The One muttered among themselves, distraught by what they witnessed. Kruutud murmured to Gevol, almost certainly weighing the chance of success against such proven feral adversaries. At Yu'ung's scrutiny, his eyes flattened, but not fast enough to trick her.

They call us Primitives, think Fierce aligning with us makes him vulnerable. They'll find out how wrong they are on both.

Kruutud raised the corners of his mouth, but any friendliness he intended fell away as Yu'ung adjusted her cudgel. She told him without words that he had met his match, and strode to Aynoh who crouched with B'o, conferring. Her mother was now an Elder of the combined tribe, considered a Lead by the Chosen. Most achieved that status by outliving their peers. Aynoh had, too, but by attrition, thanks to a difficult migration.

Once inferior because of red hair, now she is called wise.

"Do you have enough healing plants?"

Aynoh massaged her neck. "B'o and I were discussing that. I don't, but Asvulk knows where to find them. Fierce will send Braanroorv and Grub with her, with Wik who wishes to learn more about healing. When he and Shanadar return."

Aynoh scanned everywhere and nowhere, searching in silence.

Yu'ung prodded, "But you worry about the One…."

"None are trouble except Kruutud and Gevol. I worry about Asvulk's safety."

"She told you something?"

Aynoh grimaced. "She didn't need to."

Yu'ung watched Asvulk poke at the One fire, her eyes dull, hair matted and tangled. She scratched constantly because—Yu'ung assumed—she hadn't been groomed in too long. The wood she'd tossed into the flames was green. Surely Asvulk knew, so she didn't care, nor did Kruutud who paid her no attention. No one offered to collect dry tinder.

Aynoh continued, "Kruutud killed her pairmate when he slaughtered her tribe. She agreed to be his pairmate to protect her child."

Yu'ung stiffened. "A child? Where?"

Lines formed beside Aynoh's mouth. "She hasn't said."

"On the island with the others who left? Is that why she supports Kruutud?"

Aynoh stuffed herbs into her shoulder sack, the few left from treatments today. "Maybe. She does support his goal of reaching the island, though I sense not for his reasons. I think she has tired of being dominated. I can't see her allowing herself to be stuck in an isolated location at his mercy."

"She can stay with us."

"Ese offered, but she refuses."

Yu'ung had no response to that. Why would Asvulk refuse? A memory nibbled, Yu'ung and Jvelk captured by slavers. Yu'ung could have escaped, but didn't because there was more in play than just her life and Jvelk's.

Is that what's going on?

Something was off. The Asvulk she watched stabbing at the hearth didn't look beaten down or defeated, like a female at the whim of a brutal male who destroyed everything important to her. No. More like she was *pretending* to be, as Yu'ung had when she allowed ruthless kidnappers to treat her viciously, cowered at their supremacy, knowing she had a plan.

We let this play out.

B'o scrunched a brow, continuing whatever he'd been saying that Yu'ung missed, "They are labor only. They must depend upon us for all basics until we rid ourselves of them."

"Between the boats and shore is where you believe an attack will come if there is one."

"We will be ready."

Aynoh plucked a bug off B'o's shirt and popped it in her mouth. B'o returned the favor and began to pick tiny critters and debris from her hair and wraps. Yu'ung's hackles rose and she turned to the One. Kruutud was scowling at B'o's interplay with Aynoh.

Have you ever groomed Asvulk? Surely not since I've known her.

B'o turned to Kruutud and asked, "See something frightening, Kruutud?" his voice impassive. "You should."

Kruutud's jaw tightened, about to speak, but didn't.

Yu'ung mumbled to B'o, "They're planning something, in Fierce's absence."

Ocha padded over, eyes aimed at the one she determined an enemy of the pack. A quiet growl rolled from her muzzle. Her hackles popped up the same time the hair on Yu'ung's neck prickled.

I sense it too, Ocha.

Footsteps crashed. None of the One had moved but all looked expectant, and too happy. She and B'o jerked toward the sound, weapons tight in their fists. Instead of unknown One attackers, Fierce sprinted into the camp followed closely by Ragged Ear. Sweat sheathed his chest and he heaved as though near collapse.

He slowed to a stop and scanned the entourage. "Is everything all right? Shanadar warned of a problem here."

Yu'ung screamed, "Fierce! Behind you!"

He pivoted as Gevol cocked his weapon, fixed on Fierce, body tense with purpose.

Fierce roared, "You're a fool, Gevol! Kruutud will get you killed!"

"Not this time!"

A blur flashed past, and Ocha smashed into his chest. Gevol howled and crumpled to the ground, his injured ankle giving out. Kruutud cocked his lance, but not to defend Gevol. It was aimed at Fierce.

Gevol was a distraction!

Nothing distracted Fierce, though. His thin stone-tipped lance pierced Kruutud's shoulder as Yu'ung impaled another attacker. Gevol howled, which made Ocha angrier, and she tore into his dominant arm, assuring that limb would never again threaten anyone. Satisfied, she trotted back to Yu'ung.

Gevol wrapped a huge hand around the gushing wound, muscle ripped, one tendon dangling, bone exposed. Yu'ung observed without emotion.

Old One adapted to similar physical challenges, but she doubted Gevol would.

Fierce shouted, "Everyone, drop your weapons!"

Yu'ung's heart pounded as energy swamped her. Shirt damp with sweat, the world narrowed and she prepared for more violence. The buzz of insects fell away. The One's fouled wraps, now stinking of feces and fear, blocked all other odors, but not for long. She tossed her remaining shaft from fist to fist, eyes like hot coals, searching. The remaining Ones dropped their lances as though burned.

Except one. *Always, someone has to be a hero.*

Not today. Ragged Ear's massive form, bigger than most of his kind, leapt on the would-be hero, dragged him to his knees, and clamped a mighty jaw on his throat. His panicked shriek gurgled into silence as Ragged Ear shook him until satisfied the predator had been neutralized. Ragged Ear released the motionless prey, blood and tissue thick on his fangs and muzzle. Frightened voices murmured, angry at

Kruutud who cradled his bloody shoulder and Gevol, clutching his destroyed arm.

Yu'ung spoke with enough volume that all could hear, "Are you done, Kruutud? I have one more lance."

B'o muttered, "I must learn the far-throwing spear."

To Yu'ung's surprise, Kruutud grinned as though he had won. Fierce snapped his bowed spear from his back and shot. A slender fire-hardened twig sizzled through Kruutud's wrap. Fear flooded Kruutud's face when Fierce nocked another.

Kruutud whined, "You killed my tribe member," to which Fierce responded, "And you cost your band their weapons. Toss them forward."

Kruutud shook. Behind him, Gevol staggered in place, expression dark with anger, blood still dripping down his arm off his fingertips. Ump and White Streak flew in from wherever they'd been, huffed their disappointment to see the emergency over. White Streak flopped down with a moan, hackles up, tail swaying through the stubby grass, blue eyes fixed on Ump as he padded to Kruutud. He growled and snapped loudly to be sure the enemy understood, and left the way he came.

Kruutud yanked the twig from his shoulder, wincing at the sucking sound as it pulled free of his flesh, and spoke with false obeisance, "You win. Leave us sufficient supplies—and arms—to defend against predators and we'll leave."

Fierce bored into the One Leader, took his time before responding with a slow movement of his head. "My next arrow enters your throat."

"I said we capitulate!"

"Toss over your weapons or we take them."

"Who will protect us if attacked?" slipping anger into his words.

Wik tossed Kruutud a chopper. "This is all we need."

Ocha and White Streak lapped at Gevol's blood, now a puddle at his feet while Ese retrieved the One weapons.

"We now have plenty for our lessons."

Fierce spoke quietly to Grub. "Teach as quickly as possible. I know Kruutud well enough not to trust him."

Yung grumbled through gritted teeth, "They underestimate us for the last time."

B'o grunted a guttural sound of controlled rage.

"And us," came the voices of Grub, Bhidid, Eknilk, and Braanroorv.

Fierce drew a settling breath. His skin was etched with the scars that proved to all he feared no confrontation. Shanadar's musical tones floated through the air, though no one knew from where.

Fierce marched to Aynoh's side. She stopped what he was about to say. "Asvulk and I will treat them."

She would always save a life, even a treacherous one. Grub told Yu'ung how Qad had kidnapped her mother. He suffered a mortal wound during the rescue, but Aynoh stayed with him until he died.

Yu'ung studied Kruutud. Wounded, without armaments, a dead member heaped not far from his feet, still neither the One Leader nor his Lead showed any sign that the defeat weakened them. In fact, Yu'ung thought it emboldened them.

Aynoh whispered to her, "As Asvulk and I treat them, we'll listen. The departure, the strategy—someone will talk."

"Those who landed on the island assume Kruutud will come for them."

"Someone will come."

"Where Fierce thinks they landed offers many oversight locations near the shoreline. They'll be prepared this time to defend."

"But they are your kind. Why fight you?"

Fierce said, "Because Kruutud will lie to them." He clutched his bowed spear, knuckles white with the effort. "At home, I'll tell all that the People are peaceful."

"Tell them we don't wish to fight, but will protect ourselves."

Chapter 8

With White Streak, Aynoh strode toward Asvulk, satchel stuffed with treatments. Kruutud fixed dark eyes on her. Aynoh ignored him and his damaged shoulder, but withdrew stones from her satchel. She was lethal with those, more than anyone expected. White Streak bared her fangs. Kruutud shrank, eyes ringed white around black, and approached, arms wrapped around himself.

"You may pass, but because of what the predator did to Gevol and me—and others—he may not."

Aynoh paid him no attention. "Asvulk! I'll help with the wounded, from earlier and today," spoken with the People's words.

"Did you hear me?" Kruutud's voice was petulant.

Aynoh sneered. "You stop her," and she elbowed past.

White Streak snarled, this time spattering saliva on Kruutud.

"One time," he spat, and leapt back as White Streak nipped his arm, leaving a thin crimson scrape on his skin.

Aynoh tossed him a moss pad. "Press this against the scratch until the blood stops. It might help the shoulder, also. Asvulk will treat you after we care for the serious injuries."

She strode forward, unconcerned about an attack with White Streak backing her steps.

Woof!

And White Streak's mate, Ragged Ear.

Asvulk hid a giggle with a cough and then said, "Captivity with you would have been different."

Life with the One is captivity.

Asvulk gave Aynoh no time to ask about her cryptic comment.

Voice flat, but loud enough so Kruutud could hear, she said, "I welcome your knowledge and the friendship of White Streak and Ragged Ear."

They moved from one injured to another, loaded punctures with honey, slathered on mulches to stop poison, and glued gashes with bark paste. Aynoh offered commentary on treatments, always in People's words.

Aynoh gestured to the scattered dead from the earlier attack, the stench of decay heavy in the air.

"Let's take care of these before you deal with Kruutud's injury," and headed toward the bodies.

The corpses, pale and cool, purple where blood had settled, had softened from the loss of liquid and rigor, already bloating in the sun. Mouths gaped open and black tongues protruded. Cloudy eyes bulged from gray sockets. Aynoh inhaled through her damp shirt, sweet dirt replacing putrid rot. The drone of death flies increased as they approached the bodies. Tiny white eggs were sprinkled in the gashes, many already hatching.

The People placed the dead in crevasses to prevent illnesses they carried from transferring to the living and to keep scavengers away from the tribe. The Chosen shared the worry but had a different solution, one Aynoh experienced when they disposed of Qad. She wanted to honor the One customs if possible.

"The Chosen leave a weapon to assist the fallen wherever they go in death. Does the One do that?"

Asvulk slid to Kruutud's side. The words muddled, but his actions needed little explanation. Asvulk returned to Aynoh, flushed.

"Kruutud told me to let them rot because they failed him. I reminded him that we will live here until the new boat is built, which brought the reaction you saw."

Nothing.

"They are your community—"

"Not mine," she spat out. "But we will bury them as the People."

They found a fissure distant enough that the smell of putrefaction wouldn't swamp them, one so deep, only rats could reach the bodies, and then probably couldn't get out. They stripped the corpses of usable wraps and foot shields and tossed them over the edge. Then, they sat under the spreading limbs of a tree, drank from a vine Aynoh had brought, and relaxed.

"Aynoh. I scavenge, prepare meals, mend clothes, sew new wraps if pelts are available, and sharpen tools, but to Kruutud, I have no merit because I have yet to carry a child. You are a valued Elder and Healer, mother to Alpha Yu'ung. Tell me. Am I worthless?"

Aynoh answered gently, eyes damp. "Fierce's patience with Kruutud, Asvulk, comes from his respect for you. I see no children here. Where are those I saw with you earlier, when you fled the earth breaking?"

"Escaped, with parents, as I should have."

"You told me you bore a child. Is that where your child is, with these others? Somewhere safe?"

Asvulk's face crumpled and tears glistened on her cheeks. Fists clenched, she inhaled and stared at nothing.

"My child was kind, smart, cheerful despite Kruutud. Kruutud couldn't bow his spirit so he killed him, insisting we have our own. I refused though he doesn't know that."

"You weren't afraid he would kill you as he did your pairmate?"

Asvulk's shoulders shook. "The way sleep beckons at the end of a long day, so too is death appealing in place of this life, Aynoh."

Aynoh ached for Asvulk's pain. Aynoh, too, lost a partner, a Primitive who rescued Aynoh from sure death. They built a good life together in his Kith—what he called a tribe—but he died on the horns of a stampeding mammoth and his kin forced her to leave. With a child she must provide for and nowhere to go, she returned to the People where her father, Old One, was the Elder, to be again Dhar's pairmate. Yu'ung and Old One made every day worth it.

"Dhar terrorized Yu'ung in ways he shouldn't have as she grew up. It became clear no child of mine would be safe in his nest, so I took care of that in ways a healer knows. I don't know how you prevented a baby, but you did the right thing."

Asvulk's back straightened and her eyes sparkled for the first time since Aynoh had known her. "My tribe's healer was a friend."

Aynoh regarded those One squatted around the hearth, bodies tense, skin marred with white streaks from poorly treated wounds.

"Asvulk. How big a problem is Kruutud?"

"These with him are the worst of his original contingent. Tell Fierce to stay sharp. Under no circumstances should he believe any words from Kruutud. He terrorized my Clan, saying he would be fair and reasonable if we capitulated. Instead, he slaughtered us." She gulped, eyes seeing something Aynoh hoped she never would. "We should have fought."

"What was their boat like? The one that took some in search of an island?"

"A smaller vessel than yours, more inclined to float with the current than be guided, but those aboard were selected for skills at navigating and establishing a homebase. If any can make it, they did. Those Kruutud called warriors remained here to defray problems with natives."

The children's joy provided a pleasant background as they trapped fish for the meal. Asvulk fingered a collection of colored pebbles, teeth, and small feathers around her neck.

"My pairmate wore this every day. Now I do."

A shrill wind whipped through the air, scattering Aynoh's profuse mane. She knotted it into a tail and then touched her own necklace.

"Mine is from Fierce. It signifies to all that I am Chosen."

"It is like the one Yu'ung wears."

Aynoh studied the female with the weight of her tribe's destiny on her shoulders, not unlike Yu'ung though they fought different battles.

Her visage softened. "She wore mine when we separated early in our migration, as a reminder, and created a matched necklace for herself, knowing we would reconnect."

"Why hasn't she pairmated?"

"In the past, opportunities presented themselves. As Alpha, she avoids it and others avoid us."

Asvulk offered a wan smile. "Because the People are led by a female."

"A pairmate must become one of the People, which they won't. So far."

"Is she competent?"

"Stellar. The best in my lifetime. She feels her duties supersede those of pairmate and parent."

"She is young, doesn't yet know the pain of no pairmate or child. For me, each day with these One is worse than the last."

"How have you managed?"

Tears dampened Asvulk's cheeks and her features hardened. "At first, I buried the memories. Now I plan my revenge."

Aynoh exhaled. "Asvulk. How many who left are loyal to Kruutud?"

"None. As I said, they're artisans, not combatants. They won't welcome strangers. Kruutud thinks he will use that to turn them against you, to side with the One they know, but I think they—we—will do what we should have long ago."

She gave Aynoh a sidelong glance. "And you won't be strangers. I'll be with you."

Asvulk is brilliant!

Treatments completed, the dead stowed, Aynoh offered Asvulk a final gift.

"You have a healer's instinct. Your tribe—and Kruutud's—will quickly realize they die without your skill. You will no longer be forced to suffer his ire. If he doesn't understand that, follow the coast to what I am told is a monstrous rock that fills the horizon. We will be there and welcome you."

Asvulk lifted her head, a beatific smile on her lips. "Oh no. I must conclude my primary purpose. It is why I endure all that the One has inflicted on me. I thank you for the strength you give me."

Aynoh and Asvulk returned to the One camp, tucked in amongst the males, White Streak and Ragged Ear with them. While pounding tough stems, heating roots over the fire, preparing stew for an evening meal the One rarely enjoyed anymore, the females listened to the conversations of those who considered them too dull-witted to understand the meaning.

The One will take credit for the rescue, declare Fierce the enemy, and with the help of those stranded on the island, kill the real saviors.

Aynoh touched Asvulk in farewell and started toward her site. Within steps, the hairs on her neck stiffened and bristled and Ragged Ear released a low growl echoed by White Streak. Behind her, wood brushed hide. She twisted and wasn't fooled by Kruutud's grin. Ragged Ear and White Streak spun toward the enemy, but Shanadar had already grabbed Kruutud's arm, his grip so powerful, Kruutud dropped his shaft.

He stared wide-eyed at Shanadar. "I didn't see you … anywhere …."

"I am always where needed."

"Release my arm!"

Instead, Shanadar wrenched it. "What happens next depends upon what you do. Neither you nor I can stop it."

His tone carried no menace, simply caution.

"Your beast almost killed me. He must be stopped."

"As I said before, he is not 'mine,' but happily for you, he listened when I asked him to delay your atonement. It is not the time yet for you to die. That will come soon if you don't change."

Fierce barreled up to Kruutud, his face hard. "You agreed to turn over weapons!"

He snatched the lance and snapped it into pieces with one hand, flung the bits into the fire, and motioned the pack to search the Ones. Kruutud growled with each weapon discovered and finally left. Aynoh shouted to Asvulk and rejoined the People as Fierce made his way back.

Shanadar arrived. "These One belonged to a large group," bobbing his head in agreement with himself, the knot of hair behind his neck bouncing like Ocha's tail.

Aynoh thinned her lips. "As Asvulk told me."

Fierce asked Shanadar, "How do you know?'

"I found detritus of kills, enough to feed many over a long period."

Fierce watched Kruutud who watched them, seeming to know they had discovered his secret.

"Is it where those who attacked us stayed?"

"Some trace is old, probably from the now-dead attackers. More from those who left. All tracks lead here."

Fierce thought about this. "The One don't eat the soft white sea meat. It seems they always intended to steal what food and supplies they needed from natives, as they did with Asvulk's tribe." His scrutiny flattened. "This is not why Seer sent them here. Kruutud abandoned his duties, betrayed our kind. I will not allow that to stand."

Shanadar said, "I don't understand."

Fierce stiffened. "Kruutud used Mountain's anger to pretend compliance with Seer's orders, but his real goal is power and dominance. Nothing else explains what he has done. If he required another boat, Seer would supply it, but if he described Mountain's devastation, the deaths, and the consummate destruction, Seer would discontinue our interest in this land. Seer's purpose is not to conquer but explore. Kruutud couldn't return to our home without a plausible solution that allowed him to remain here. He decided to wait out Mountain's anger on an island beyond its reach, return to our homeland when the threat had ended and not reveal what happened here, just that he needed new supplies and warriors. The arrival of my Chosen with tales of Big Rock and plans to build a vessel became a better solution."

Yu'ung said, "But it isn't working as he'd hoped."

"Because he found out why I am here. Seer sent me to find the other explorers, ensure they were following instructions. In all we did, Seer counseled me to trust my instinct, make good decisions, and avoid violence against the natives."

Aynoh said, "Kruutud calls you explorers."

"He expected that to mean weak, but he couldn't defeat us as he did Asvulk's tribe. He'll try to ingratiate himself with you, Aynoh, and Yu'ung."

Yu'ung snorted. "His body speaks louder than his words. It never lies, and now, screams danger, to stay away." A snore at her side reminded her of Ocha's presence. "As do the Canis."

"Kruutud convinced the new arrivals to the One band that you beat him only because you surprised him." Aynoh described what she and Asvulk heard around the hearth fire. "They will try to take over when the vessel is rebuilt. Until then, she says to never trust him. Kruutud will take any opportunity to further his goals, regardless of who is hurt."

Grub beamed as he chewed another mouthful of a raw duck leg. "Tell her we love to fight. Nothing would make us happier."

Yu'ung tightened her mouth, raised her brows, and blinked. "Can they swim?"

Chapter 9

Kruutud's shuffled arrival delayed a reply. His arms hung loosely at his sides. He forced a smile across his lips, the look of one who feigned defenselessness. Yu'ung saw it among those ingratiating themselves to Dhar when he was the People's Alpha.

She chuckled. *All see his weakness!*

Kruutud's warriors fanned out around him, cautious of the Chosen fighters but disdainful of the so-called Primitives, Jvelk and Laak, who purposely slouched in their positions, adopting the lazy attitude of bored subadults. They were so convincing that all the One warriors moved on with nothing more than a glance, missing the far-throwing spears each carried in hands thickened by practice, wrist cords bulging like tree roots, the confidence radiating from their unlined faces. Jvelk's Tall One father taught him skills he honed with Laak until the youngsters became the People's secret weapons, more surreptitious than the Canis, to be unleashed when least expected with devastating effect.

As anticipated, today, the youths were dismissed as inconsequential.

Another mistake that will secure Kruutud's defeat.

The other highly effective weapon in Fierce's arsenal was the Canis pack, this one no secret. All had seen or heard of their ruthless attacks, so when Ump slunk forward, hackles stiff, blue eyes focused on Kruutud, not a male among the One didn't take him seriously, including the Leader. The color drained from his face and his words tumbled out as he careened through a poorly thought out explanation.

"You and I, Fierce," his voice graveled with dread, "were the best."

Fierce cringed.

Kruutud hurtled on. "You risked your life to save mine, long ago. I owe you! How do we re-establish the trust once so easy for us?"

"We can't."

Fierce had told Yu'ung the story to explain the culture of his kind. Where most predators marked territory with urine, the Chosen did so with blood. Bands fought to the death over too few resources. Kruutud was one of the worst. He claimed any territory, forcing natives to choose between life as slaves or annihilation. Only Fierce was exempt because he matched Kruutud's power. Each allowed the other to live in peace.

But to "live in peace" wasn't in Kruutud's nature. As soon as the warriors reached the agreement, Kruutud set about to find Fierce's weakness. It wasn't hard: morality. Fierce gave his word and believed it inviolate. Kruutud considered it a means to victory. In this case, he warned Fierce of a formidable adversary set to destroy both of them. To stop the enemy would entail their combined strength. Fierce refused to participate, so Kruutud arranged a faux ambush on a tribe that had nothing to do with either Kruutud or Fierce. The purpose was to draw Fierce into a defense of the innocent.

It worked. Fierce and Kruutud partnered, fought the supposed enemy of both their tribes. Much later, word reached Fierce through a reliable friend that Kruutud had staged the attack. The experience made Fierce doubt his own instincts and he accepted Seer's offer to explore distant terrains. He didn't know Kruutud had been sent much earlier to explore, never returned, and was considered lost, until he ran into him.

"Kruutud turned my honesty against me once. I won't fall for the same trick."

A harsh wind roared off the frigid sea and thrashed the adjacent brush. Its force bent trees, whipped the bare branches like angry lashes, and slashed anyone within range. The chill ate through wraps no matter how securely the seams were sewn until joints ached and breathing seared the lungs. Only the Canis didn't suffer, protected by overlapping layers of fur. Shanadar should have been cold, standing in the open, one layer of wrap over his undernourished body, but he long ago adopted his pack's attitude of ignoring what he couldn't affect. Kruutud tugged his shirt more tightly around his torso as he waited for Fierce's response. Yu'ung could see his thoughts. If this didn't stop the only one who could ruin his plans, Kruutud would devise another hoax.

Yu'ung silently cheered as Fierce crushed Kruutud's hopes, or at least, crippled them. "You taught me the importance of relationships. Nothing I see says you changed."

Kruutud jerked. "I have—"

"You haven't. You are unable to be fair to friend or foe or even see the difference."

He waved an arm through the air. Grub, Eknilk, and Braanroorv trotted over, lances in both hands, cudgels and bowed spears on their backs. Lips blue, bristling with energy, skin vibrant with health. The Ones with them were empty-handed, shirts tattered. Their gaunt forms shook with cold and hunger. Brave words aside, their eyes were worried, faces bleak, which told Yu'ung their primary defense was Kruutud's bravado and even they could see that crumbling.

I see what Fierce is doing. Remove the fake aura of strength Kruutud assembled and his tribe will turn on him.

Fierce studied Kruutud under hooded eyes. "The battle has yet to start and you are already defeated. You wasted your one chance. Leave."

Kruutud's jaw tightened and his dark skin paled. He wrenched Asvulk to his side as a shield, as though that would change Fierce's mind. Yu'ung flinched. Fierce yawned.

Kruutud grinned at Yu'ung's reaction and directed his next to her. "We have nowhere to go. Asvulk will die."

She flattened her voice. "You understand so little, false Leader."

Fierce crouched by the hearth and popped a sizzling meat chunk into his mouth. "Leave with your group. Asvulk stays."

The One as a group gawked at the steamy chunk of flesh and Fierce's glistening digits dripping with fat. He scanned the clearing under lidded eyes and swiped away the juice that spotted his chin, its succulence a call to everyone it was time to eat. All the One drooled except Asvulk. Kruutud chuckled at the twinkle in her eye.

"My dutiful pairmate," he said, misinterpreting her reaction.

Ump snarled, as did Ragged Ear. Kruutud swallowed, throat bobbing. "Where you and I live, Fierce, you did the same as us when faced with enemies."

Yu'ung clenched her fists and scowled. Did Kruutud think any would find truth in his words?

Fierce's response echoed hers. "You tried to convince others. No one believed it then and won't now."

"Then you changed!"

Fierce helped the toddler, Ruk, pour stew into a gourd, reminded him to let the liquid cool or burn his mouth. Then the child scurried up to the overwatch where the scouts awaited.

Fierce pawed through the pile of weaponry taken from the One. "Your tips are dull, Kruutud, shafts rough. You are weak! Any of our kind can build a water-safe craft, but you can't."

"How can we without our weapons? And what risk are we disarmed? Let us help you rebuild your vessel."

Fierce arched a heavy brow. "Describe the process."

Kruutud's chin raised. "Strap logs together with cordage and guide them with paddles."

Yu'ung snorted. "That's what you sailed over the horizon? My People built similar platforms that soon fell apart under the violence of the sea."

Kruutud flushed red. "We wish to assist Fierce, offset the … damage … caused by our ... mistakes."

He clutched Asvulk tighter to his side, bruises already dimpling her skin where his fingers pressed, spoke in hushed tones to Gevol positioned behind his shoulder, weight on his good ankle. The wind's howl drowned out his words, but Asvulk slyly leaned into the conversation. He didn't notice, or if he did, didn't feel the threat. As they murmured to each other, Ump intermittently licked Asvulk's hand and snarled at Gevol. The Lead glared at him.

"Stay away!" he shrieked, voice edged with panic, brandishing the palm-sized stone Ese had tossed to him with his uninjured arm.

Ump snatched it from his finger, as well as the tip of the digit. Because of his bad ankle, he toppled over, fell on the wrecked arm and squealed a high-pitched, fear-soaked wail. Ump nipped the wrap on his chewed foot and then breathed wet, noisy pants in Gevol's face. No one tried to help. Ump and White Streak padded away, a final warning snarled over their shoulders.

Wind shrieked across the shore, and sent the sand swirling in cyclones. Fierce squelched a grin. "Your intentions are clear even to the pack."

Gevol pressed his bleeding hand to his stomach. Face pale, dimpled with sweat, he made no effort to help his Leader. Kruutud raised his fist to Asvulk, but dropped it, and with it, his anger.

"I give up," Kruutud murmured. "All we want is to help our missing tribe members."

Fierce asked everyone without words. No one objected.

"You get no weapons, no access to our food though there is plenty in the sea. We will deliver you to the island where we believe your members landed. What you do next is up to you."

Kruutud pawed with his foot. "We need blood meat, not the white flesh."

"Of course. Throw stones at birds or animals. Surely you know how." He started to turn away, and then added, "Or make new lances. I won't stop you."

Ruk had returned from his chore and took Kruutud's confusion at that statement in true youngster fashion. "I can help if Fierce allows it. I will cut branches, smooth the bark. Glue stone tips in place. I've made many—"

Fierce interrupted. "Ruk won't help you, but he's made his point. The youngest among us can do this. So if your decision is to remain here, replace your tools. I won't stop you."

Kruutud dragged his foot through the dirt, crossed his arms and uncrossed them, eyes slit at being upstaged by a child.

Fierce said, "If you become a nuisance, we abandon you. You aren't vital to any part of our journey. In fact, you are in the way."

Kruutud drew himself to his fullest height and sucked in a breath between gritted teeth. "You have my word. Teach us to build a vessel, sail it, skills we will need in our new home, and we will behave."

Fierce leveled him with an icy stare. "You misunderstand. Again. Purposely, I suspect. You will do only ancillary tasks like collecting vines, stripping bark for glue, and gathering beeswax. We do the rest."

"Because you don't trust us."

"I *trust* you will again attempt to steal our craft, lie to us, and prevent our progress. This is how we stop you."

Yu'ung spat out, "As will I." Ump and White Streak snarled. "What is your pleasure, Kruutud?"

Kruutud bristled. "Why help us at all?"

"Better to strand you on an island with no means of escape than in a position to stalk our steps."

Kruutud recoiled. "You are unfair."

"You crashed our vessel. Why risk your treachery again? Leave any time—"

"Without weapons!"

"With the weapons you can make. There is plenty of time. The warm air is almost here. Animals have their cold air pelts. Kill them. Turn them into wraps. Prepare for the return of the cold."

Kruutud huffed. "If no one is on one island, you will take us to another?"

Gusts of sand swirled, slung grit and pebbles against exposed skin. Fierce was laughing too hard to notice.

"You get one stop. We don't care if it is inhabited."

Yu'ung leaned into his ear. "Will they follow us later?"

He shook his head. "I have passed the island most likely to be where the One is. It has sufficient vegetation, insects, wildlife, and enough trunks for a raft but not a vessel such as ours."

She grinned.

Dusk settled. Night sounds replaced the day's. Exhausted, all ate hastily and slept deeply.

Except the scouts. They stayed on watch not only to search for danger but to protect against each other.

Chapter 10

Daylight dawned brightly without the hills, cliffs, and forests that blocked Sun in Yu'ung's former mountains. The gusty wind blew itself out overnight and the frigid terrain warmed bit by bit, cold sunbeams sparkling off the crystal sea as the yellow ball made its relentless climb out of the deep well of the night's brutal cold.

Yu'ung added another layer of wraps and joined Fierce, already with Grub, to discuss the upcoming day. The crisp air and clear sky energized her thoughts.

Grub was explaining, "We exhausted our salt supply."

Fierce dismissed the concern, his words a white cloud in front of his lips. "I can fix that while Braanroorv and Bhidid find the makings of a new craft." After a pause, he added, "Take Kruutud to keep him out of my way, and Ump."

The Lead chuckled. "To keep the One in line."

Yu'ung's eyes flashed. "I am eager to see your secret."

Kruutud was sanding a bent branch that would never fly straight no matter how much grit he rubbed over it, but he didn't notice. His purpose wasn't to engineer a useful weapon. It was to spy.

Fierce yelled, "Waste time later, Kruutud. Go with Braanroorv and Bhidid," and then, "Wik! You have overwatch, with B'o!"

Wik rushed up the hill and stretched out prone by B'o, prepared to glean what she could from him. Her pairmate, Grub, had already turned her into an expert marksman with the far-throwing spear. Now, she was absorbing everything B'o could teach her about scouting.

Kruutud trotted toward Fierce. "What are you doing today, Leader Fierce?"

"Replenishing salt supplies."

"I can help. I'd like to learn...."

Fierce stopped him with a smile. "No one cares what you'd like to learn."

Yu'ung giggled when Kruutud said, "Without weapons, we are no danger to you."

Fierce's eyes narrowed. He touched the worthless knob beneath his mouth. "I don't have time for your speculations. We must deliver you to your stranded tribe, the People to a new home, and return to our homebase across the sea before the cold air returns. You do not want to cause our delay."

Where the sea ended, before it merged with what Fierce called the Endless Sea, was the People's destination. Fierce called it a peninsula surrounded by water on all sides, except one, and that a steep uncrossable range. Valleys, relentless hills, boulders, and dense copses had always marked Yu'ung's territory and softened Sun's heat. She couldn't see far unless she climbed to the canopy of the tallest tree. From there, she could check the movement of other tribes, herds, animal families, returning hunters, and the clouds that announced impending storms.

Every coast on the shoreless sea is craggy. Always a hill screens what lies out of sight. A tingle rushed through her. *Fierce assures me Big Rock is nothing like this or my homeland.*

She looked forward to the boundless open space, endless horizon, and high overwatches where no one and nothing could hide.

The command in Fierce's voice broke through. "Take your males, Kruutud. The trunks are heavy."

"Where—"

"With. Bhidid. He will show you the logs we need for the hulls."

"Some are injured. They can't work—"

"They can harvest bark, vines, and sap."

Yu'ung snickered. To ensure that this enemy didn't see how water was turned into salt, Shanadar sat overwatch, prepared to alert Fierce with his flute if any snuck too close.

All left to their work. Kruutud hissed in Asvulk's ear as she crouched over a pile of roots, then he trotted serenely in the direction Bhidid had taken, but stopped. As though confused, he studied the trail, looked around, and scratched his head.

He's pretending he can't find Bhidid.

Proving Yu'ung's observation, Kruutud squatted, pulled out a cobble and a striking stone as though to knap, settling far enough from Asvulk she wouldn't ask his assistance. He needn't have bothered. She ignored him. He wasn't fooling anyone. All knew his real purpose was to spy.

Roots softened, Asvulk pulled a pelt into her lap that Aynoh gave her.

Yu'ung beckoned, "Help us, Asvulk."

A frown drew the corners of Kruutud's mouth down, like a stubborn child who wanted his way.

He scowled. "Asvulk is a Primitive," he said as though chewing a rotten fruit. "She—"

Asvulk interrupted with a smile. "I am coming, Aynoh."

Her confidence has grown since we first met.

Yu'ung slipped between Kruutud and Asvulk. "We ask Asvulk because she *is* a Primitive. Our memories are better."

Fierce said to B'o, "Wik is comfortable on overwatch alone?"

"Her comment as I left was, 'Why am I always the one expected to have a partner?'"

Fierce grunted. "Good. Take your time on this task. Keep them away as long as possible."

B'o shouted to Kruutud, "Since you didn't go with Bhidid, you and Gevol come with me," and sprinted out.

Kruutud shouted that Gevol must protect Asvulk, but B'o snapped, "Ump will do that."

As they departed, Fierce called to Eknilk, "Take whoever remains, including the injured, to collect fish. If there's more time, sap and bark. Don't return until," and indicated a spot in the sky a finger above the horizon.

Eknilk shot a look at the One, the males expectant, accustomed to being told what to do. "They say the slimy squishy flesh weakens them."

"They don't have to eat it."

Eknilk motioned to those crouched, eyes haunted, and bellies grumbling. "Come. Do the work. I'll feed you."

Everyone hustled without question. Kruutud made no effort to disguise his disgust at being ordered around. If not for the desperate circumstances, Yu'ung had no doubt the peevish, self-important imposter would refuse. Today, though, out-manned and out-weaponed, he sensibly pretended commitment.

But you fool no one, Kruutud.

Aynoh beckoned Asvulk. "Come. Help us remove salt from the sea."

Asvulk trotted over. "Wherever we end up, this will be valuable."

Fierce shouted, "Ese. Keep the fire strong! Everyone else, bring an organ sack or gourd to hold water," and he crouched by a shallow spot along the coast to wait.

Yu'ung asked, "Can we drink the liquid?"

"It can be distilled, but there is no need. We have plenty."

When everyone arrived, he said, "Fill the gourds and pouches with the sea water. Place them in the fire by Ese until they bubble."

Ese asked for everyone, "The water becomes salt?"

He grinned. "You'll see."

The water soon boiled and steamed until none remained.

Ese rolled back on her heels. "Now what?"

"Look inside." White crystals sparkled at the bottom. "Taste them." Everyone did.

"Salt!"

The process was repeated again, and again until Ese's salt carrier spilled over. By the time Shanadar announced the return of the cutters and scavengers and sea hunters, all trace of the procedure had been stowed. Kruutud tried to discover the method, but no one involved would talk about it. They stammered mumbles about "you had to be there to believe it." Kruutud yanked Asvulk aside, intending to force her to describe everything. Muscles rippling, she tore her arm away.

"Don't grab me ever again," and she stalked away.

Kruutud had no time for a nasty reply because Laak and Jvelk hurried in. "We bring a treat!"

Their hands were coated in honey, palms overflowing with a well of the sweet nectar.

Jvelk couldn't contain his enthusiasm. "Laak is fearless."

Everyone slurped at the treat while Jvelk described how Laak managed to steal honey from a hive full of bees.

"He hit each trunk we passed with a stick until bees flew out of a hole high above our heads. Laak shimmied up to the hive and snatched every comb he could, but the bees returned faster than he anticipated. Laak sure can run fast!"

Laak grinned. "The last time I did that was as a child."

This was a rare treat, one everyone enjoyed. Kruutud refused the honey, using the distraction to peer inside Ese's carrier.

"Is that salt?"

Kruutud stuck a finger toward the gourd, but an ominous growl stopped him.

Yu'ung smirked. "The pack takes guard duties seriously."

Kruutud slapped his thighs and stomped toward Fierce. "Where's our portion? We also ran out."

Fierce continued to knap the hard stone that would find new life as the penetrating tip of a lance. "You didn't do the labor. You only receive some if Asvulk shares her allotment."

Kruutud barked, "Her salt is mine. She is my pairmate!"

Fierce grabbed his arm. "If you or any of the One take her portion, they will not come with us."

Kruutud clenched his jaw. Throughout the discussion, Asvulk ignored him. If she felt responsibilities as his pairmate, she didn't show it.

Chapter 11

Yu'ung, Aynoh, and Fierce lay atop the escarpment, Ocha snoring by their side. A bird's beautiful song called. The Moon bathed a murky figure in dim gray light.

"Shanadar is studying Moon."

Fierce said, "That's Shanadar? I can't tell the difference from a live bird."

Yu'ung could recognize Shanadar, but not by sound. She had what Old One called extreme sight. Where most saw a blurry, distant image, she identified clearly the injured or aged animals in a distant herd so the People's hunters knew the most likely prey.

Nevertheless, she answered what Fierce hadn't asked. "His flute has slight differences from the real bird."

While Fierce scrunched his eyes closed, concentrating, Yu'ung searched far down the cliff's crest and picked out Shanadar's lean shape, a Bear femur in his hands, fingers curved over the top and bottom. The flute sang. Moon replied. Shanadar answered.

Fierce opened his eyes and scratched his cheek. "We play tones, too, when we sail without Sun, but not bird music." He studied the night sky.

Yu'ung scrunched her brow. "What do you see overhead, Fierce?"

"I track the stars, the fluctuations in the shades of darkness, how the night wind vacillates, and changes in a myriad of skymarks."

"Skymarks?"

"Like a landmark, but overhead."

She shuttered her eyes, heard the soft night breeze, the chirrup of insects, the scrape of a snake through the grass, the swoop of wings that ended in Owl's victory cry, and fell asleep.

Muted voices woke her. She pushed to her feet, surprised to be inside.

How did I descend the bluff in my sleep?

Outside, Sun's first rays spread a glow over the earth. She approached Fierce as he examined the trunk that would become a boat, eyes lit with excitement.

"This is perfect, Bhidid. It is straight, broad enough for several to sit abreast."

"Pressed shoulder to shoulder!"

"We need another like it."

"Another?" From Yu'ung, mouth wide in a yawn.

Bhidid padded in place. "This is the only one we could find. The rest tapered too quickly."

Fierce pivoted to the side. "I saw some in the opposite direction. Bhidid, come with me. Braanroorv, gather a group to hollow this trunk."

Kruutud chased after him. "Gevol and I want to help."

Fierce funneled him toward Ese. "Ese! Kruutud and Gevol offered to collect vines with you and Asvulk. Take Ragged Ear and Ump, too."

"Vines!" Kruutud growled. "We don't help with vines!"

Gevol brandished his crippled arm. Before he could make excuses, Ese said, "That arm will never heal back to a normal appendage. Get used to the idea that you now have only one arm. That means working one-handed. You might as well start now."

Gevol squeaked, "How?"

Ese squared her body to him, the surprise obvious on her face. "Our kind climbs anything, any height, carrying tools in one hand." When he looked even less sure, she glanced at Asvulk. "Does he really not know, or is he acting dumb to get out of work?"

Asvulk shrugged. "He hates work, but in this case, I think he's telling the truth."

Ese huffed and turned back to Kruutud. "Wrap your legs around the trunk. Grip with your good arm and scoot up." Then, she turned away, bored and disgusted with this male, done providing assistance he shouldn't need.

Fierce added, "The vines are high."

Kruutud flushed red. "I don't climb, even with both arms!"

Ese glowered. "He'll climb."

Fierce hid a laugh. "Once in the canopy, chop only the sturdiest vines. If they tangle on the way down, untangle them as you descend."

Ese scowled at Kruutud. "If you're nice, Asvulk will take care of what you can't. Do you know how to be nice to her?"

He sputtered, raw wounds on his cheek pulsing with every blink. As Yu'ung asked Asvulk where to find vines, Kruutud edged toward a boulder bed, maybe thinking Yu'ung couldn't talk to Asvulk and watch him simultaneously, hoping to hide and be left behind. Yu'ung stepped sideways and blocked him while continuing her conversation. He blustered his annoyance, shouted to his band, but no one paid attention to him. Those capable were hurrying to catch up with Eknilk who headed to the sea with a harpoon. Apparently, they were more hungry than disdainful of the supple white meat with the mild flavor.

Ocha and Ragged Ear lay on their backs, legs dangling, looking sound asleep to those who missed the twitch of their brows. Kruutud did, sidestepping out of Yu'ung's line of sight which made Ocha's ears perk. Then Ragged Ear's lips parted to reveal fangs bloody from a meal. Kruutud fled, calling to Ese. Yu'ung never changed her attention from Asvulk, never thought the Canis wouldn't take care of the problem.

He and Gevol are like those who enslaved Jvelk and me.

Fierce, B'o, and more Chosen strode down the shore.

Our traditional raft serves limited travel and simple waterways. Because Big Rock is almost surrounded by water, we will need a vessel like the Chosen's to hunt food.

Asvulk raced off with Ese and Yu'ung caught up with Fierce as he entered a copse. The trees soared, high enough for an expansive view if Yu'ung wanted to sidle up to the canopy. Which she didn't. Not today. Fierce brushed his hands along the trunks in search of a future boat. He halted by a tall, straight beauty with few low limbs, its stalk thicker than himself and another Chosen side by side.

"This is it."

With choppers glued to the end of husky arm-length shafts—what Fierce called an "axe"—the Chosen set to work. The axes bit into the hard wood, digging wedges out from opposing sides. Chips flew in every direction, to be collected later for kindling. The Chosen worked on one side, Yu'ung and B'o on the other. The Tall Ones were faster at first, but with each swing, Yu'ung and B'o's strokes bit deeper, the power from their muscular shoulders, chest, and arms far exceeding the rest. Under the assault of their exceptional strength, the tree splintered, cracked, and finally crashed through the nearby layers of foliage. A flurry of birds exploded into the sky with loud, displeased squawks as the noble giant hit the ground with a deafening thump, bounced, and then settled.

Fierce paced the length. "I will even the crown. Bhidid will cut off the roots. Yu'ung, you and B'o chop limbs off."

Individual jobs completed, everyone spaced themselves along the trunk and lugged it to camp. Yu'ung panted, but soon caught her breath. She routinely carried heavy carcasses alone. Not so the Chosen used to sharing labor among larger groups. Their arms trembled from the exertion and they all gulped air into starved lungs. Yu'ung and B'o drank their fill of water, ate chunks of fresh hot meat, and waited for the rest to recover.

"B'o," she asked between chews, poking her lips over to the wheezing, exhausted Chosen, "What is wrong with them? Are they sick?"

He shrugged. "They all act odd."

As the Chosen recovered, Grub marched into the camp with the One helpers. His scowl told Yu'ung everything about the group's success. Before Grub could rid himself of his work team, Fierce sent them on another chore.

Grub's nostrils flared as he good-naturedly snapped at his group, "Come on, everyone!" and sprinted away at a ground-eating pace. Fierce watched until they disappeared down the shore.

The boat builders commenced the tedious task of stripping bark and hollowing the new log's interior. This must be done carefully, without damage to the wooden walls that made the vessel waterproof.

Sun dipped below the horizon. Tools were stowed. All gathered to eat, exhausted but relaxed in the way of those who have worked hard and successfully. Yu'ung crouched by B'o.

"Where's Ese?"

"Not back."

Did Kruutud cause problems?

Yu'ung rose, intending to find out, but B'o's pairmate trotted in beside a striding Asvulk, in front of a scowling Kruutud and a wobbling Gevol, the last leaning heavily on his spear, damaged arm cradled to his chest.

He won't survive if he doesn't force the healthy hand to take over the work of both, as Old One did.

The impairment to the Elder's arm had been extreme, but he never complained. In time, switching tasks to his healthy limb enlarged it to the size and strength of his thigh.

Kruutud tried to join the People's fire, but Fierce blocked him.

"That's where you go." He pointed to the One hearth, barely embers.

Gevol and Kruutud shambled away without argument.

Fierce asked no one in particular with only the slightest concern, "What happened to the Lead?"

Asvulk said, "He fell. Ese and I treated it."

Asvulk visibly drooped at the sight of the One's dark fire pit and the hollow-eyed gathering who tracked her movements. If she sat by the fire, they would expect her to take care of their meal so she headed instead for a smooth cliff wall warmed all day by Sun.

Ese shouted, "Come eat with us."

Asvulk needed no encouragement and changed her direction.

"It's time they grew up, Asvulk. If they want your help, they must deserve it."

The People already crouched by the fire, rubbing their hands and arms over the heat. The day had been cold despite the hard work. All ate whatever was left from previous meals, too tired to be picky.

Meal over, Asvulk straggled back to the One camp. She offered to check Gevol's wounds. He brandished his weapon awkwardly at her with his non-dominant hand which she easily slapped away. Kruutud raised a fist, threatening to unleash the bully that always worked in the past, but this time, his former pairmate snarled, kicked dirt at him, and marched across to the People's cave.

Her days of being intimidated are ended.

Ese welcomed Asvulk inside. Message transmitted, Kruutud glared. His pairmate had her own strength now. Soon, exhausted snores mixed with the purpose and rhythm of rock against stone as axes were sharpened for the next day's work.

Chapter 12

The smoky tang of fire woke Yu'ung. She trudged outside, shaking the fuzziness of sleep from her head. The boat builders were managing the fire burning inside the prepared log while the harvesters hurried away to collect the wood chips left behind when the tree was chopped down. Ese and Fierce squatted at the exterior hearth instead of the warmer one inside the cave. From here, they could block the One from observing the boat preparations and watch for their trickery. Gevol glared at them, hissed to Kruutud, and limped away on a raw stricken ankle.

Yu'ung bent to warm her hands. "They're up to something."

Fierce rose gracefully. "They think they can outsmart us. Gevol will find out soon that they already failed. Excuse me while I prepare a welcome."

Fierce's cleverness always amazed Yu'ung. She shot to her feet. "I'll join you."

Fierce dipped his head and trotted over to where Jvelk, Laak, and Wik seemed to be waiting for him. After a quiet conversation, they hurried off in one direction, Fierce another. He caught Yu'ung's eye and they silently took up the trail of the One Lead.

Gevol's injuries meant he moved awkwardly, no matter how quiet he tried to be, but he made an effort as he slipped behind the camp's overwatch hill into a shallow valley that was hidden from the People's camp. This route led to a waterhole, but Yu'ung doubted he was thirsty. Fierce and Yu'ung glided soundlessly behind him along the twisting path, stopped every time Gevol did, and froze if he glanced their way. It was easy to see moving prey. Motionless, everything blended together. Because twitching on his ankle and moving his shattered arm made him wince, he quickly accepted that no one followed him and stopped paying attention to his backtrail.

Another mistake.

The Canis showed up to the trail's side, moving like wraiths through the long grass, lips and fangs tinged with blood. They somehow knew their part in this adventure more than Yu'ung did.

Well out of the camp's sight and sound, Gevol sped up. His direction validated what Yu'ung already suspected: he planned to climb the overwatch hill's backside. It was steeper, but invisible to the camp.

Gevol hobbled on, oblivious to the enticing scent of his soggy pink bandages. He fell on his injured hand, hissed, tottered onward, finally giving up and balancing on a spear-turned-walking stick. At the cliff, he picked a trail he must have laid out earlier, one Yu'ung could see kept him hidden from view of all the camp's work areas, and began the climb.

He has grit. Too bad it's wasted.

Gevol's one-armed hand- and toeholds meant uphill progress was slow, accented with the frequent sharp intake of breath, but if Yu'ung was right about his goal, speed didn't matter. Yu'ung glanced at Fierce to warn him, but his grin said it was unnecessary.

"There is a surprise for Gevol at the top."

After extended heaves and huffs, his bandage now soaked crimson, he summited the hill. His smile of success didn't last. Jvelk, Laak, and

Wik blocked his way, in the high grass on the precipice's edge, where Gevol had meant to ensconce himself to secretly study the construction below, then return to the One camp under cover of darkness.

Jvelk laughed. "There's not enough room for you."

Yu'ung called from behind. "Those injuries gave you a lot of problems, but congratulations for not quitting. Too bad it won't matter."

White Streak must have sensed trouble from Gevol and placed herself between the One Lead and the People. Gevol snarled, lost control, and charged, arm cocked to throw the only weapon he could manage.

Yu'ung shouted, "What are you doing? You can't win with a stone!"

Fierce guffawed. "Another in a long list of mistakes."

But he threw anyway. White Streak had no trouble snapping the stone from the air and then ploughed into Gevol, crushing the surprised male beneath her body. If not for that, his crazed charge would have hurtled him off the cliff to his death. Something crunched. Gevol wrestled his way free of White Streak while howling in pain and frustration. Everyone watched as he crawled to his feet, bloody hand with its dripping wraps clutched against his chest, and staggered back the way he had come. No one said a word, nor did they follow. His progress was loud and obvious. The group reached the camp well before him, and had begun to think he'd died out there somewhere, when he finally arrived, falling as often as he stood. He glanced around, saw no one coming to his aid, and collapsed by the dark hearth.

Yu'ung and Fierce left to complete chores in preparation for the migration. Ese remained, watching.

Yu'ung and Fierce returned much later to find Gevol in the same desolate position and Ese arguing with Kruutud.

"No one rides who doesn't help."

Kruutud strode toward Ese, shoulders tense, mouth a tight line. As he approached, his feet flew out from beneath him and he landed on his back. He thrashed to his feet, stomped one foot and then the other, mud thick on his sides and arms. Red drops dripped from his mouth down his chin.

Yu'ung mumbled, "Missed that sludge hidden beneath the branches. You should be more careful."

Fierce commented, "Bit your tongue when you fell? Oh-h…."

No One made a move to assist Kruutud or argue his case with Ese. It didn't take long for his defiant expression to be replaced by exhaustion and bitterness and defeat.

He finally responded to Ese through gritted teeth, "Whatever you wish."

"We need cordage. You can soak bark and vines, twist them together."

Kruutud asked mildly, "Where's Asvulk? She is good at that—and Gevol is hurt. Why isn't she helping him?"

Yu'ung responded in a way calculated to annoy him, "She is building the replacement for the boat you destroyed. Everyone is other than you."

"We will help, too, of course," he said, and started toward the People's camp.

Ese stopped him. "Stay. We'll bring materials to you."

Kruutud blurted out, "They're too heavy," but Ese and Jhat had already left to return with armloads of vines and softened bark.

Kruutud muttered, "You're strong. Why isn't Asvulk?"

Yu'ung wanted to snap at him, but settled for, "Stop talking before we dislike you even more. Separate the vines into strands. Twist them into cords."

Yu'ung headed for the partially completed boat, stuffed a handful of last night's leftovers in her mouth, and said between chews, "Let me help."

Bhidid said, "B'o and I finished digging a trench the length of the log's interior. Now, we'll burn the inside."

Fire destroys forests! Why not the hull? But no one worried as the flames licked the sides, blackening the hollowed-out log. The pleasant aroma evoked memories of cooking and camaraderie. While the fire dried and hardened the shell, Eknilk and Braanroorv shaped the front to drive the craft through water in a way similar to how the tip on a shaft does. Yu'ung helped Bhidid mix resin with beeswax and created a sturdy glue to seal cracks caused by the work or natural knots.

As the vessel took shape, Jhat and most of those not involved in the building collected travel food for the extended journey—fish, stems, insects, worms, small birds, eggs, and tubers—and preserved mussels, clams, crabs, tortoises, and other seafood. The People had always consumed fish, though less than now. The Chosen learned to eat it in quantity while exploring. Carapaces, at times, proved as difficult to penetrate as animal hides. The trick, according to what Fierce learned from the Clan, was to heat the shell until it darkened and popped open.

Daylight ended and the tired group ate a varied banquet of white meat, seaweed, eggs, and frogs scavenged throughout the day. A favorite for Yu'ung was a brown-shelled spider with crusty legs and a round body. Fierce said what the Big Rock lacked in herds was offset by the sea's white meat. They wouldn't go hungry, but their diet would be adventurous.

Asvulk officially dissolved her broken pairmate status and slept with the People. Yu'ung invited her to be one of the People, but Asvulk insisted her tribe would need her.

"You have no doubts this will work."

"No, of course not." She glanced to the side, then back at Yu'ung. "And thanks to you, the ache inside my body no longer cripples me. The scars won't heal, but I see my purpose."

She fingered the necklace and turned to Yu'ung in a daze. Deep anguish showed in her eyes, a thick stew of unforgettable memories.

Yu'ung spoke Asvulk's name, but she didn't seem to hear, so Yu'ung remained with her until Asvulk rose with a strained effort and made her way back to the One camp.

The day prior to launch, leaks in the hull were mended and the boat tested for seaworthiness. Night fell. The moon's dull glow silhouetted the overwatch hill where Wik, Laak, and Jvelk lay. Coyotes yipped, quieted by a mournful howl.

Kruutud and Gevol spoke to each other in muted tones, glancing often at Fierce. Asvulk resumed living with the One, far enough from the rest that no one asked her assistance but close enough to hear conversations which she shared with Fierce. Shanadar and Xad resurfaced after an absence of days, resplendent in freshly painted stripes, long Canis tails tied behind their necks. Shanadar had added an Eagle's feather to his, Xad, a young bird's plume. The youngster carried himself with pride. He toted a bleached femur the same length as his mentor's flute, without the holes, but shaped the same.

They squatted on the overwatch hill. Shanadar played his beautiful music, both a goodbye to their past and a welcome to whatever came next.

Chapter 13

Fierce's familiar scent of dust, sweat, and the earth itself had come to mean wisdom and thoughtfulness to Yu'ung rather than stress and danger. On the cusp of this massive change in circumstances, Yu'ung could think of no better person to ask her question.

"Fierce. Kruutud failed his supporters. They must be furious, maybe enough to take it out on us."

"But he didn't fail them. He achieved what he promised, just not the way they expected, and the cost was high."

"So, they might turn on Kruutud."

"Because he proved untrustworthy. Asvulk has shown how one can stand against evil. I don't believe Kruutud can recover his authority.

That chunked a piece into place for Yu'ung. She stood still and ran everything she knew through her thoughts. Something inside told her whatever was going to happen would be before Asvulk and the One separated from the People and the Chosen.

Everyone stuffed themselves with food and drink in case provisions were lost to the sea. Ridding themselves of the One wouldn't take long, but the trip to the Big Rock would. The People could manage for days without food. Water would be available if necessary onshore, but scavenging plants or hunting would take time the travelers didn't have.

Fierce called the travelers together. Most mixed companionably, but that didn't mean trust. The One whispered among themselves, cast furtive, confused glances at those who had taken their weapons, but rescued them from a fatal situation.

No one followed those who kidnapped Jvelk and me out of loyalty. Nor do they Kruutud.

Quiet settled over the assemblage. "Bring only a satchel. No weapons. We will protect you if necessary. There is little room for provisions so expect to provide for yourselves on the island as we will on the way to our final destination."

The Big Rock.

Yu'ung peered into the distance, where Sun slept. What would be worthy of such a grandiose name?

A high-pitched voice she didn't recognize whined, "What if that is impossible?"

Someone else added, "He's right. What if there is no food?"

Fierce wasted no time on the answer. "Then you die."

The People required no reassurance. They came through foreign terrain with little food and less water, led by one who relied on a Canis pack, a smooth rock with a face, a bone flute for advice, and an unseasoned Alpha.

Kruutud barged forward, fists clasped. The One fell silent, some scowling that they listened to him a Moon ago. Others looked away.

It starts.

Aside from a clenched jaw, Fierce ignored Kruutud.

The One Leader spoke as though an equal member of the journey's leadership. "We have complied with all your requirements. Let us bring our weapons. We will assist against attackers. We've said often—"

Fierce brushed him away before he completed his thought and Yu'ung spoke for the group, "If we are attacked, we toss you into the sea regardless of where we are and then we leave. There are no marauders on the shoreless sea unless they are part of your group, Kruutud."

Ese marched toward Kruutud, brandishing a palm-sized missile. "Your enemies aren't just Fierce and his warriors. Test us, the People. Start with me. Please."

Fierce shouted to the One. "Don't misunderstand. We wish to be friends with any on the island. If they are as friendly as Kruutud has promised they will be, we will moor our boats and replenish supplies."

Devious pleasure flitted across Kruutud's face, there and gone, but Yu'ung saw it.

"I will ensure they are, Fierce. I am Leader. I will tell them how you have helped."

The tiniest smile lifted Fierce's lips, one she suspected Kruutud misjudged.

Fierce asked, his voice too pleasant, "Where did you send your boat-raft?"

Kruutud pawed at the dirt. "Sun's strong side, but waves and tides could have pushed the craft anywhere."

Fierce bobbed his head pleasantly. "There is one island in that direction. Your group will be there or nowhere."

Worry tinged Kruutud's response. "We check all—."

"No. The raft you described is not sturdy enough to go farther."

Kruutud glanced from Gevol to Fierce. Desperation ratcheted his voice higher. "You cannot leave us if we are alone."

"We can and will."

"But—"

"Or stay here. Mountain's anger has abated."

Yu'ung jerked upright. "I prefer they stay. Then we could go directly to our new homeland. We would like to reach it before the cold air arrives."

Kruutud stomped his foot. "It is dangerous here."

"Dangerous?" Fierce's voice was gritty. "B'o, Grub, Yu'ung—have you seen any threats?"

B'o scratched his head and then moved a hand's width from Kruutud, gaze fixed on the One Leader. "Only them, Fierce."

Kruutud paled, his cheeks mottled a blotchy red. "We killed most of the enemies. It is safe for you, but those victories expended our supplies. You give us no choice but to accept your terms."

"It is a better choice than you intended to give us." He motioned to Grub. "Put them in different crafts."

Kruutud jerked as though slapped. "No! Gevol assists me—."

Yu'ung interrupted, the strength of fire-hardened wood in her voice. "Get in or stay behind. Those are your choices."

Without further discussion, the Canis herded the Ones into place, then bracketed them. Asvulk pushed up behind Kruutud, acting the loyal pairmate. If Kruutud had even glanced her way, he would have seen not a dutiful pairmate but an imminent threat. Instead, he ignored her, missed her clenched hand hidden by her wrap.

Fierce mumbled to Aynoh, "What does Asvulk hold?"

"The guarantee for her future."

Aynoh caught Asvulk's eye with a quizzical look, received a nod. *She knows what she's doing.*

Fierce grinned. "Ump. Ragged Ear. Ocha. White Streak. Toss any who cause trouble—for us—into the water."

The travelers were arrayed to balance the crafts and the boats launched. The sailors paddled aggressively through the pounding surf toward where Sun slept. Their muscles bulged with the labor, dripped with sweat. They tackled each wave with gusto, no matter how monstrous or high. By the time the tide could no longer pull them back to shore, those on the paddles were short of breath but wore wide grins. As the land melted from sight, progress became easier.

Everyone took turns rowing, their strong uniform strokes synchronized as a team.

They moved through the water efficiently and speedily. Fish of all kinds leapt in the sea, curiosity greater than fear of the huge, odd intruders to their habitat. Every area they passed through was different from the last, sprinkled in varied shades of blue and green, filled with life that dove, swam, flew, and slithered. Serpentine forms splashed in the wake. Grub in Yu'ung's vessel—with Wik—said the sea's colors were caused by the depth and the fauna beneath the surface. Occasionally, Yu'ung dipped her finger into the water, sucked, but spat the liquid out. It always tasted of the poison.

Gray foam coated the turbulent, blue-black flecked expanse. The odor of wet fur permeated everything.

Yu'ung asked, "Is the storm going to be a problem, Grub?"

"The wind blows toward the darker shades. The tempest will drift away."

Familiar birds circled overhead.

Yu'ung tingled with excitement. "We are close."

Loud voices broke through the susurrus sea breeze and waves lapped against the sides. Kruutud was arguing over something Yu'ung couldn't make out. He emphasized with the flap of arms out of sync with his words. Gevol stiffened.

She murmured, "Kruutud's plan is about to start."

She studied the One Leader and his Lead, separated too far for talking, so why did the hair on her neck rise?

She asked Grub, "Are we prepared?"

"Have been since we left," and he roared. "I love a good fight!"

Chapter 14

The fog lifted and revealed craggy beaches edged by high cliffs. A sandy inlet provided a safe harbor. Yu'ung studied the length for life signs.

None.

Fierce motioned the rowers in both boats to stow the paddles and arm themselves.

Gevol sputtered, "Why stop? Plenty of daylight remains."

Grub said, "The storm will arrive at any time. Without full light, we could be stuck on a shallow sea bottom or hidden shoals."

Yu'ung huffed. "How will the inhabitants react to armed intruders?"

Grub's gaze remained on the island. "Our experience exploring with those we've met is natives are patient. Curious. Weapons aside, they don't start out expecting a fight because we don't present one, but this could be different. These natives may know Kruutud's tribe, may hold grudges for being stranded here or whatever treatment they received at the One hands. No. Fierce won't take a chance."

They halted beyond the tides. Everyone ate except the One—they would find their food tomorrow ashore—and then split up the nightly guard duty, including the pack. The One watched them eat, begged fruitlessly with their eyes, and then went to sleep, all except Kruutud and Gevol, ever watchful for opportunity to seize control. That wouldn't happen.

Yu'ung scanned the dark stretch of land within range of a well-made raft or a desperate attack from far-throwing spears. Moon was full tonight, the sky clear, but a damp chill hung in the air. A cold rain was coming, if not tonight, then tomorrow. She stared out at the glossy black water, sparkling under the twinkling stars, unprepared for such flat emptiness, broken by the rare white splash in Moon's light.

Eyes adjusted to the dark, she squinted, searching, and picked out a dark strip that separated the island from the sky.

"Trees, Grub. They grow on the summit. That means those that live here—and you, Gevol—can build rafts."

Gevol narrowed his eyes, a furrow between his brows. "How do you see that?"

She didn't explain.

A slight glow on the horizon, the muffled sound of the waves, and the caw of morning birds stirred the sleepy travelers to life. A low growl reminded the One they were prisoners, not passengers, but didn't dampen their excitement. They chattered among themselves, eager to reach a new homebase. In the emerging light, the isle was taller and broader than it appeared in the dark.

Yu'ung leaned forward, drawn to a bright spot. "Someone set a signal fire."

Fierce called loud enough for both boats to hear, "One! Gather your belongings. We'll deposit you offshore. From there, swim or walk to the flames onshore and make your case. This is your adventure."

Kruutud blinked to clear the sleep from his brain. "These could be enemies! Come with us!"

"No."

"You said you'd go ashore if the reception was friendly!"

"I lied, a tactic you taught me." Kruutud opened his mouth to object, but Fierce talked over him. "Shall we test your trustworthiness? One question: Do you intend to tell them you are a captive or that we saved you?"

Kruutud protested, "How can you ask that? You know me!"

"I do, which is why we will not beach the vessel."

"No—you must! I can't swim!"

Aynoh laughed. "You swam, Kruutud, in your failed effort to destroy Fierce's vessel."

"Others can't!"

Fierce's words were quiet, but Yu'ung easily could tell what he said. "Carry them."

The rowers pulled to a halt well short of the beach. As the blue water lightened, Asvulk called out, received screams in response, then leaping and bouncing.

She yelled to Aynoh, "It is our tribe! They made it!" all the while waving and leaping, the response no less enthusiastic.

Kruutud rasped, "Stop! We must act like captives!"

His commands came too late. The former tribe mates had already made their decision, screaming to each other what sounded like, "She did what she promised—she found a way to rescue us! Who would have thought it possible!"

Fierce and Grub started to push the One from the crafts. "This is as far as we go."

Kruutud squealed one last plea. "Replenish your water!"

"No. Get out."

"Fierce!"

He jolted toward Yu'ung's voice. Kruutud used the distraction to grab for Laak's spear, might have succeeded if not for Asvulk. She crowded into her former pairmate. He tried to push free of her girth and then lurched.

Yu'ung couldn't believe what she was seeing. *Asvulk stabbed him!*

Yu'ung had seen Asvulk use a long dagger to cut open deer and Oryx. Now, it was buried to the hilt beneath Kruutud's ribs. His arm froze in place, confusion and then shock as he gasped, "Why?"

Yu'ung couldn't hear the words, but there was no doubt what Asvulk said.

"You really don't understand, do you? For my son."

He tugged feebly at the weapon, but his hand shook so hard he couldn't make a fist.

Asvulk hid what was happening with her body, speaking into his ear.

Yu'ung moved her lips with Asvulk's, "Let me do that for you."

A twist to the weapon enlarged the mortal wound to the size of an acorn. Then, Asvulk yanked it out. With it came tissue, gore, and a fountain of bright blood.

"Oh! I should have asked for help," she said in a voice as cold as ice in a stream.

Kruutud tried to speak, but the words were softer than a whisper. He stumbled toward Asvulk. She grabbed him as though to steady him. Others might think she was helping him to balance. She shuffled him to the hull's edge. He looked confused, eyes dull, so she smiled.

"Careful. You're dizzy." She pressed his weakened form to the side and then—

Yu'ung screamed to distract any who might have noticed the drama. "Fierce! We made it!"

He looked at her quizzically, quickly figured it out and moved to block Asvulk and Kruutud, but needn't have worried. No one paid attention to anything but the tribe members on shore. Asvulk leaned her body, both hands against the One Leader's torso, and pushed. The killer of her pairmate and child tumbled into the water so quietly, Yu'ung doubted anyone noticed.

Grub did, though, and covered a congratulatory whoop to Asvulk with a cheer to the One survivors onshore.

Yu'ung motioned, "We checked everyone for a weapon."

He shrugged with a grin. "We did."

A scream erupted.

Gevol saw, too.

He aimed a stone at Asvulk, but he had no throwing skill and less power with his weak hand. The stone hit Wik's back as Yu'ung swung her cudgel. Gevol's chest collapsed. Wik growled at being hit which diverted attention to her, letting Yu'ung shove Gevol overboard to join Kruutud. She watched until he sank beneath the waves.

Oblivious to Gevol's death, Wik asked Yu'ung, "Why did he attack me? We are almost where he wanted to be?"

Yu'ung shook her head and moved them both away from the blood-stained sea. Asvulk caught Yu'ung's eye, content with how it ended. Clearly, vengeance agreed with her. A final smile and she dove into the shoreless sea. Uprights lined the shore, brandishing weapons, but out of excitement. Yu'ung guessed they had learned a lot since allowing Kruutud to take over their tribe based on lies and promises. Asvulk aimed for the entourage. She was a strong swimmer and soon, the One trailed at a distance, many floundering, a few helping others who couldn't swim. Yu'ung watched the faces of those ashore harden at the sight of those who had treated them as enemies.

Yu'ung said, "It looks to be a good home. Asvulk will be happy."

Fierce thinned his lips. "Not so sure that will be true about the One."

As Asvulk reached the sloping coast, she strode toward her tribe. Voice keening with pleasure, she shouted how those in the boats freed her. Everyone waved their thanks. As the One approached, they received no such welcome. In fact, led by Asvulk, they were driven back into the sea. A few tried to fight their way ashore and died with the effort. When Kruutud's former loyalists realized the island was no safe landing, they tried to return to the boats, sure they would be received.

Not so.

Yu'ung squared herself to the first of the struggling One, face impassive. "Go. There is no room for you aboard these vessels."

Fierce spoke, "We do not forgive the many deaths you caused, among them Asvulk's child."

The One tried to clamber up the sides of the Chosen's crafts and were repelled or killed.

Fierce called out, loud enough that everyone in and out of the water heard, "Paddle. There is no time to waste. We have far to sail."

As Asvulk and her tribe disappeared behind them, the boats stopped at a small atoll to rearrange seating with so many gone. For the remainder of the day, rowers hugged the shoreline, not returning to the sea's center until the next day.

Yu'ung asked why. "From here on, the beach bends around inlets and hollows. A straight line through the middle of the sea is faster."

"How do you know where to go without landmarks?"

"Sun's nest."

The edges of a gray promontory appeared ahead in the mist. It wasn't long before it dominated the horizon, silhouetted by Sun's brightness. The mixed browns and greens of hillocks on one side, dry stunted trees and scrubby brush on the opposite, soon funneled the travelers to the timeworn behemoth.

Fierce spoke softly, almost reverently, "The Big Rock. Your new home."

Part 3

Return to Big Rock

Chapter 15

Kazeb and Turk, all that remained of the once-vibrant Clan, crouched behind the prickly bush on the promontory's highest point, staring at the approaching apparitions. Buffeted by the wind, always strong at the top of Big Rock, they barely noticed the growing chill that marked the departure of daylight. Usually occupied seeking herds on the distant plains or fish swarms out on the sea that bordered their home, today, as Sun prepared to sleep, flotsam in the water disrupted the waves and disturbed the gulls. The birds circled and then returned to their nests on the promontory.

Kazeb pulled a tuber from his shoulder sack and took a bite. "Whoever it is, their boat is big. See how the current avoids it?" Kazeb stared hard.

"Maybe it's a Clan member returning on their raft?"

Kazeb didn't think so. He'd never seen the Clan send rafts out together. Besides, the waves were wrong for the Clan's platforms

"They don't fish here, haven't since the deaths."

It must be who I thought I'd never see again.

Turk rose to his knees. "Whoever it is, they won't reach us tonight. Let's go."

"Wait." Kazeb couldn't leave without being sure.

The odd waves formed into a fuzzy shape, logs, hollowed out, with blurry bodies moving within their hulls.

"They're paddling towards us, Turk, but they don't match the Tall Ones' vessel." *Similar but not the same. Is it another of their kind?*

Soon, the crafts were close enough to see the figures bustling throughout the interior, stem to stern. They thrust paddles in the water, muscles glistening, damp with sweat and sea spray. A burly but slender male with striped cheeks dominated the prow of the front craft. A stocky red-haired female occupied that space in the other, her light-colored skin a contrast to his deep black, both muscled in all required places.

Kazeb liked her instantly. Maybe it was her surety of movement or how she scanned the surroundings without fear, demeanor confident that whatever she saw she could handle, or how the rest drew on her strength for the final strokes to a shoreline some knew nothing about.

She scanned from the promontory's craggy footprint to its vaulted crest. Kazeb stopped breathing, didn't twitch to the tickle of ants crawling over his bare skin. She stuttered at the bush where the brothers hid and passed on.

Did she see us? No. That is impossible.

Turk said, "We'll know soon enough. Only the Tall Ones know how to avoid the shoals, beach safely on this shore."

Turk was right. Any boat wishing to land at the foot of Big Rock must deftly avoid the underwater rocks. If they saw them—which they could, the water was so clear—they would continue down the shore to a spot without risk.

Kazeb switched his attention to the striped Upright in the front boat to see what he would do. He talked to the rowers, voice commanding, his familiarity with the cove overwhelming the doubts of his fellow travelers. He yelled to the other—Yu'ung, it sounded like—and gestured toward where Kazeb always beached his raft, the lone spot without hidden shoals.

He knows!

The rowers sliced expertly toward the meagre section of sandy coast safe for landing and grounded the crafts with the skill of those accustomed to water travel. When they disembarked, he caught his breath.

The red-haired Yu'ung isn't the only female!

All the sailors squiggled into the soft warmth of the sand, unsteady on their feet as Kazeb would be after a long ride in a rocking craft.

The next to exit the vessel jolted him.

"Those are Canis!" and natural enemies of Uprights.

One had mottled shades of brown, one black, another with a white streak across its crown, the last older with a muzzle speckled heavily with gray. They all pranced through the cluster of Uprights, licked a few hands, then tipped their muzzles upward and howled.

One-called-Yu'ung followed the black Canis' line of sight to the top of the huge outcropping. The brothers ducked.

"They found us, Liis!" Turk used Kazeb's Clan name, the one he preferred.

Kazeb scowled. The brothers meant to reveal themselves, but in their own time. It seemed the Canis pack outsmarted them. He peered between stalks of dry grass under hooded eyes. One-called-Yu'ung seemed to catch his eye and shouted indistinct words to another of her kind. The black Canis stared, tail swaying, mouth agape in fast pants. The one with the gray muzzle trotted over to a slender male, long smooth hair pulled into a good replica of a Canis tail. Tucked into it was an Eagle feather. He squatted and ran his fingers through the bristly fur.

Kazeb switched back to One-called-Yu'ung. Something about her fascinated him. There was no energy wasted, her every movement graceful. She talked to each in the entourage with respect that was returned. She exuded confidence and assurance over the complex blend of People and Tall Ones who burst from the vessel.

Turk spoke in hushed words, "The one painted like you acts like Alpha, or Leader."

Never had Kazeb seen a female Alpha. His brother must be right.

The animal with the glistening black fur and prominent tan muzzle nudged Yu'ung. She murmured. The creature yowled. Yu'ung nodded, he suspected to affirm whatever the Canis sensed.

We're far above and well hidden. No one could pick out our scent, not even a predator.

As though Turk heard his thoughts, his brother stammered, "They know we're here, Liis. The Canis told her."

"That's impossible."

"I would agree, but the black one—she seems almost sentient!"

Kazeb snorted. "Let's say you're right, and I think you are, why wouldn't we be on guard by the arrival of armed invaders?"

Turk grunted agreement and returned his attention to the spectacle below. Kazeb studied Yu'ung, the changing expressions on her face, how her eyes missed nothing, the way she carried both spears above her shoulders, balanced and ready, level with the ground.

"She wonders how to approach natives on this foreign shore. She doesn't know if we are many or few, scouts for a large group or the entire tribe, friend or foe."

Yu'ung's innate caution made Kazeb respect her even more, and something else he couldn't explain, an emotion he thought died with his pairmate poked back to life. Was this real or just the hope of a tired spirit?

Turk stiffened. "I recognize them, Liis."

Kazeb scoped in on the rowers.

"Yes, brother, their stripes are similar to the Tall Ones who visited long ago, but this isn't that group. There's a young adult and an Elder also wearing the colors."

Kazeb watched as everyone coalesced around one central figure, probably the Alpha—

Fierce!

"Fierce!"

It was Fierce who gave Kazeb his Chosen name, his stripes, and asked him to guide the explorers. Excitement tightened Kazeb's throat and twisted his stomach.

Turk flushed, seemingly as excited as Kazeb, but the cause was different.

"This is our chance, Liis, to make amends for why we lived and the rest died."

Kazeb groaned to himself. The death of Turk's pairmate had changed him. Turk had always been the selfless one who laughed over mistakes, finished Kazeb's sentences, but bitterness filled what had been their perfect homebase. Bad memories tainted everything that had been good. Turk believed the Tall Ones had never been loyal no matter what the Leader Fierce said. One named Qad had called the Clan Primitives, a term to denote inferiority, those who didn't think clearly. Kazeb brushed it off, saying Qad was always angry, but Turk said he spoke for the band.

If Turk was right, why did Fierce leave the gift?

But when they failed to return, Kazeb worried he was wrong.

"Turk. This is our chance to find out if it was them who unleashed the illness on us, and why," but his brother was too busy seething to listen.

"The one with red hair that flows past her neck, your color, Liis–"

"They call her Yu'ung."

"She is our kind. Why does she help him? We will warn her that they tricked us and will do the same to her!"

Kazeb watched as Yu'ung stutter-stepped, flung the Tall One's far-throwing staff expertly and impaled a shorebird mid-flight, a serpentine shape wriggling in its mouth.

Turk gulped. "She throws with assurance, moves with the grace of a Canis, and sees with Eagle's eye."

Kazeb remained silent, afraid his voice would break. Why did he feel off-balance around her?

Finally, he choked out, "If they intended to kill her, they would have by now, and if they are guilty of slaughtering our kind, why lead others to where we'd reveal the truth?"

"I don't know, Liis, but neither of us should forget that it is because to them our pairmates—and most of our Clan—are dead."

The outsiders heaved the vessels higher on the shore, where eager waves couldn't drag them back into the sea. A poignant song called, but from where? And to whom? Kazeb scrutinized the surroundings.

I don't recognize that bird. Did it too travel with them?

He studied the male who held what could only be a chopped femur.

He is our kind, painted with stripes, but I don't recognize him from the last time.

The male placed the bone between his lips and patted the smooth sides with his fingers. Suddenly, a lonely bird called its flock. A subadult at the striped male's side lurched to the music. His eyes were shuttered, hair also gathered behind his neck and adorned with a small feather. One stripe slashed each cheek. He held a bone similar to the one held by the taller Upright at his side, but he fisted it.

Kazeb didn't know what to make of that. Yet.

Turk hissed, "They must be finished exploring, but before returning home, will ensure their duplicity is hidden."

Kazeb touched the lines that memorialized his friendship with Fierce and hoped his former friend had a different explanation. Each time the stripes chipped away, he pulverized the requisite rocks, mixed in fat or oil to the right consistency, heated, and repainted his cheeks. With little to do each day, keeping the stripes fresh gave him purpose. And hope.

Turk ignored his hesitancy. "I want these enemies to suffer as we did."

Kazeb peeked at him from the corner of his eye. Regardless of how often they discussed the past travesty, neither could deduce any reason that strangers who showed no lasting interest in the Clan's territory or food, no animosity toward the tribe, would wipe them out. He could not kill them until that was clear.

Kazeb reverted his attention to the intruders. Yu'ung, still comfortably carrying both a thrusting and a far-throwing spear, scanned the surroundings as a scout would, or a hunter, neither job usually done by females. Fierce's word for that bounced through his memories.

Is she a warrior?

The new arrivals proceeded to the cave where the strangers long ago lived. Fierce lingered outside, studied the ridge from one end to the other, surveying the area's vastness. He turned to follow Yu'ung into the cave, but she was already rushing out, an object in her hand, hidden by her body so Kazeb couldn't see it. Fierce inspected it, turned to scan the landscape, and Kazeb saw what he held.

"My bowed spear."

2 years prior

"Fierce! That bent shaft you carry with the sinew tied to either end—are you supposed to throw it?"

Without waiting for an answer, Kazeb flung it. The curved shaft bounced, no further ahead of him than his shadow. He giggled. Fierce retrieved it, caressed the wood spine.

"You don't throw it. *It* throws an arrow."

He snatched a straight, smooth twig the length of his forearm from a holder by his shoulder, nocked it to the sinew, pulled, and let go. It flew across the field and penetrated a trunk at the field's end.

Kazeb's mouth dropped open. "How does that work?"

"Fire hardens the wood. Sand smooths it." He grinned. "Be our guide as we continue our journey. I'll teach you how."

Kazeb had agreed, but his pairmate became sick. Fierce gifted him a bowed spear with arrows, his way of affirming they must meet again so he could teach Kazeb to use them.

"I'll leave cairns. Come when you can. Until then, bring to mind memories of me shooting. Practice. By the time you catch up, all I'll have to do is clean up bad habits."

Kazeb never followed, and practice with the bowed spear brought bad memories. Despite that, he couldn't destroy the magnificent weapon so he kept it at the beach grotto Turk never visited, a place where he contemplated happier times.

Current time 75,000 years ago

Turk's voice pinched. "You use Fierce's gift. That's why debris doesn't cloak it."

"I don't use it. I don't know how. I hold it because I never thought they would return!"

He panted, angry at himself for losing his temper with his only friend. A sideways glance said Turk took it in stride.

"You're right. I didn't either."

"The happiness on Fierce's face—that is not guilt. He is eager to reconnect with us. I would guess he doesn't know why I never caught up to him, and is here out of concern for our welfare, not to wipe out survivors."

Turk clenched his fists. "Don't be naive, Liis!"

"This shore was the first stop outside of his homeland. Maybe it's his last stop on his way home, nothing more."

"I gave up my pairmate, my children. They won't take you! I will kill him first!"

He started to rise until Kazeb snagged his arm, firm and unhesitating, and dragged him deeper into the scrubbrush.

Turk growled, but softly, "He can't see us! He is turned the wrong way!"

"Not Fierce," and turned Turk's attention to the Canis with a gray muzzle, staring at them, hackles raised.

He growled.

Long ago, in a dark musty chamber, an instinct about danger, beyond the reach of logic or learning, had saved Kazeb's life and taught Kazeb a life lesson about trust. Today, despite these Canis being natural predators of the Clan, Kazeb found himself trusting them.

How did both the gray-muzzled Canis and the black one find me, so far away?

"We should have coated ourselves in mud or dung," *but we didn't think it necessary.*

Kazeb squinted his eyes as both Canis approached Yu'ung. They spoke in huffs as she studied the entirety of the soaring rock wall.

She takes them seriously.

The brothers agreed to remain hidden—even if they weren't—until they could devise a clear plan to approach these possible enemies, hoped-for friends. It felt good to work out a solution with Turk, as though they took a shaky step back to what they once had.

The strangers spread out along the coast, checked in recesses and under ledges. The black Canis and the older one, ears stiff, tongue lolling, trotted along with Yu'ung but seemed to herd her to one cave.

Where I usually stay when I'm on the shore.

They reached the mouth. The black one darted inside, quickly reappearing.

"Ocha!" Yu'ung called.

Ocha. Its name.

Ocha dropped a long object in Fierce's hand.

My spear, the one I was making in the image of Fierce's.

Kazeb scratched the nape of his neck, plucked a tiny critter out and flicked it away. He and Turk hadn't groomed each other in too long.

Fierce examined the shaft, smiled as Kazeb remembered he often did at Kazeb's flawed efforts to throw the Tall One spear, stitch hides together, and cook glue. He mouthed something to the older animal who huffed at Ocha and flattened his hackles.

Did he just tell them I was a friend?

Yu'ung pushed against Fierce's side, inspecting the lance, pointing to his efforts at smoothing the shaft and creating a firm hand hole.

Is she Fierce's pairmate?

Another female approached Fierce, this one with a rounded stomach. Fierce softened as those do around pairmates who carry babies.

So Yu'ung is not his pairmate.

He said to Turk, "They have acquired a band, pairmates, and the prospect of babies. They have changed since we met them."

Kazeb poked a thin spike at food lodged between his teeth. Relief told him he succeeded, though his focus remained on the scene below.

"I will wait to kill them, Liis, but only until they admit their treachery."

Which was why Kazeb slipped away without another word. When far enough for his steps to be hidden, he ran.

Chapter 16

Yu'ung set her feet onto the sandy shores and felt the world burst open. The massive Big Rock, a stone's throw away from where they moored, blocked sight of everything except a short expanse of boulders, scruffy greenery, and spots of scrub. Life's energy exploded in every direction. Rabbits bounced between their burrows, goats bleated to call their siblings, and birds cawed to announce intruders. The squishy sand was unlike anything in the mountains she left behind. It cleansed her thoughts of what she knew and prepared her for what she would learn. Scree piles and boulders littered the beach, tumbled together over time. Inside, below her ribs, a tingle told her the People were fated to be here.

She straggled along the shore, past clefts and cavities that invited her in, many with narrow mouths that would be easily blocked.

The Chosen with B'o, Laak, Jvelk, and Wik had already gone to overwatch spots while Yu'ung and Fierce searched the soaring flanks for a new homebase. Yu'ung trotted to where Ocha uncovered the lance. Fierce had been shocked, but quickly recovered, offered no clarification. The overhang was sufficiently large while small enough to warm quickly in cold times, and high enough off the beach to avoid floods even at the sea's maximum. Its swollen outcrop would well protect a hearth fire from rain and wind. Numerous dark tunnels disappeared into Big Rock's depths. All must be explored for rear entrances. A faint moistness in the air promised that one led to a stream. She lapped with her tongue.

No salt.

Since Fierce indicated the nearest stream he recalled was a distance away, water inside the shafts would be valuable. Bones from deer, cave bear, wolves, and ibex speckled the floor, as well as Giant Pig, Boar, and mountain sheep, but no Rhino or Mammoth with the oversized pelts required for outside homebases.

We will find them.

She explored many of the caves along Big Rock's base. They were laid out in the way of the People with hearths in front to vent outside and intimidate predators. Nests were along back walls, out of fire's light but still warmed by the heat. Yu'ung backed away from the Rock's towering shadow, found herself in the warm sea with a broad view of the shore's length.

A welcome earthy aroma wafted across her nose, damp dirt and life. *Grass! From where?*

The shore was sand and gravel, the cave floors dirt and debris. The rear tunnels were too dark to support life. Only one place remained. She backed up further until she was knee deep in the warm salt water and saw it, high above, a green fringe dripping over the Rock's summit.

If vegetation grows up there, sheep and goats could feed on it!

She held a hand up. The space between fingers, Sun, and horizon said there was enough time to check.

The flank was steep, but not the most treacherous she'd climbed. The sides offered numerous holds hued by those before her. Stretching one to the next felt good after the tight confines of the sea craft. She crested what should have been the peak but turned out to be a broad plateau stretching from the cliff to its flank. From the edge, rolling hills spread below, broken by silver strands of water, colorful fields of flowers, and lush knee-high grass spotted liberally with saplings. Offshore, swarms of fish left white trails in the blue-green sea.

She stretched, feeling the last vestiges of exhaustion lift away, replaced by a rare sense of contentment. For a moment, she simply took it in, the mellifluous coos from the far wall where a dense flock of fat, brownish pigeon-birds roosted, making room for new arrivals who shared scavenged food. Each greeted others with musical voices not unlike Shanadar's flute.

It would be pleasant to work among these birds, a fire warming the scarp's face when the air is cold. The adjacent areas are level enough to stake hides to dry and cut into wraps.

"Yu'ung. I have something to show you."

"Shanadar! I didn't see you behind me."

His step stuttered as he evaluated her question. "Because I was in front. Come to my homebase so you know the way."

"You won't be with us...."

"Xhosa asked me to guide you. Being one of the People is not my future."

He trotted past the pigeon-birds, stopped along the soaring rock wall at a spot like all the rest to her eye, and climbed.

As with the pathway to the plateau, finger- and toeholds festooned it.

Someone already marked this route for Shanadar.

He scampered upward, not slowing until he reached the topmost peak of Big Rock. The openness here of the weather-battered cleft made her dizzy, but the cool air soon calmed her. Shanadar strode onward toward a break in the solid rock where he disappeared. Yu'ung traipsed behind. Each stride kicked up dust whorls from the dry, packed surface.

No one has been here in a long while.

She entered a large cave. A fire crackled in an old hearth. Xad settled beside it, feet crossed over thighs. He looked content in ways she almost envied. The expansive grotto included nooks on the sides, a vent to the sky, and dark stygian tunnels in the back.

"This is my homebase. Close your eyes. Breathe. Listen. Sense what surrounds you."

Yu'ung settled on her bottom as Shanadar did, legs crossed, and inhaled … the flames crackled … sap in dry wood popped…. She exhaled. Bird calls drifted in … the beat of a stick on a dead trunk.... The mellow sound saturated her chest and flowed through her insides. Voices filtered through the emptiness, muddled words, stories of times past.

One is Xhosa. Does she live with Shanadar when not in my dreams?

Another misty voice, older, confident.

Old One? Is that you?

Shanadar asked, "Do you hear them?"

Eyes sealed shut, she whispered, "Yes."

A feather tickled her cheeks.

I fell asleep.

Eyes slit, she peered into a rat's whiskers.

Shanadar stroked its sleek fur. "He is a new friend. In return for food, he reveals tunnels where our predecessors etched memories."

Yu'ung stretched, shook away the haziness of sleep. "I must go."

"Will you bring us food and water? Xhosa and Seer provide the rest."

She wobbled upright, wanting to ask what that meant, but shadows outside were already long. If she didn't go soon, she would have to descend unfamiliar trails in the dark.

She backed toward the mouth. "Everyone will worry."

"Tell them not to. I will share more when I am prepared." Then, he seemed to forget about her.

Without another glance, she scampered down using the same ledges and protrusions that worked for the ascent. Darkness took over by the time she reached the shore. Flames danced ahead. She cricked her neck upward. Somewhere high above, Shanadar and Xad moved, but she saw only gray shapes in the fire's light, a blink of eyes, and then they disappeared.

She entered what had been selected to be the People's homebase. Fire sparked, fueled with dung and debris left by previous inhabitants, the interior walls already warm. Alcoves broke off the front. Each could have its own fire pit with smaller sections for tool knapping, food preparation, and hide work.

B'o approached, tense. "No one's seen Shanadar."

Yu'ung tilted her head upward. "He created a homebase at the top. With Xad."

B'o exhaled. "Of course he did."

Few talked while they ate, too busy listening to the sounds of a new life. Finished, they scraped pelts to replace those worn by sailing. The hunters sharpened tools. The subadults gathered around B'o for a lesson on how to work around the fissures that weakened the tips.

Day dawned early with nothing to block Sun's rays. There was something wondrous about waking up at the first hint of dawn, lying in a soft bed of grass in a homeland Yu'ung had spent far too many Moons to reach. She went outside to relieve her morning water, found Fierce, satchel secured over his shoulder, preparing for the day's tasks.

He called to her, "B'o, Jvelk, myself, and others will scout out waterholes, other tribes, Upright trace, find out who we share this area with—"

Aynoh interrupted, "And find healing plants."

"Yes." Then he looked at Yu'ung.

His words said one thing, but his body another which Yu'ung didn't understand.

"If you're going to a quarry where we can mine hard stones, yes. We need those. Otherwise, tell me how to get there."

"The route we'll take for the rest of our chores crosses by a quarry I visited on my last trip. I want everyone to know where it is."

Aynoh slashed a hole through the pelt she was scraping. Yu'ung glared at Fierce. He frowned, knowing he missed a clue but not what it was. Aynoh refused to look at him, so he stooped, pressed his palms against the sides of her head.

"Something is wrong here on this Big Rock. Kazeb should have greeted us. He knows we landed. Something changed since I left, caused problems. I must find out what that was and resolve it before placing you—and the others—in danger."

Aynoh picked at her wrap. "Before you leave—"

"You don't follow what I'm trying so awkwardly to say. If I leave, it is with you. If you stay, it is with me. Whichever it is, regardless of my band's decision, I will be with you."

"But we can't stay here if it isn't safe. Is that what you mean?"

"That's what I mean."

"And we can't leave the People in danger. Now I understand."

Yu'ung didn't believe what she'd just heard. Males didn't stay with a female's tribe. Always, it was the reverse. Before she could unravel enough to ask a question, someone shouted that they wasted daylight.

Yu'ung murmured, "Go. Aynoh and I will find the healing plants. You do the rest."

Fierce started to leave, turned back. "Until I am sure you are not endangered, never travel or work alone. Eknilk and Braanroorv will go with you and whoever is scavenging plant foods. They can scout at the same time."

Fierce and his group left. Ocha trotted out of the cave. She'd spent the night alone in the Canis' den. There was still no sign of Ragged Ear, Ump, or White Streak.

Probably investigating their new home, too.

But something inside told her it was more than that.

If they left us, would they not take Ocha?

Sun announced day's end. On cue, the hunters and scouts, scavengers and foragers straggled into camp, tired from the day's labors. As promised, food was abundant. The subadults blocked the entrance with a bushy screen. Nests were established, refuse dumped far enough from the homebase to keep scavengers away.

Everyone gathered around the hearth, helped themselves to the plethora of food while reviewing the day's activities. Little trace of Uprights was found, mostly one tribe of the People's kind. They'd found the quarry for hard stones and would mine it soon, but no water holes though there were animal trails Fierce was sure would lead to water. More importantly, the area held no surprises, no hidden dangers, nothing that would rule it out as a homebase.

Despite that, Yu'ung slept poorly, thoughts spinning about this long-awaited destiny.

Chapter 17

Wet, rough licks covered Yu'ung's lips and nose.

"Stop, Ocha!"

A voice said, "It's not Ocha."

She jolted. "Shanadar?"

Why is he here?

She forced her eyes open. With Shanadar was a large dirty Canis, crawling with ticks, fur thick with debris. His yellow eyes appraised Yu'ung as though deciding whether she was worth his time. A black strip stretched across his skull where White Streak had a light one. He howled—had Yu'ung passed?—spun a circle, and leapt, settling huge paws on Shanadar's bare trunk.

"It's good to see you, too, Blaze!" He rubbed his hands against Blaze's sides and nuzzled into the white fur. "Where have you been?"

She gaped. "This is the pup you've mentioned?"

"Now an adult."

Shanadar moved gracefully, unhurried yet with purpose. His tail fell past his shoulder, feathered with additional plumage.

Yu'ung said, "If he's part of Ocha's pack, they still aren't in the den. Only Ocha slept here last night."

Fierce slipped in, a frown across his visage. "Shanadar. Are Ump, White Streak, and Ragged Ear all right?"

Yu'ung subtly shook her head to remind Shanadar that Fierce knew nothing about Xhosa.

Shanadar said, "They are where they must be. All make their own choices."

Yu'ung's thoughts flashed over compact muddy trails, pendulous branches, steep inclines she'd seen in her dreams with Xhosa, enemies that left the furrow on White Streak's crown from a significant injury. Blaze sat on his haunches, panted, alert, knowing that whatever happened, whenever it was, Shanadar always would rescue him.

But if he knew the location of the rest of his pack, he wasn't saying.

Shanadar shrugged at her confusion. "He will tell you what he can, when he can, which isn't now, though you can ask."

Blaze flattened himself to the ground and squinted between his paws. His tail swished through the dirt.

How would I ask? I don't speak his barks, woofs, howls, yaps, and calls.

Ruk raced in, chubby legs churning, and wrapped his arms around Blaze's thick furred neck. Jhat barged in, steps behind her child, heaved a sigh at the surfeit of adults and the grubby furred creature Ruk hugged.

Fierce turned to Shanadar. "You and Xad live at the top of Big Rock?"

"Yes."

"You are more like Seer each day."

His words carried no judgment, despite the inference that Shanadar wouldn't assist in daily chores from the rock's lofty height. Seer didn't either. The Chosen had Lead Warriors, Hunters, Scouts, and also, what they termed a "spirit Lead"—Seer. His job was to make sense of the nonsensical, provide optimism when none existed, and devise solutions no one would think of.

Like traveling to unknown lands in search of new homes.

Jhat asked Fierce, "Where does this one called Seer live?"

"Like Shanadar, not with his tribe which is the Chosen. Days go by we don't see him. If I go to his cave, he may be cooking mulch for his visions or sitting trancelike, oblivious to my presence, a vine around his neck strung with pebbles and teeth, feathers in his hair, stripes on his shoulders and face. He has no Xad so goes without food or water or sleep until he awakens. Then, he eats with us at our hearth, face haggard, but eyes sparkling with the wisdom he's acquired. He will prance around, twirl and spin, then predict where to find a herd or migrate. The Elders at first argued about his pronouncements until they found they were always accurate.

Shanadar murmured, "Living apart serves us."

"What have you learned?"

Shanadar canted his head upward. "I will reveal it soon."

Jhat asked, "Why does Blaze have yellow eyes, the rest blue?"

Yu'ung waited for Shanadar. It was his tale, but he remained … distracted … so she replied for him.

"Let me tell you a story Shanadar told me." She flicked a glance at Shanadar, to see if he didn't want to tell this himself.

He plucked ticks from Blaze's coat and began to speak. "I had the good fortune to save the pup, Blaze. I was traveling from my former home with Ump, White Streak, and occasionally Ragged Ear—"

Ruk interrupted, "Not Ocha?"

"Not yet. She would come later." Shanadar rubbed a callused hand down Blaze's back. "One night, a pup appeared at my fire. He lay across from me, chewing a gazelle haunch with the pack. He still had soft fur, paws too huge for his body, ears that reached his neck, and absolutely no fear. Wherever he came from, he had been protected and cared for."

Shanadar fell silent and Yu'ung took over. "Blaze left while Shanadar slept. Shanadar didn't worry until coyote calls announced cornered prey. Ump and White Streak recognized Blaze's pitiful howls and raced to his rescue. He had trapped himself in a crevasse, a vine wrapped around his foot. Ump and White Streak held the coyotes off and Shanadar cut Blaze loose."

Shanadar took over again, his voice faraway. "That was the first time. The next time, he'd decided to nap on a sunny log and awakened to find it hurtling down a river toward a waterfall. His pack again called me to help."

Yu'ung chuckled. "They don't swim, nor does Shanadar, but no one considered those impediments!"

"Ump and White Streak stayed onshore. I attached one end of a vine to Ump and dragged the other out to Blaze. Then, Ump dragged both of us to shore. I didn't think it would work, but he was never supposed to die on that log. I haven't seen him since. Until now."

The ticks and the sharp stubble bit through Blaze's layers of fur to the delicate skin beneath. Shanadar spent a long time pulling all the debris and critters from his fur. Then, he massaged a foaming root over his body. It cleaned the remnants of dirt and mud away while soothing the raw skin beneath. He finished by washing him with water Xad brought in gourds. The clean Blaze was pure white, no longer a dirty brown.

Yu'ung tasted the sudsy substance and didn't recognize it. "What is this, Shanadar?"

"I cut myself crossing an arid desert on my way to you. It festered and the natives gave me these leaves. The exterior is spiky with painful barbs, but that doesn't stop them. The plant is useful for many purposes—a sturdy cordage, the flowers as food, and in my case, a disinfectant."

"How did you prepare it?"

"Removed the bark. Ground the interior pulp into powder. Mixed the shavings with small amounts of water until they produced a frothy substance that cleans and sanitizes."

Shanadar rolled back on his heels. "Has anyone fed Blaze?"

A whispered, *Of course he's hungry,* made Yu'ung giggle. She tossed Blaze a snake killed earlier, a treat he immediately devoured.

"How did he find us, Shanadar, this far from where we last saw him?"

Shanadar petted Blaze who purred happily. "He followed our scent."

"Across the water?"

"Of course not. Have you forgotten already that he can't swim?"

Shanadar fingered his flute with one hand and rubbed Blaze's side and back with the other. Xad pulled a replica from his pouch, one also whittled from a cave bear bone with holes drilled on both sides in a rough approximation of Shanadar's flute.

Grub called from outside the cave. Fierce barked back and then, to the group, said, "Animals or Uprights denned here for extended periods. They couldn't have done so without water. We'll find it today."

Shanadar rose, leaving Blaze asleep. "I will go with you." He turned to Ruk. "Would you check on Blaze when you can, make sure he doesn't need anything?"

Ruk responded by curling between the Canis' legs. "I can do that."

But it was not to be. As soon as Shanadar left the cave, Blaze scrambled to his paws and dashed after him.

Yu'ung passed on joining them, curious about a small cave at the base of the People's with a fig tree at the opening. She kept smelling water from it and wanted to see if there was enough to matter.

Fierce and Blaze led B'o, Shanadar, and a few others on an animal trail that was more suggestion than decisive, then diverted through unbroken scrub. Too remote to benefit from the sea breezes, they sweated beneath the blazing sun, hemmed in on one side by precipices, on the others by hills. Shanadar squinted against the wind's hot breath, pulled his shirt over his mouth so he didn't choke on the dust. They lapped up trickles of water from a few mostly dry streams and underground waterholes that bubbled up enough to dampen the soil. This was not unusual for them. There were times when everyone woke early to suck the dew from grass and leaves, lick depressions where moisture collected overnight before Sun evaporated what water remained.

Today, the group tramped over low slopes and along a dry river bed, faster than a walk, slower than a run, hoping the river bed had water farther up. Blaze raced ahead. Fierce caught up as the Canis sniffed prints that looked like the People's.

He said, "No surprise others would come here. Ahead is where I mined the hard stones the last time. It definitely has water."

Shanadar squatted. "He knows the odor from these prints."

"How can he?"

Shanadar murmured, "He waited for us a long time."

Fierce might have asked questions except Blaze growled and took off, chasing through a rugged, pockmarked field into a small forest. Past its far edge was a pool fed by a waterfall, surrounded in misty rainbows as it cascaded over a high cliff. The slap and plop of its descent drowned out all sounds. Shanadar lapped the air. The waterfall was fresh and clean, tasting of the plants it fed.

Heavy branches dipped into the pond which rippled with life. Fish darted through the shallows, insects skittering just out of their reach. The shores burst with wildflowers, scrubby stunted saplings, and brush that clung precariously to the steep grades. It flowed past the sunlight into the grotto's dim interior. How far Shanadar couldn't tell because everything below the surface was hidden by froth.

The group satisfied their stomachs, dumped cool water over their bodies, fed on cat-tails and roots, and tried to figure out if there was a reason other than water why Blaze brought them here.

B'o poked his lips to the precipice. "A river must feed the waterfall, at the top, likely connected to a lake. There's a scant route that leads to the waterfall's bluff. Does Blaze want us to track the stream that feeds the falls? Does it lead to a tribe he wants us to meet? One he stayed with while awaiting our arrival?"

"Let's find out," and Fierce trotted toward the trail barely evident beneath the pounding water.

Blaze didn't. Instead, he disappeared into the grotto.

B'o said, "I guess we go in there."

Fierce diverted his path, now stepping carefully on the slick surfaces. "I think this is where Kazeb and I found the hard stones last time, though we entered through a different access. He described the waterfall, wanted to show me, but we ran out of time."

There were old prints which Fierce ignored, but fresh sets stood out, the broader sole of the People's kind overlaid with Blaze's. The Canis barked from one of the tunnels at the rear, ears perked, eyes on Shanadar.

"We're coming." Shanadar lit a torch from his carry sack and followed Blaze's lead down the passageway.

Soon, the only light came from the torches. The hollow echo of water dripping blocked out the sound of their steps. The tiny stream that ran beside the trail, fed by the waterfall pond, disappeared. The tunnel floor was smooth in spots, jagged elsewhere, sometimes so twisty they fit through only if they canted to the side. The waterfall stream sporadically resurfaced to provide them with welcome liquid and then, again, submerged.

Fierce said, "I remember this. The air was always cool and damp because of the waterway, and there were springs, too, here and there. If we were stuck down here, we wouldn't die of thirst."

Blaze picked his way through a labyrinth of tunnels, vast chambers, subterranean lakes, and thick stalactites as though he knew the route. Suddenly, he barked into the dark. A shout responded.

Grub jerked. "Someone is stuck!" Then lurched as fast as possible through the murky darkness toward the call. "Whoever you are, we can help! Hold on!"

Fierce muttered, "That voice is familiar," but said nothing more.

The course constricted, a wall to one side, a deep fissure to the other, the tunnel's floor ever narrower. It became more slippery the farther they went. Everyone leaned into the wall for balance while making way intermittently for a bevy of critters drinking the water that clung to the rocks.

Whoever was trapped called out, "Be careful. There's a crack you have to jump over. If you don't, you'll end up down here with me!"

They navigated the fissure he warned of and stopped just above his position. Shanadar's last torch dimly illuminated a figure below, too deep to crawl out, but not so far that a vine wouldn't reach him.

Grub dumped one down and yelled, "Wrap this around yourself! We'll pull you up. If you're injured, one of us will come down!"

"I'm fine!"

With everyone's effort, the stranded male was extracted in no time. As a torch lit him, Fierce grinned and the dusty, disheveled male groaned.

"You! I am indebted to the one who cost my pairmate's life!"

Fierce paled and fell silent, but Turk crouched over Blaze, rubbed his open hands down the Canis' sides. "But it was you who led them to me."

He nodded to Shanadar and scowled at the rest of his saviors. "If you're out of torches, I have more," pulling a handful out of his shoulder sack. After passing them around, he said, "I'll show you the way out."

Fierce said, "We know—"

"It's a shortcut," and he charged off.

He was right. In no time, they reached sunlight, the access point Fierce remembered taking with Kazeb.

Outside, Turk asked, "Where is my brother?"

Fierce scratched his side. "Kazeb? Why would I know?"

Shanadar noted Turk's sightless eyes, fixed on Fierce but not seeing him. Despite that the Chosen Leader had saved Turk's life, the heat of fury leaked from his pores, the swell of doubt from his eyes as though what he thought he knew, he no longer did.

"Because of the female Yu'ung—never mind. Go back to your homeland, Tall Ones. You are not wanted here," he said and sprinted away.

Blaze moaned.

Shanadar watched Turk fade into the dusk from the canopy of a small copse. Even from this distance, his long thumping stride made him easy to follow. Sharing the limb with Shanadar was a gray squirrel intermittently eating an acorn and chattering nonstop at this massive furless creature disturbing the forest. Shanadar had seen none of the Giant Apes here that had populated select jungles and forests along his journey to Yu'ung's former homeland, so the Clan might be the largest tree-climbing animal the squirrel had ever seen. While it groused at Shanadar, it tracked Turk with its unblinking eyes, a torn ear twitching, no doubt glad the huge Upright left, taking with him the stench of evil that encased him like a fog.

You fought and won, earned your scars and indifference. We could be friends.

That was not to be. As soon as Turk disappeared, the squirrel switched its enmity to Shanadar. Its paws dropped and tail raised. Mouth open to display formidable incisors, it yowled a long, defiant call. Done, dominance established over this branch, this tree, this copse, it scampered away.

Fierce called up, "Shanadar! We'll nest inside for the night, mine rocks tomorrow."

Blaze left to catch his meal while others gathered tinder for a fire. They were eating travel food as Blaze pranced in, blood on his muzzle. Before the hearth's embers died away, Blaze fell asleep next to Shanadar, quickly followed by the rest.

They dropped armloads of stones into the camp's communal pile as Sun peaked overhead.

Aynoh approached. "I thought Yu'ung was with you?"

A chill ran through Fierce. "No…."

Ese huffed. "Then she's missing."

Chapter 18

Yu'ung

Before he died, Old One had told Yu'ung of an unusual way to find water, taught by the elders in his boyhood for desperate times. Never had she been in a situation to use it until now. She hoped the secret would work.

A leafy fig tree grew at the mouth of a nearby cave. It was too early for the sweet fruit, but that's not what brought her here today. She wrapped both legs around the fat, open roots and slid into a murky, submerged grotto until her feet touched damp ground. Within steps, she drank pure, clean water, and then paused, sniffed, and glanced around.

The Upright from above has been here. I wonder if he—or she—left a message.

Tribes etched or painted messages onto the flat surface of shaft walls to advise those who came later what predators to be wary of or where to hunt.

She lit a branch with tinder stored in her satchel and entered the only tunnel that had been recently disturbed. One torch after another fizzled out, which didn't worry her. She'd brought plenty. Finally, there it was, an expanse of rock decorated with the squares, circles, triangles, and dots. She fingered the indentations, the curves and swirls, deciphered what she could, and stored the rest in memory.

The People's journey will be a commendable addition.

She chipped her own lines, circles, overlapped triangles, and other shapes to reflect the People, most of them unlike those already in place. When the torch sputtered out, another replaced it, then another. Satisfied with the indentations, she extracted a concave shell from her shoulder sack where she could mix ochre, cinders, or charcoal with sap, bees wax, or animal fat to create the right shade of red, orange, brown, or yellow. Shades differed depending upon the message, but always started with ochre. If her torches weren't low, she'd cook them to darken the hue. Today, she settled for the natural muted red, used fingertips for broad strokes, a flat-tipped bone and a sliver for detail.

Another torch expired, and she completed her work with a circle of dimples created with a porcupine needle. The message glowed with import. She packed away the materials, lit the last torch, and hurried on her backtrail. A study of the other walls would have to wait for a later trip.

She stumbled to a stop at an unfamiliar intersection as her final flame expired.

I don't need light. I can follow my own scent.

But it was hard to find, melted into the musty dampness. Earth mixed with decay was far heavier than her odor. She picked the most likely tunnel and dragged her fingers along the rough wall. The passage tapered to a ledge about the width of her feet. She didn't remember this.

I picked wrong. Better to retrace to the alternate tunnel.

Which she did, but the intersection had disappeared.

She shambled forward, unraveling the problem. Light appeared ahead, but turned out to be iridescent fungi spotting the tunnels walls and casting an eerie, green hue unlike anything she'd encountered coming in.

What's going on?

She crouched, exhausted, sipped water. If not for that moment of quiet while her mind mulled through options, she would have missed the yip. The hair on her neck stiffened and her heart beat wildly. She slouched against the rough wall, cold with fear as the yips grew louder.

How could a predator track me? But who hunts down here?

She sucked in air, finally identified the hunter.

"Ocha!"

Within breaths, Ocha was on her.

"You tracked me!"

She grabbed the nape of Ocha's neck, and the Canis led them past the message wall—how did Yu'ung miss it?—to the fig's base. There, Ocha stopped, slapped her tail against her sides. She'd committed to rescue Yu'ung with no plan for how she would climb out.

"I have an idea, Ocha."

Yu'ung piled the spent torches by the chute which left room for Ocha in her shoulder sack. Then, Yu'ung wrapped the Canis' arms around her neck. Ocha was heavy, but Yu'ung was strong. She jumped, grabbed the roots, wrapped her legs around the corded stem, pulled with her arms and pushed with her feet against the roots. Like a worm, hand over hand, she slithered up and then out.

As they exited, a flicker from the distant hill caught her attention. The blink of eyes.

I am being watched.

Kazeb

Kazeb wasn't ready to reveal himself to the newcomers. He wanted to watch first, determine their intention, see if those of his kind were captives or willing participants, and find out if the return visit was a health check or to eliminate a problem, as his brother said. He'd spend today, maybe longer, snooping, and then talk with Turk.

No surprise, despite the lengthy travel, they started with Sun. One group trundled off to forage. Yu'ung and several females went with a

Chosen male. Another mixed group led by Fierce went the opposite direction, probably to explore.

He froze.

The white Canis was with them, the one he and Turk found wandering the foothills and nursed back to health.

All groups passed out of his sight. Kazeb had just decided to follow Fierce, to see if there was an opportunity to catch him alone and talk to him, when Yu'ung returned by herself. Instead of going into the tribe's cave, she stopped at the grotto guarded by the fig tree.

Does she smell the water?

Kazeb visited the hidden pool when it was the closest water source. Of greater interest was the message wall. He'd been there only once, to read the stories etched into the stone, intended to add his own, but had lost the desire to do more than survive after his tribe's destruction.

She has enough torches to find the water, but not to investigate the etchings. Without light, she will be lost in the tunnels, and no one will know where to search. I'll stay until she returns, make sure she is safe.

He wriggled into the thatch, used the time waiting to take note of the newcomers' overwatch positions and clumsy trawling efforts, their camaraderie, and the fullness of their carry-alls. Then, the scouts plodded in, jabbering at each other, a wild boar slung over one's shoulder as though it weighed nothing.

They act like a tribe exploring, not one looking for trouble or retribution.

High above, a fire burned in a cave. A figure scuffled through the shadows and glanced at him before melting into the shadows.

Who is that? And where is Yu'ung?

She should have returned by now. She must have discovered the messages, decided to decipher them, and leave her own. As he tried to decide whether to go after her or continue to wait, a black Canis jumped onto the exposed fig roots and dropped into the dark.

Is that the one they call Ocha? She can't climb!

He wanted to ensure Yu'ung found her way out of the maze, but with the dying daylight, Turk also concerned him. He'd left to mine hard stones at the opposite end of the peninsula. The only danger up there was that he must crawl deep into the cave system to reach the quarry. Any misstep could land him in a yawning crevasse difficult to climb out of, especially in the pitch dark.

I'll check our homebase. If he's not back, I'll find him if need be, then see what happened to Yu'ung.

The homebase was empty. Turk hadn't been there all day. Kazeb wasted no energy on a fire, ate only a handful of nuts, and fell asleep, planning to wake with Sun and find what happened to Turk and Yu'ung.

He awoke to Turk's snores. His brother stunk of dirt and crud. New scrapes and gouges blooded his skin as though he fell into a crevasse and fought his way out. Kazeb wouldn't question him. Injuries were common in their physical lives. The hard stone pile remained empty.

Kazeb kindled a cinder in the hearth fire, then reheated leftover stew. While he ate, Turk awoke and groggily told of being trapped in a gorge, doomed until he heard the Canis' barking mixed with Tall Ones and Clan voices. They pulled him out.

Kazeb stuffed his satchel with torches and vines, what he might need. "Who rescued you?"

Turk grumbled, "Fierce and his band. I didn't expect that."

Kazeb wanted to discuss that, but didn't have time, not if Yu'ung remained missing.

"If they were with you, they don't know Yu'ung may be in trouble."

Turk rubbed sleepy eyes. "Yu'ung? I'm sure she's fine."

Kazeb wasn't. "You sleep. I'll be back when she's safe."

Turk grunted, toppled over, and was asleep before Kazeb left.

The sky was already low and gray, dark black clouds overhead a warning. As though fulfilling a promise, sky fire struck the earth, exploding in a waterfall of sparks and flames, one tree and another sending a plume of fire upward. Kazeb sped up, but carefully. The ground was already slick with a soggy matting of dead stems. He reached the woods above the fig cave. The rain was steady and cold, but not under the welcome canopy. He searched the surroundings, saw the line of worried faces in the mouth of her cave.

She hasn't returned.

The shafts in Big Rock flooded in heavy storms. If Yu'ung got turned around, she could be lost in those and Kazeb was probably the only one who could track her. He found a spot where he could see both the newcomers and the fig tree cave where he had last seen her. If she didn't show up soon, he would descend into the warren of tunnels and find her.

He didn't have long to wait before she straggled out. Hanging around her neck was the black Canis Ocha. She squirmed free of Yu'ung's grip, twisted to face Kazeb, and howled.

Chapter 19

Yu'ung

What had been a blue cloudless sky when she started this morning was now a black rumpled pelt of clouds as far as she could see. Thunder boomed, roaring claps broken by spikes of fire.

The same red-haired stranger she'd seen earlier stood on the overwatch hill. Rivers of water poured from his hair, his breath a diaphanous cloud. He rubbed his arms to stay warm. When he caught her eye, he didn't look away. Nor did she.

Who are you? And why are you here? Did you know I was lost in there?

He brightened at her appearance.

Why?

Her curiosity was sidetracked by a panicked voice. "Yu'ung!"

When she turned back, the stranger was gone. She ran toward Ese. Rain came down so hard it almost hurt, stinging her skin and blowing into her eyes and nose and mouth as she sped toward the distressed call. A tree burst into flames. Rain doused the fire, but left the trunk to smolder. She splashed through ankle-deep puddles, drops blurring a world she was just getting to know. Ocha snorted happily, and bounded forward from one puddle to the next, lapping droplets from the air as she bounced up.

She dove into the People's cave through a curtain of water that fell in a waterfall. Inside, a warm fire crackled. Tribe members crouched in front of the heat, wagging chapped hands over the fire. Wet pools formed beneath them. Blaze sniffed and turned to her.

Yu'ung roughed the creature's white fur. "You smell Ocha. She's … outside.... She'll come in when ready."

Grub growled. "Glad you're here. No one wanted to search for you in the storm."

"I was investigating a pond at the fig's roots."

Ese and Jhat shuffled past to collect the water that flooded over the mouth.

B'o shouted to his pairmate, "No need! The storm will restock the ponds!"

Blaze bounced at Yu'ung's side, his yellow eyes anxious.

Fierce approached. "Where is Shanadar?"

All turned to him. "With you."

"He came back with us, but I haven't seen him since."

Yu'ung murmured, "Maybe that's where Ocha went," which didn't make sense if Shanadar was in his cave.

Xad paled. "He wanted to be left to himself. I asked...." He picked at the skin on his arm until it bled, then switched to the other one.

"Xad. Don't worry."

But that was impossible for the boy-male whose life seemed to begin when Shanadar saved him. Without his liberator to tell him what to do, Xad was lost.

Ocha darted into the cave, froze in the mouth, silhouetted against the black storm by sky fire.

"Ocha! Blaze was worried! Stay here."

But Yu'ung glazed over, remembering another time she and Ocha raced into a storm to save a tribe member. Ocha charged Yu'ung, ran in circles, and sprinted back out into the storm. Blaze howled and raced after her.

"It's Shanadar," and Yu'ung scrambled to her feet and chased the Canis, fearful that he, like Old One, was in mortal trouble.

"Shanadar!" she screamed. A bay from both Canis affirmed her thoughts.

"Ocha! Blaze! Where did he go?"

They howled again, muzzles tilted up, voices haunting in the gale's roar. Reflexively, she tilted her head to match the line of Ocha's muzzle. There Shanadar stood, on a ridge well above her, silhouetted against the sky as fire shot through the darkness.

"Shanadar! Get back! It's too risky!"

He was soaked. Water streamed down his wrap, plastered to him like a skin. Arms up, head back. If he heard her, he didn't acknowledge it. An expanding puddle covered his feet. He must be in a hollow of some sort.

He'll slip in this rain!

Yu'ung raced up Big Rock's flank using the cracks and protrusions she remembered from the last time. Ocha pawed at the rock face, leapt, but slid down. She wailed, unhappy to be left behind. The narrow ridges worked for digits but not for paws. Yu'ung clawed up the slippery surface, past the flat plateau she had imagined as a work site. The birds huddled, protected by the overhang. They cawed their annoyance as she rushed past. She couldn't see Shanadar's trail in the dark so found her own. It had no natural protrusions, but Yu'ung could leap untethered by hands or feet from one ledge to another farther than she was tall. This she did, exploding forward, toward ledges she couldn't see but recalled from memory.

It worked until it didn't. The crack that should have been there wasn't.

On instinct, she slammed against the clammy bluff, clung to the tiniest of grips to steady herself, then, foot wedged into a crack, scrabbled with her fingertips on any available edge as she yanked a foot free and found another crack. Pain seared through her ankle.

It cleared her mind.

The sky roared, a warning but not to her. The tenebrous clouds fired a fiery bolt. Shanadar's limbs froze, his scream soundless as fire outlined his figure. Yu'ung shrieked.

His knees buckled. He tumbled. Ocha howled. Yu'ung flung herself toward him, gripped the wall with her weak hand, stretched the other to Shanadar as he toppled past. She snatched his arm and locked her elbow. He jerked to a stop, almost dislocating her shoulder, but the thick muscles held. The water-slick hand started to slip free, so she clung tighter. With a hiss, he slapped against the escarpment, his fingers and toes clambering for any hold to take weight off the arm, and found one. Shanadar was a good climber. Yu'ung too pressed into the craggy surface and they both rested.

She needed to unravel this mess. How could she lower him safely if neither of them could see the small edges in the dark? Was he conscious? He'd said nothing since the sky fire lit him up.

I can do this.

Her arm trembled violently, but she refused to loosen the grip.

He saved me once. I can do no less for him.

Shanadar's calm voice broke through the raucous deluge. "Close your eyes. We're almost to my route. You know that one."

The din of rain drowned out every sound except Shanadar's words. Carefully, she did as directed, eyes blind, mind seeing each toehold and ridge. Cold penetrated the saturated pelts, chilled her limbs and torso, but she paid no attention. She almost cried when she felt a familiar edge.

"Yu'ung," the word faint but clear. "You did it. I'm fine now. You can let me go."

She surveyed his injuries, what she could ascertain in the rain-drenched gloom. The fire charred the entire side of his neck, scalp, and arm. His free hand gripped a ledge, feet on a tiny shelf she recalled from her first ascent.

"Are you sure?" He sounded sure.

"Of course."

She released him.

He offered a minute smile of appreciation and lowered himself with an alacrity even healthy Clan members couldn't match. By the time she touched ground, Shanadar was consoling a distraught, quaking Blaze. Xad crouched by the side, hunched into a ball beneath a jutting stone ledge, knees tight against his chest, damp wrap glued to his torso.

A glance—Xad was uninjured, just distraught.

"Come, Shanadar. I need to treat those burns."

"They're fine," he said, but she didn't believe him.

Everyone scurried out of the way as she dragged him inside the cave. Xad trailed behind, whimpering like an injured animal as tears mixed with rain on his shirt.

The bolt scorched Shanadar's skin where it entered and exited. One eyelid was crimson, the orb milky. The burnt hair and singed wraps painted him with a noxious stench. He struggled to make out Aynoh's words and blinked his one good eye often as though to clear his vision, but whatever discomfort he felt—which must have been debilitating—he refused to give life to. All made room for the healers to work. Aynoh pounded herbs until sufficiently soft, then mixed them with honey and applied the mulch liberally to the burns, scrapes, abrasions, and cuts. Yu'ung and Ese rubbed the burns with mucus from a fat green leaf.

Aynoh said, "I have flowers for the pain…."

He looked befuddled. "Pain?"

Aynoh huffed in annoyance. "Xad." The subadult scurried over. "Take these." She handed him smooth leaves. "Apply the inside slime to the burns as often as possible. If you run out, I will tell you where to harvest them."

As Aynoh talked to Xad, Yu'ung asked Shanadar, "Why did you stand on that ledge in a storm?"

"I had to call the sky fire—" he said and passed out.

"Well, you did," *but why?*

Yu'ung hunched by the fire, pelts steaming, hair dripping a steady rhythm that sent chills through her chest. She tried to stay awake, but tipped into Aynoh's lap. She didn't notice Shanadar rise, missed Xad's squeal as he stuffed Aynoh's fat leaves in his satchel and sprinted outside.

Aynoh muttered, "If he is intent on death, we won't stop him this time," and she called to Xad, "Tell Shanadar to return tomorrow so I can check his burns!"

Xad bobbed his assent and continued the chase. Yu'ung never opened her eyes.

Yu'ung. Wake up.

Xhosa?

Shanadar seeks truth. Leave him to do so.

Can I help?

He needs mushrooms and flowers.

To heal these burns?

No. To become himself. The broth imperils any but Shanadar.

Shanadar will know where to find them?

I've told him. He must access the sentience in all life.

Sentience? What is that?

Shanadar must talk to animals, hills, plants, peaks, and valleys as Seer and I do. Listen to what he tells you.

Listen…. I will….

Now, sleep. You need rest.

Chapter 20

Yu'ung intended to finish what she didn't get to yesterday by scouting the opposite direction Fierce had, and see if there were any camps or trace that should concern her. First, though, her patient.

"B'o! Have you seen Shanadar?"

"Not since last night."

Ese dropped stems on the hearth to soften and asked, "Will he recover?"

Yu'ung told the truth. "A few do."

B'o barked a laugh. "Nothing as simple as sky fire will kill the Shanadar I migrated with."

Yu'ung sighed. The demands of a new homebase, the confusion of Xhosa's words last night, and the stress of a threat made her skull pound.

"He's driven by forces I doubt he controls."

B'o snapped stone against hammerstone. A sliver chipped away, thin and sharp enough to cut.

He said, "Shanadar was … normal … at first. He only became … strange … after you and Old One left for the mountains … as though he didn't know how to be part of a community. That mystified me. I assumed over time, he would adapt."

Aynoh asked, "Did his former tribe reject him?"

Xhosa had told Yu'ung sketchy details about Shanadar's life prior to the People, that his former tribe treated him poorly, didn't understand his oddities, even encouraged him to leave. Xhosa's offer provided purpose to his life. That he had gathered his own pack—the Canis, the Wise Stone, the bone flute—to guide him was all the proof Yu'ung needed that it worked. Mentors and friends need not be tribe members or even Uprights. The Canis were proof of that.

But those were Shanadar's secrets to tell.

"He never said. I am scouting today, where I planned to go yesterday."

"Did Fierce tell you about rescuing Turk from the cave?"

At the shake of Yu'ung's head, Aynoh told the story briefly. "He thinks it will make Turk safer to be around because at least he'll think before reacting."

Yu'ung stuffed a water-laden vine in her shoulder sack and hurried down the coast, cautious of the scree, until she arrived at a spacious field where she'd seen toe- and fingerholds cut into Big Rock. They must have been created by former inhabitants, and Yu'ung wanted to see what view from this edge of the Rock was important to them. She stretched from one to another without difficulty, summiting in time to see Sun crest the horizon.

One sloped side dumped into the vast endless sea without shores, not even a brown stretch of land on the horizon. To the other side was lush grass spotted with saplings and brush, swaths of prairies laden with berry bushes, broken by low hills and bottomless crevasses.

Those would be good for the dead …

There was a small quarry closer than where Turk was rescued, but maybe too small to be reliable. She saw rabbits, ground birds, a brown bear well off in the distance, and predators, Canis or hyaena. The latter wouldn't be there without meat prey. No mammoth, rhino, or other large animals.

As she prepared to turn back, she dropped. Someone was there, at the edge of her extreme sight.

Is this the male who spied on me yesterday? Or one of the brothers Fierce met on his first trip? Or are they the same?

She studied the fuzzy figure, searching for any abnormalities—a shadow that didn't belong, a strange hump or movement the breeze didn't cause—and found nothing, just the lone figure who might or might not have burnished hair. Since she'd never asked if both brothers were red-haired like herself, it didn't matter. She backed away from the crest, sure he hadn't seen her, but with the unsettled feeling that he was stalking her.

Why do I always see a similar lone figure where I am?

She returned to camp, but the entire way, felt eyes on her back, though not enough danger to raise her hackles. By the time she was within sight of the camp, they faded away.

At the clearing in front of the cave, Ese called, "Shanadar brought eggs."

"How is he?"

"Other than a black stripe on his side festooned with raw, raised blisters, fine. He admits to no discomfort."

Yu'ung saw Fierce hardening the tip of a lance in the fire and trotted up to him. "I scouted the reverse direction you went yesterday. An Upright shadowed me."

"I don't think either of the brothers is cause for immediate danger, especially not after we rescued Turk," he said, but called to Grub.

"Did you or Eknilk see any unexpected trace yesterday?"

"Old prints and one set like the People."

He grumbled, "Yu'ung thinks someone is stalking her. It is odd that the brothers haven't made themselves known since our landing. I won't count the accidental meeting with Turk. They knew as soon as we beached our vessel last time. I have no doubt they knew just as fast this time."

Yu'ung stabbed her spear's round end into the ground. "I found Upright prints by the fig tree. When I descended, they were also by the pool that watered the fig as well as in one of the tunnels."

She skipped the details about following it, leaving a message, wandering hopelessly and Ocha's rescue, ending with, "When I climbed out, an Upright—probably our kind—with red hair was watching the cave's entrance. Fierce. When you leave the Big Rock, will these former friends reveal themselves as enemies?"

Fierce's gaze shifted. "We left on good terms," but he sounded defensive, and his hands fidgeted. "At least I thought so until seeing Turk yesterday."

"I think it's Kazeb who has been watching me, but why?"

Fierce marched in a tight circle, shoulders tense, hands fisted. "I told them I'd return. That's one reason I landed where my band did the first time." Confusion flushed his face. "Something happened when we left to explain why they avoid us now and Turk was so unfriendly."

Fierce shucked his satchel to his shoulder. "Show me where you saw them today, Yu'ung. I'm going to confront them."

"We'll go, too," and B'o said as he motioned to Laak and Jvelk.

Laak preened. Jvelk blinked. Wik grabbed her far-throwing spear as though also invited. No one argued.

Yu'ung slowed, allowing the rest to move ahead. "He is behind us. Can you tell if it is your former friend?"

Fierce huffed, face forward as though nothing about this scouting had changed, but he gripped his spear more tightly and shucked his shoulder sack to place his cudgel in a more accessible position. Yu'ung did the same.

Fierce murmured, "If it is, he'll show himself."

"We agree to let him say his piece, find out if he's friend or foe."

She raised her voice now so the spy could hear, forced calm into it she didn't feel. "Yes, everyone is happy. Ese arranged areas for sleeping, knapping, cooking, and deboning. She and Wik want the cave uncluttered, waste-free, unattractive to predators. She established a midden and a location to stretch and dry skins."

Fierce responded calmly, as though a normal conversation, "New wraps signify to Seer and the rest of our tribe that we had a successful quest."

Yu'ung scowled. "I prefer this be deemed a failure, to discourage your kind from returning."

The ropes in Fierce's neck tightened. "I tried to talk to Aynoh about my departure and she asked about cordage. Every time I raise the topic, she avoids it."

"Of course she does. Aynoh wants to stay. She has become the People's Elder. She waits for you to commit before choosing between obligations."

Dry thatch crunched as though whoever followed tried to get closer to hear. Both ignored it, pretending to be involved in the conversation.

"Wik will go as Grub's pairmate. Others who carry Chosen babies will make their own decision to stay or leave. Too many joining the Chosen will decimate the People."

They fell silent, and Yu'ung strained for sounds of their spy, but he was cagey. Just the one hint and now, nothing.

Did he purposely step on twigs, tell us he is here, now, nothing? Not nothing. I feel him disrupting the air around me, his odor mixing with the otherwise prominent dirt and rock aromas.

Yu'ung and the rest stopped by a pond. She sucked in water, fresh from yesterday's rain, and dumped handfuls over her head and neck, then scratched her arm and thigh, visually eyeing the bend of a river through the shallow valley.

At least, he will think that's what I'm doing.

The corner of her eye caught him—a young, muscular male, sure in a way one is who's made difficult decisions.

Has he placed himself this way so I don't feel at risk? Or so I do?

Why her? Why not Fierce? She sniffed. It matched the aroma by the fig.

Time to put him on notice.

She jerked in his direction. He ducked behind the boulder, but not fast enough.

"We know you are here. Show yourself."

Chapter 21

One-who-tracked them stepped into the open, arms loose, face inquisitive not intimidating.

It's the one with ochre hair.

Fierce released the tight wrap he had on his shaft. "Kazeb!" his voice happy but cautious.

Kazeb smiled, which did little to ease the tension. "It's good to see you," his voice cautious.

Yu'ung wanted to ask why he hid when the group first arrived, and again when she explored the fig grotto. Was he the one to leave the messages in the tunnel? Spy on the People? Was he trying to resolve his difference with Fierce or get rid of him? But she didn't have a chance. Kazeb had his own agenda.

"Do I still call you brother, Fierce?"

The voice broke through her thoughts, a hard edge to the words.

Fierce started toward him. "Of course. Why not?" He motioned. "Yu'ung is Alpha for those I travel with. Angry Mountain destroyed her home. She hopes this will be a new one."

Kazeb turned to her. "Yu'ung. My brother said you were fiercer."

"And Fierce said you were friendlier." She shifted her weight to get a better view. "Guess we're both disappointed."

He couldn't squelch the smile that reached his eyes. "Good. You are worthy of one who leads hunters, talks to Canis, and fearlessly explores what you have never seen. What is this Angry Mountain?"

Yu'ung squinted at the Sun, reveled in its warmth. "Boiling lava and cinder buried everything in my home territory. Ash saturated the air and hid Sun and Moon until all life died from lack of heat and light. We had to breathe through our wraps much of the time. We scavenged carcasses, but soon, those were gone and we survived off our travel food, tubers, worms, and the pulp inside bark. The trail to reach this peninsula was laid out by Shanadar and Fierce. Much of it was as desolate, barren, and lifeless as what we fled. I began to wonder if we would ever escape far enough to survive. Then gradually, over what felt like many Moons, enough improved that we could scavenge."

Kazeb wrinkled his brow. "Are you referring to the white snow-that-doesn't-melt? Not enough fell here to cause problems."

Voice measured, words labored, his smooth red hair, fresh stripes, rich brown eyes, solemn and guarded, he asked Fierce, "How far did you travel after leaving us?"

Fierce spread his fingers. "Both handfuls of Moons. I lost track."

Yu'ung asked, "And you? Where did you first call home?"

He smiled at her, something it appeared he hadn't done in a while. "We came from over the mountains. It is a treacherous climb that makes them almost unbreachable. I often wonder how we survived the migration."

"How did you?"

"Instead of over, we traveled around. That was moderately less perilous."

Yu'ung stifled a giggle. "Fierce says you are Alpha?"

A shadow crossed his features, lingered, and melted away. "Turk and I split those responsibilities. When we arrived here at the Big

Rock, we solved every difficulty that came up, thrived on the newness, as you have. It was only the latest we were unable to surpass."

Fierce stiffened. "Latest?"

Surprise and then relief passed through Kazeb. "You are unaware?" His question hopeful, which surprised Yu'ung.

"How would I know? I have been gone. Before I left, you were a strong, vibrant Clan with a positive future." His enthusiasm tapered off and he blinked. "Did something happen to change that? Related to your pairmate's illness?"

Kazeb brushed his hand through the air. "A discussion for later. Or is there no later? Are you leaving soon?" An edge to his words.

Fierce bobbed agreement, absentmindedly, missed the anger in the question. Yu'ung didn't.

Kazeb directed his next question to her, "You carry a Tall One spear."

"They long ago intrigued me, what could be accomplished with them. As a subadult, I retrieved one that had been abandoned, taught myself to mimic how it was used."

His face lit up. "Tell me the story!"

She studied his eyes, filled with excitement, the honest lines framing his mouth. "Another time, I will. Today, we must hunt."

"There are no herds, not now, but there are other food sources."

She didn't expect that reply. "What do you use in place of hides and organ sacks?"

"The occasional small herd suffices and we are judicious with the resources. Large herds arrive rarely but systematically. Those, all locals hunt together, then each tribe takes what they require to last until the next large herd makes its way through. If we are friends by then, you may participate."

He lingered on her and she on him. Was he who he seemed or trying to trick her? She ran into the latter too often on this journey. Appearance, actions, and instinct identified them, but not always soon enough. Kazeb inspired none of those instinctive tingles.

I'll check with Ocha.

"Your People call you Liis. Fierce calls you Kazeb. My mother also has a different name among the People and the Chosen. We called her Kriina. Fierce calls her pairmate and Aynoh, which means—"

"Spirit. An unusual choice."

She studied his earnest way with a level gaze, how he wrinkled his brow or laughed at the right times.

"You backed out of guiding the Chosen because your pairmate grew sick."

A storm brewed in his eyes. Normally, she avoided someone's painful memories, but she must know. If he blamed Fierce, would it carry over to her? Something told her they were less about what *had* transpired than what *hadn't,* but she wouldn't know until she poked.

Fierce beat her to it. "Where is Turk?"

"If you ask whether he endangers you, no. If that changes, I will tell you. Until then, he trusts me to ask the questions." His voice cracked. "For one, why did you leave, Fierce?"

"We waited for you whenever possible, left a trail of cairns. We never abandoned you."

"The day you moved on, our world exploded. Sickness felled many, including my brother's and my pairmates."

And they blame Fierce.

Fierce rubbed his hand on his hips. His voice was so quiet, Yu'ung practically missed what he asked, "Where is your Clan?"

Kazeb hunched as he told the sordid tale of his Clan's demise.

"Turk and I never suffered. The healer suspected the poison that caused the illness came from the water or food that everyone ate. Intentional or accidental, he wouldn't commit. He warned us that the mysterious individual hid among us and would continue until stopped or he ran out of victims. When the healer died, we encouraged whoever survived to leave until the mystery could be solved."

His voice stuttered, hands twitched as he fought past horrors. Yu'ung feared that without a lifeline, if he couldn't rid himself of these toxic memories, he would disappear.

Why do I care?

But she did.

She touched his arm. A jolt hit her, like skyfire but without the misery. She kept her hand in place. He must have felt it, too, solace in the simple contact. She could see the pain loosen its grip, as bark does when boiled.

She said, voice soft, "The preponderance of our adult males died from Mountain's anger. Those of us who survived, mostly females, did what we must without hesitation or question. No one expected such horror, but we figured out how to continue. Together."

His voice pinched, but he forced a response. "You—almost all females—managed alone?"

"We do our duty. Today, it's to help you."

Yu'ung and Fierce left Kazeb to think through all that he had heard and returned to the camp. Over the night's meal, they shared Kazeb's story.

Yu'ung proposed, "A member with a grudge administered the poison. His intention might have been to kill or to debilitate and he administered the poison wrong, or something else."

Fierce stiffened. "Seer warned me, but it made no sense."

Shanadar smiled weakly. "It matters that those responsible feared you enough to wait for you to leave." He rose. "Be cautious. The past isn't over."

Yu'ung stared at Shanadar as he and Xad returned to his cave.

The killers escaped, but may still live here. The question is, do they imperil the People?

Chapter 22

Yu'ung rose quietly, scanned her surroundings as she released early water. No surprises, all normal activity. Today, she would unravel the truth behind Kazeb's story. Instinct said the People were safe with him, but did it include his Clan? After a quick word with B'o, she headed for Kazeb's homebase. It didn't matter she had no idea where that was. The young Alpha with the wounded eyes, lined from squinting into Sun, would cross her path.

I have questions for him, and he wonders how the People's intentions fit his. In his place, I would.

She heard and dismissed the usual chirps and rustles. Squirrels flicked their tails and ran up trunks. Birds flitted through the branches, but beneath it was the pressure that someone was watching.

His appearance didn't surprise her.

"Can I help you find something?" His voice was calm.

"I could ask the same." Her stomach churned. "You're always around."

"In case you have questions."

She responded, "One is whether this is the home my People seek or a stopover. Is it safe here?"

He looked away. "That depends in part on your relationship with Fierce."

"We have traveled with Fierce for as many Moons as you have digits. He and the Chosen are as intent on fulfilling promises made to us as we are to them."

"Did he mention an illness?"

"Not Fierce. Shanadar. He obliquely referenced deaths, but without context."

"Shanadar—"

"A free-thinking, independent-minded Upright who helped us migrate."

"Many of my Clan claim Fierce unleashed the illness that destroyed us."

"Why would he?"

Kazeb took a shallow breath. "I don't know, but he left when our misery arrived as though to be sure his Chosen didn't catch it. I say this as a warning. Be careful of what you don't know, or think you do."

Yu'ung's eyes popped open. *If he thinks Fierce killed his tribe, how can he act so calmly?* But she knew. *Because he doesn't believe it.*

A low voice interrupted them. "You should have told me. I would have stayed to help."

She jerked toward Fierce, prepared to confront him about following her, but all thoughts of anger dissipated at the sight of his pale visage and wobbly stance.

"Why would I do as you say, Kazeb? We were—are—friends," his voice strangled. "I admit my kind can be vindictive. Yu'ung ran into several."

"One enslaved me. One killed Jvelk's father. One group destroyed Fierce's boat, slaughtering many in the effort." She drifted with the memories. "So yes, some Tall Ones care only for themselves. Fierce isn't like that. For example, when he first met the People, he brought an armed contingent not to attack us, but to warn of danger. One of our inexperienced subadults, Laak, saw it as a threat and charged. Instead of killing Laak, Fierce saw his courage."

Fierce clenched his fists, his voice thick with stress. "I will prove to you in any way I can that someone other than my band caused your catastrophe. Then, we will figure out together who benefited. That will be who carries the guilt. We are friends, Kazeb. I will talk to any of your Clan, convince them."

"Everyone is gone."

Yu'ung interjected, "Including Mook who tried to kill you?"

Kazeb snapped, "Who told you?"

"Shanadar. There are no secrets from him. Don't even try. But he won't tell me if there are other would-be murderers and if they are a threat to the People." She scowled. "Something about me being fully capable of figuring it out on my own."

"Mook is … around, ingratiating himself to Turk. I hope you never meet him. He is evil." Kazeb exhaled a satisfied huff. "I believe you, Fierce. Turk may not."

Fierce lit up. "You're a good start."

"You saved Turk's life. He will have to figure out why you would do that if you want him dead. Since we are again friends, I must show you the traps we set, for protection. There wasn't enough daylight to find food and scout for intruders, so we placed the pits on well-traveled passages, as silent scouts."

Fierce leaned forward. "I know about them, Kazeb."

Kazeb gritted his teeth. "How could you? We created them after you left."

"Credit Ocha." He regarded Kazeb briefly, rubbed a palm across the top of his head, and spat out, "Something you need to know, but first, a question. Why was Turk in that cave where we pulled him out?"

Kazeb's vision narrowed. "You know because you and I went there for the same reason on your first visit. Certain hard rocks—for specialized needs—are found only there."

"I remember that, but Turk had none with him when we rescued him. He did have something else that concerns us, both of us." Fierce pulled a withered plant from his pouch. "This. I've seen it nowhere else on this promontory. It must grow in those tunnels."

Kazeb glanced at it. "Why do I care?"

"It causes the illness your Clan suffered. Why would your brother carry it? My first thought was to show you because he thinks we were harvesting it, but he doesn't know I've been in that cave. Is there another justification?"

Kazeb glared, eyes no more than slits. "Right now, it's as believable to think you were there to harvest it and ran into Turk. How do I know you found it on Turk?"

"If we harvested it, why would I tell you? And why would I save Turk's life?"

Fierce's voice drifted at the end, to give Kazeb time to make sense of the bits and pieces of evidence, but Kazeb was too upset to do that.

"Turk was there to mine the hard stones. Why were you?"

"We were scouting with the Canis Blaze. He led us to the cave, to that entrance. You and I didn't enter through the waterfall, but Turk did and Blaze picked it up, tracked him to where he fell. If not for Blaze leading, we wouldn't have found Turk.

"We didn't know about the plant until back at our homebase. Shanadar found it stuck to our wraps, probably from the passages we squeezed through to reach Turk. He warned me how toxic it is. If Turk wasn't harvesting it, he might have brushed against it and transferred it to us as we pulled him out—"

Yu'ung interjected, "By accident."

Fierce bobbed his head. "Yes. I don't believe Turk realized its toxicity or he would have hidden it." Kazeb said nothing, so Fierce did. "But someone knew, and knows. Who else frequents that location?"

Kazeb stared at nothing, lips slightly parted. "It also grows where we buried those who died of the poison. That would explain Mook's presence and why Druyl seemed so familiar with the tunnels."

He sucked in a breath. "And Mook helped with treatments. Does it have any safe purposes, maybe that he tried to apply to sick Clan members?"

"Shanadar didn't mention any."

Kazeb scratched the nape of his neck, again, this time extracting a tiny critter.

Yu'ung said, "I'll groom you later, or another of the People will." She tugged her lip. "By the way, the traps—Blaze knows where they are."

"But he came out of the mountains after we dug them, and he wasn't at your boat with the other Canis."

Yu'ung eyed him. "That was you watching when we landed."

Kazeb didn't deny it, seemed relieved the secret—if that's what it was—was out. "Why didn't Blaze travel with his pack on your vessel?"

Rather than try to unwind those details, she responded simply, "There are explanations," without clarifying. "The pack is also why I am not suspicious of you. When you spied on us, Ocha showed no concern so we assumed whoever watched was a native checking to ensure we were friendly, not intending to cause trouble."

Kazeb responded to her forthrightness. "Another of our kind arrived with you, an unusual male, wiry rather than brawny, who speaks the words of a bird."

"That's Shanadar, the one I mentioned."

"But he lives away from you, at the crest of Big Rock, with a youngster. Turk and I saw him collecting roots and flowers when we climbed to the overwatch."

"Yes." Fierce tugged on his chin. "It is their choice to live separate. Shanadar is … unusual but similar to one of my band who … advises the Chosen on … events."

The tension that bracketed Kazeb's mouth melted away. "I'm relieved. How does he know the words of a bird?"

"They come from a bone flute he produced by hollowing a cave bear thigh. It is similar to the whistle some tribes employ to announce their return or call for help. Shanadar drilled holes into the sides which he covers and uncovers to coax the bone to sing."

"The beauty of his bird words matches any I've heard."

Blaze appeared out of the scrub and padded up to Kazeb.

Yu'ung asked, "How did you and Blaze meet?"

Kazeb poked his lips toward the high range. "He staggered—literally—out of the foothills at the base of that range. He was nothing more than abraded skin, ratty fur, and pain. He was so hungry his ribs etched ledges in his trunk. He'd been bitten, clawed, mangled, his paw pads worn away, and every part of his body gouged by fights. He shouldn't have been alive, but there he stood, yellow eyes clear, sure he should be with us. I couldn't leave him, not one who fought off predators and survived with no food or water, all to reach us. Turk argued he was our natural enemy and would turn on us when he regained his strength, but I didn't believe that, so I patched his wounds, fed him until he could get his own food, and found myself talking to him as though he understood." She saw excitement in his eyes. "Here's the strange part. I'm sure he did. I wondered if this was how healers feel who say they talk to all life forms."

His words faded as he lost himself in his thoughts.

Just as I do.

Then, he came back. "Even after he healed, he spent most of his time staring out to sea. We kidded that he waited for his pack. I guess he did."

Yu'ung said, "He often traveled with his mother, Spirit. When we left, far from here, all but Blaze and Spirit joined us."

"Spirit?"

"Another with him, with light gray fur, white to her knees. Did you see her?"

"With blue eyes. I assumed it was an apparition."

Yu'ung straightened. "No. That's Spirit, the Alpha of her pack."

"Turk and I are solitary. With Blaze—as you call him—we no longer felt that way."

Someone moaned.

Yu'ung asked, "Have you met Ocha, too?"

He turned to the new arrival. "Yes. She and Blaze touched noses. She has blue eyes, like Spirit. I guess the gray wasn't an apparition."

Yu'ung leaned into Ocha, head cocked, and said, "Ocha says something is in your traps."

Ocha raced forward as they approached the first pit, slapped the edge and growled. At the bottom, Giant Pig snorted, tried to rise on a broken leg, one bone protruding through the skin. Despite its imminent death, Pig still bawled a warning to its killers. Yu'ung's stomach twisted.

How long has it been in misery?

Any amount was too long. Fierce flung his spear. It penetrated the throat and broke Pig's neck, ending its pain. With vines, the Uprights and Ocha dragged the carcass out.

Fierce shouted, as loudly as any whistle. "The hunters will be here soon. They'll take the carcass back while we check your other pits."

The next held an Ibex, also alive.

Kazeb said, "It's good that Giant Pig and Ibex survived the falls because we rarely check these pits. If they died falling in, the sacrifice would be wasted."

Fierce shucked his satchel higher on his shoulder. "I'll let the others know about this one, too."

Yu'ung and Kazeb chopped the carcass into pieces, careful to preserve the fullness of the hide.

She swiped sweat from her brow, breath barely elevated, and commented, "Aynoh will be happy with this pelt. Any others?"

He trotted to a heavily traveled intersection. A brush pile blocked it which Yu'ung would have avoided, but Kazeb kicked it away.

He grinned. "Another Ibex."

When he bent forward, the dirt crumbled beneath his bare feet. He yelped, flailed in a botched effort to regain balance, and crashed atop the panicked Ibex. Despite being injured, the trapped creature launched its healthy hooved leg at Kazeb, backed by a headful of lethal horns, missed him both times but not by much. Blaze howled and leapt into the pit, landing on Ibex's vulnerable throat. The animal died quickly.

Kazeb shouted, "Get a vine. Haul us up, then we'll do the same with the carcass!"

The next pit held another Ibex, this one dead, but recently.

Kazeb grinned. "This time, I'll secure Ibex with one vine, myself with the other."

"I'll pull you out. We'll work together to drag it up."

They finished skinning the carcass as more hunters arrived.

Kazeb motioned, "There is one more pit," and sprinted forward.

Yu'ung raised a brow at Fierce and chased Kazeb. She breathed a sigh to see the final pit empty, and scratched at critter bites that had responded to no treatment.

"You've met our smallest annoyance."

"They itch for too long."

He broke a branch from a low-growing shrub, crushed it in his palms, and rubbed it over the welts on her arms.

"The critters don't like the smell."

"This meat and the hides will bring joy to the People, Kazeb. You are appreciated."

"Do you not enjoy the white flesh?"

"Yes, but we need pelts, tendons, and organ sacks."

Fierce stood at the first pit. "Bhidid and Eknilk are hauling the Giant Pig to our camp. I'll help carry the Ibexes to yours, Kazeb, then come eat with us. Food should be ready by the time we reach our cave."

Kazeb shook his head, but Yu'ung stopped him. "This is meat you trapped."

"We have more food than we need. Tortoises, hares, rabbits, birds as well as fish. You will see. Food is abundant here. Besides, it's time I talked with Turk about our situation. Past time."

Yu'ung bent down with her cutter and started on the Ibex. "We'll skin it, disembowel it—"

He waved her off. "We have plenty." Then he faced Fierce. "What do I tell Turk? Do you stay this time or again leave?"

Fierce flushed, but not in anger. "We must continue home, but after I clarify a few issues...."

"A few issues…." From Yu'ung.

He sighed. "Aynoh and I…."

Kazeb set his lips. "It is good your stay is temporary. My grudge is gone, but Turk's, maybe not."

Yu'ung watched Kazeb hurry away, conflicted. Blaze seemed to be also. He huffed, tail stiff, then raced after Kazeb. Ocha sat with Yu'ung, one leg bent beneath her, blood crusted on her fur from the brush with Ibex. Yu'ung followed Kazeb's progress until darkness took them.

Inside the People's cave, the hearth glowed warmly. A stew bubbled on the fire. Roots and leaves sizzled. Ese and Wik had already sliced chunks of meat and placed them on slabs to cook. Long bones were disarticulated and handed to each adult carrying a child. They hammered them open with an anvil, then inserted a twig into the center, twirled it to collect the nutritious marrow, and they feasted on the blood-rich food.

Fierce huddled with the Chosen, voices low, words hidden but not their bodies. Yu'ung glanced at Aynoh and Wik. They were the only pairmates of Chosen, but Jhat might go with Bhidid. They spent nights together. Yu'ung feared her loss. Besides being industrious, clever, and optimistic, she would take the People's youngest child.

Yu'ung turned back to Aynoh, shoulder to shoulder with her pairmate, laughing about something as he slurped a mouthful of stew. What would the People do without her if she left? Everyone relied on the Elders to connect the past with the present. Aynoh was now the oldest of the People because of the difficulty of the migration, so that responsibility rested on her. Plus, the child she carried must be part of the decision.

Meal over, the subadults twisted bark fibers into cordage to sew wraps once the pelts were cleaned, cut, and pierced. Ese scooched sideways to make room for Yu'ung.

"If we work together, we can clean these pelts tonight, stretch and dry them tomorrow, and cut them into wraps for those in great need."

Snug wraps kept them warm but provided a perfect habitat for the tiny bugs that lived in their hair. As warm as this area was, that wouldn't be required. Together, the adults held the hide by the edge between their teeth, pulled the skin tight with one hand and scraped away the bits of meat, blood, and connective tissues with a flat, sharp-edged tool. They would be softened later.

One by one, all those not tasked with keeping the fire alive or scouting fell asleep.

Chapter 23

Shanadar

The night was clear and crisp. Shanadar shoved his nest to the ledge outside his cave, stretched out, and noted how far the stars that looked like a scoop had traveled since Sun disappeared. Moon, the color of foam on agitated water, had yet to slip into sight above the ridgeline. A rat scurried through debris behind him. A large fish broke the sea's surface, hung above the water, and then dove back into the depths. A hyaena yipped. Blinking eyes told him it was the one who visited him.

You too feel the power of the wilderness, its ability to strip away what doesn't matter, sharpen the senses, and remind us—you and I—how vast the world and how small we are.

Tomorrow's tasks spun through his mind. Strategy confused him, but Xhosa guaranteed that what would happen paved the way to his future, and hers. As though in confirmation, a howl broke the night's silence, and then another.

Thank you.

Shanadar slept fitfully in the cool night air. He scratched his burns as bugs drank the blood he required to survive, their nips so annoying, he finally gave up. With Sun's first rays breaking the horizon, he nimbly dropped down Big Rock's flank. Aynoh had offered a treatment to tamp down the itching. Today promised to be long. He couldn't afford distraction. She salved him with the same mucus she had the prior night, told him to keep the wounds layered with it. He muttered agreement with no intention of following through.

Ese called as he strode outside, "Come back tonight. We need everyone to help prepare the skins from Kazeb's pits. One of the new wraps will be for you!"

He doubted he'd finish what must be done by then, but nodded as he trotted away, listening to the conversations as he passed.

Bhidid: "The Ibex in the traps—we can track its herd!"

Yu'ung: "Kazeb said we will meet the local tribes during a hunt, but not for a while."

Jhat sharpened a harpoon tip. "Sea-based food is abundant and easy to catch. Why risk injury from horns and hooves?"

Bhidid's mouth drooped. "On our first visit, we ate mostly white meat. It has little blood."

Finally beyond the group's sounds, Shanadar reveled in the solitude, the rhythm of life, the peace absent outside his cave. He had tried to adapt to the People, be what Yu'ung needed and Xhosa expected, but abandoned the effort when Xad arrived. Xad was like him. Each experienced a calm in the other that was lacking elsewhere. Shanadar had no doubt Xhosa sent Xad because Shanadar was struggling.

Still, without the People, life would be impossible.

Today, Shanadar trailed Eagle's spiraling journey through the sky. He eased over humps and trenches, potholes and stone rivers, bashed through the scrub where the trail was blocked, powered up and down steep eroded banks, all the time hoping the splendid bird headed for where it roosted, not where it hunted. He needed a feather for his tail, another for Xad if possible, but it must come willingly from Eagle.

When it finally disappeared into the heights of a tree, Shanadar relaxed.

Its nest is up there.

He layered himself with mud, climbed the stout tree trunk, carefully wriggled out on the limb that led to Eagle, trying not to move the branch. Eagle was busy feeding its brood and the wind was in Shanadar's favor. He wasn't noticed until he plucked several feathers for his necklace. Eagle screamed. When it spun to claw him, Shanadar pressed the massive wings to the formidable bird's sides and tossed it into the air to stop its panicked attack, hoping for enough time to flee.

But the noble fowl seemed stunned. Instead of flight, it plummeted to the ground right where Coyote waited. Shanadar leapt down to protect Eagle, but because of his bad eye, he crashed atop its fragile frame. The scavenger scurried away, frightened by the predator from above. To Shanadar's horror, he crushed the magnificent bird. His vision blurred as he cradled the frail form, apologized for his mistake, but it didn't revive. Finally, he did what he could to honor it, gutted the carcass, tossed the innards where scavengers would gain power from their consumption, then lugged the bulky body as carefully as possible homeward. He devised and rejected one idea after another on how to get the unwieldy fowl with its massive wingspan up the promontory's steep face.

Only one solution passed the test of logic. He strapped the wings to his arms with vines, positioned the beaked skull on top of his, and climbed. He didn't worry that the People would be delivering food or wraps, something they did for him, because they had made that trip yesterday. Otherwise, he rarely saw the tribe, most of his time spent deep in Big Rock in his sanctuary. Shanadar necessitated privacy.

The climb was awkward at first, but he found his rhythm moving along the memorized hand- and footholds. Soon, it was as easy with Eagle's weight as without. The day was sunny, breezy with a chill in the air. He glanced down to the shore occasionally, to see if he was noticed, but everyone worked, either away scavenging, heads down scraping, or doing another of the myriad chores that never seemed to run out. No one looked up Big Rock to check on his cave so no one noticed the spread-winged Eagle climbing rather than flying. If they asked about it later, Shanadar would shrug.

He scrambled over the final lip and paused to glory in the empty quiet. Xad must be in the sanctuary preparing for the tribe's impending visit so Shanadar wouldn't have to explain about Eagle's final flight. Food lay by the fire. Shanadar ignored it.

He strode to an alcove toward the back of the cavern. Here, he laid the bird down, stretched the feathered arms to simulate flight, as it would want. The shiny dark plumage fringed with shorter quills was glorious, white neck topped by a soft crown almost Shanadar's size. Devastating talons were attached to formidable legs, to capture prey. None witnessed Eagle attacking without being awed by its mastery.

Tiny flames lit the alcove, far enough from the entrance to be hidden from those below. The fire popped as a stone exploded. Xad entered the recess only to feed it, make sure it always burned, because Seer or Xhosa never advised Shanadar when they would call. He needed them to contact him now, tell him how to properly honor Eagle.

Shanadar freshened his stripes in preparation, then donned the necklace crafted for these events. This one included shells, round pebbles, mammoth and rhino teeth collected on the journey, and claws. Each memorialized incidents that guided conversations. He sat cross-legged, placed Wise Stone to one side where he could hear its counsel. The rock befriended him at the journey's start, its guidance invaluable throughout. On his opposite side lay the flute.

In his last vision, Xhosa told him he passed sky fire's test. Next, she would tell him what that meant. Maybe.

The fire hissed as the log shifted and sent a shower of sparks into the air, and charred new holes in Shanadar's wrap and the skin below, though Shanadar barely felt it. He tossed a sizeable mushroom on a smooth rock, flattened its yellow cap, and flayed the stem. Nothing was wasted.

Xhosa provided specific instructions for the preparations—

Eat one raw. Chop the rest. Drop them in hot water. As time decelerates and your heart speeds up, as euphoria overtakes your senses, drink the liquid.

Shanadar popped one into his mouth and chewed as he prepared the concoction. When his hands separated from his limbs, he drank the liquid, ate the soggy mushrooms, and let it dribble down his throat. The staff, a stalagmite smoothed and shortened, adorned with shells and feathers, warmed in his fist as broken questions flooded his mind, followed by blurry disconnected answers as he slid into darkness.

A thump assaulted his ears, steady, like a tree limb against a hollow trunk, mournful and primal. The beat washed into his blood. The solid surface beneath him evaporated. The strikes fused with his ever louder pulse and connected him to a world outside of the People and the Chosen. He absorbed the energy, fed off it, and grew stronger for having done so. Only then did he feel the presence of those gone. Today, it was Xhosa.

She spoke without words. "In my lifetime, on the sea's coast, hunger drove a starved eagle to scavenge a deer carcass splayed in the grass. The great bird crouched, gripped the dead animal, and its curved beak tore into the flesh. Intent on the unexpected food, it missed the brawny figure—your kind, Shanadar. He rained heavy blows onto the frail physique. Assured it was dead, he carried the carcass to his cave, respectfully as you did, careful not to bend or break the feathers. He, too, admired the substantial hooked talons, massaged their length with his thumb. They would be polished and strung into a necklace. The true power lay in the tools of Eagle's flight. Any who saw him in the wings would respect his dominance."

Shanadar asked, "Did they?" But Xhosa was gone.

Sun had vanished into muted purples and blues by the time the vision ended. Shanadar blinked, stiff, feet numb, but consumed with empathy. Eagle gave its life for the People. He now knew how to honor it.

To both Yu'ung and Ese's wide-eyed amazement, that night, Shanadar squeezed into the circle next to Fierce. He skillfully stretched the hide and staked it as tightly as possible to prevent shriveling while asking the Chosen Leader about Seer.

"Seer considers everything and everyone connected. Plants, insects, herds, animals—all are part of a collective sentience."

Yu'ung jerked toward Fierce and muttered, "Sentience again, that word," and listened more intently as she worked.

Fierce continued, "He accesses this vast living ecosystem by consuming foods from a special grotto. When finished what he calls a 'trance,' he prophesizes what will confront us, offers suggestions and solutions. For example, he sent me here to find Aynoh. Her power to heal crossed the vastness of time and place to touch Seer's consciousness. You, too, Shanadar. Your genius is not to treat illnesses, but to live visions. Seer wishes both of you to be part of his sanctuary if you desire."

Shanadar tugged on the hide as he scraped away bit after bit of fat. "Is he also an explorer?"

"In a different way. Seer often leaves with daylight, returns with darkness."

"Does he have a pairmate?"

"He does, to provide children, but they live separately."

Yu'ung could see Shanadar's confusion chunk into place, why he preferred Blaze's company, the flute's voice, Wise Stone's guidance, and Xad's companionship.

He murmured to himself, "Occasional mating events to do my duty would be acceptable. Even tolerable."

Fierce took that as a question. "It is enough for Seer."

"Does Seer have animal companions like the Canis, or play music? Or converse with a Wise Stone?"

Fierce shook his head. "He wants to hear about those from you."

Shanadar nibbled at shreds of meat. "I glimpsed impending death, but I don't know for whom. How would Seer respond?"

"He would remind you that death visits everyone. No prediction lies in common visions."

Shanadar rested his hands in his lap, labor forgotten, searching the dark outside world. He rubbed his palms against his thighs, opened his mouth to release another question, but Fierce stopped him.

"I have no more to tell you. The rest is yours to discover."

Shanadar trundled to his feet and shuffled into the dark.

Chapter 24

Yu'ung

As Sun cast its first ray over the glorious landscape, Yu'ung wriggled onto a narrow ledge high above the beach. Eagle's feather, a gift from Shanadar, fluttered in her hair. The cavern behind her had room enough only for a small fire, which was fine. Here, separated from the noise and chatter, she wanted to be alone, to think.

Below, the day's work was well underway, scavenging plants and sea food, knapping a myriad of stone tools—scrapers to skin, cutters to deflesh carcasses, and choppers to hack the abundant rabbits into manageable pieces. Hammerstones, critical in the past to release bone marrow, were now employed to crack open the shells of sea animals.

She let her mind wander. Life for the People had fallen into routines, for some, settling into the new home, and others preparing for departure. Both would require a visit to Shanadar's sanctuary and that before the communal hunt. Fierce didn't object, saying it was what Seer would do.

Some days, instead of seeking solitude on this high ledge, she traipsed over the boulders that sprinkled the sand to a walkway that led into the shoreless sea. At the far end of this stone path was a tall spire. From its top, surrounded by water, Yu'ung watched the fish outsmart the white caps, then vanish to wherever they spent their days. She felt at one with them.

Today, though, she needed a long view of the peninsula to search out natives other than Kazeb's fragmented Clan. Muddled prints indicated someone other than Kazeb and Turk was monitoring the People. Kazeb assured her the People were safe, that these were former Clan members who lived separately. Yu'ung the tribe member might take his word, but Yu'ung the Alpha—never.

Which was why she sat in the shadows on this high overwatch, studying the surroundings.

Who spies on us?

Whoever it was left a trail. Most would miss the prints, but they were clear to her extreme sight. The tracks wandered over a shallow stream, then through a channel that paused at a pool, dry now, but awaiting rain. Bluffs and crags materialized ahead, splashed with green and purple lichen and unusual spiky molds she would ask Aynoh about later. Almost to the extent of her extreme vision and well past Kazeb's probable homebase, was where she saw the fires last night.

Who built those? Are they to guide others here or simply for warmth and protection?

All this flashed through her thoughts in an instant, the way things do as a crisis unfolds, because it was—the crisis. Her brain sharpened. She crawled forward and dangled her legs over the edge. She couldn't see anything, but the pigeon-birds exploded from their wall down Big Rock's flank in a flutter of fragile wings, a raucous squawk of high-pitched calls to announce their distrust of whoever passed by their senses. Shanadar, who had just returned from a foraging expedition, certainly heard the ruckus but couldn't see the platform from where he sat. He settled on his ledge with his bone flute and quieted the frenzy with soothing bird calls. A few below swayed and bounced to his flute. The pigeon-birds settled into their nests, satisfied they'd neutralized the intruder, and cooed to each other.

The music stopped, then began again, but without the realism. Yu'ung glanced up. Shanadar was standing on the rim of his ledge, arms raised, turned toward the location of last night's flames. Behind him in the shadows, Xad was practicing.

Shanadar's burns are less raw, but the milky eye is still cloudy. He ignores discomfort as Old One did, lives with the consequences of a life lived aggressively.

Shanadar talked often about meeting Seer. She didn't want him to go with the Chosen, had come to respect his odd approach to life, to rely on him.

A joyous whoop below and B'o raced into the camp, shouting, "Kazeb and I stole an Ibex from a Leopard!"

Red meat! A welcome change from the white. Anyone not working gathered round the hunters, slapping them on the back. Kazeb beamed, eyes finding her on her ledge. She ran through their last conversation.

"Turk is suspicious of the People because they—you—help our enemies." At her surprise, Kazeb clarified, "The Chosen, no longer my enemy, but I didn't correct Turk," then reddened. "He has become wary of me because I talk about you too much!"

Her mouth fell open. "Well, Fierce says he and Turk weren't friends, but respected each other. It seems Mook has effectively chipped that away."

"It's not as bad as he thinks. Turk won't attack, but Mook might. I'm glad Fierce is training the People with the far-throwing spear."

"Those who wish to learn."

"How does he do that?"

"He says it is done with drills where he lives, but here, with our kind, he uses contests. For example, he attaches a vine to a gourd and swings it to simulate the flight of prey. Participants try to spike it with the throwing spear as it moves. If they succeed, they back farther away. The winner is whoever strikes the gourd from the farthest distance. So far, Jvelk wins, though Laak is close."

They will soon be worthy Leads for the People.

Yu'ung glanced back at Shanadar. He had disappeared. She turned her attention to the shoreless sea, the direction of Fierce's home. Did his band wonder about his extended absence?

"Yu'ung!" Grub pointed to show he would leave to hunt on the water when Sun reached that spot.

Another skill Fierce insisted the People conquer to thrive here was catching fish offshore, from a raft.

Kazeb yelled, "Come with us!"

Which she intended to do until movement beyond the camp made her scoot into the shadows.

A tribe I've not seen carrying thrusting spears. Kazeb promised us his excess pelts. Are these former Clan bringing them to us?

She leaned forward for a better view. *I don't see any hides. Has this group come because we're new? Are they armed in case we aren't friendly?*

Yu'ung caught Grub's attention and thrust her lips out, then descended and strode to where Wik gathered with an assemblage preparing to forage. No one had noticed the strangers. Wik greeted her and indicated when they would be back.

Yu'ung murmured, "Go prepared. An assemblage armed with thrusting spears heads this way."

Wik shrugged Yu'ung's concern away. "I'll tell everyone, but if they try to intimidate us, it is they who will suffer."

She juggled a handful of missiles. Wik threw with incredible speed, force, and accuracy, lethal if she chose.

Yu'ung grinned. Wik had lived where the Chosen went to harvest salt. She had no spears so stones became her reliable offense and defense. Thrusting spears were no match for Wik and her stones.

Wik chased after the rest of her group as Yu'ung trotted up to Fierce.

"Someone comes."

"Turk?"

Ocha blew past them, legs stretched out, tail stiff behind, joined by an enthusiastic Blaze.

"Could be. Kazeb says Turk wears no colors."

Kazeb trotted up to her. "What's going on?"

"Someone's coming."

He sucked in a breath. His chest heaved as words spilled out. "Many came to me last night, with Mook, angry at your return, insisting you leave. I told them you claimed innocence and I believed you. We had additional … discussion, but some couldn't tell truth from falsehoods."

Kazeb jerked when Shanadar touched his elbow. "I thought Yu'ung was going to hang noisy shells on you that bang together every time you take a step."

"I'd like that."

He asked, "How do you materialize out of empty air?"

"I watch where I can blend into shadows and natural movement, where I'm part of normal activity—"

Yu'ung stopped him. "Later. They are here."

A rowdy, raucous assemblage broke through the brush. Kazeb and Shanadar blocked them, Kazeb stiff with anger. Shanadar, though, smiled.

This is who I first met, sure of himself, fearless.

She joined the gathering, her lance prominent, attitude unmistakable. "I am Alpha. Why do you flourish spears at us?"

One who must be Mook said, "We have no interest in you—"

She stopped him, her voice bland, face hard. "You should. You must go through me, my pack, and my fellow warriors to get wherever you're going."

Evil billowed from him like dust in a storm, his hate like sand scraping her skin. He was Kazeb's size, but there the similarity ended. His hair was ratty and unkempt, pelts too shredded for even meager protection, with one front tooth broken and another dark. He approached not as a friend or to seek conciliation, but to wrest control from an inferior.

"We want Fierce, not you. He tried to destroy us!"

Fierce shouldered his way to the front and spoke to the group. "You're listening to the wrong people. Someone you respect, lean on, did that." He fixed a hostile glare on Mook. "Maybe you."

As he spoke, the rest of the Chosen gathered behind Fierce, Yu'ung, Kazeb, and Shanadar, spears fisted, prepared for whatever was necessary.

Crimson with rage, Mook snarled, "Why, Tall One? We treated you well, offered friendship!"

Despite the fury and lies, Fierce remained relaxed. "Have you told your followers you tried to kill their Alpha, Kazeb?" He spoke calmly, but with an edge to his voice, then peered past Mook. "Flint and Gik? You travel with this false leader?"

Fierce's eyes crinkled with pleasure, quickly matched by Flint and Gik. Greetings from Grub and others of the Chosen, with smiles, relaxed what had seemed tense and stiff, a battle brewing.

"You haven't forgotten us, Leader Fierce?"

Fierce clapped them on the back and turned to Yu'ung. "During our stay, Flint and Gik often came with us to explore and share ideas."

Yu'ung studied Flint, stockier and better muscled than Gik.

Life has presented challenges for him.

He gestured to Fierce's arms and thighs, white scars fresh enough to still be raised. "Fights won, I see."

"We traveled far through areas not always friendly. Now, we are on our way home."

"Wish I hadn't missed it." His gaze flicked through the gathering, stuttered at Jhat and Ruk in the background.

He gulped. "You are not alone now."

Jhat called out, "I'm Jhat."

He mumbled, "Jhat?"

"And my son Ruk. You are?"

Yu'ung flicked between Jhat and Flint, couldn't stop a smile that pulled at the corners of her mouth.

"Fl-flint!"

"Flint. When you finish, can you help me carry this?" She flourished a small gourd.

Yu'ung guffawed as Flint bobbed his entire upper body. "Of course I will! If it is … acceptable," asking if she had a pairmate somewhere.

Yu'ung waved. "Jhat is stronger than anyone you'll meet. She wants to befriend you before others have a chance."

Flint mumbled, eyes glued to Jhat. "They won't…."

Yu'ung chuckled. "The Chosen leave soon. Without them, we have few males."

Mook stomped up. "Enough! Why did your good health persist while we perished?"

"I'll answer Mook. Do I have your name right?" Yu'ung didn't wait for his response. "I also serve with Aynoh as Healer." A glance confirmed her mother was with the gathering. "She is Fierce's pairmate. Illness isn't fair or equitable, and death is part of life. Surely your healer explained."

"But no Chosen died!"

Fierce responded, his quiet voice brimming with power, "A similar illness attacked my home. It killed with abandon, spared few. Most lost pairmates or mates. We found out that it was caused by a disgruntled band member. Maybe someone like you."

Yu'ung fixed Mook with a dark stare. One look suggested he wasn't to be trusted. The sheen of moisture on his lip, the evil flashing across his face every time he mouthed his transparent lies confirmed it, but besides all that, there was the history.

He'd tried to kill Kazeb.

No, Mook was not a friend.

Mook reddened beneath his brown visage. "You lie!"

Yells increased, mostly by Mook. Every time the throng quieted, he riled them again. Blaze growled, angry that One-called-Mook yelled at his pack. Shanadar pressed his hand firmly on his packmate's crown to prevent him handling this the Canis way. Instead, he rested his head on his paws, tail tucked, and moaned. Shanadar scratched Blaze's hackles, his stripes fresh, knotted hair resplendent with the Eagle's feather. His necklace jangled with feathers, shells, and newly acquired bird claws. He was of the People but different. Everyone among Mook's group stole glances at him as his eyes flitted through the crowd, taking as long as required to connect with each face.

He spoke into a lull in the battle. "You worry that if we stay, you will be sick again."

A chorus mumbled yes.

Shanadar smiled, his face alight. "My former tribe lives a Moon from here across the snow-capped peaks. A similar illness to yours, to Fierce's, also infected us, but we suffered no deaths."

He extended his palms. In them were thready white patches similar to bark.

"This pith arrested it before it killed anyone. If I lie, take my life in compensation."

He passed it around. Yu'ung hadn't heard pulp as a cure for any disease, not from Aynoh or Old One or any other healers she'd met, but she kept that to herself. A disgruntled Mook, mostly because his followers seemed satisfied with Fierce's rejoinders, wandered away, the direction of Turk and Kazeb's camp. Shanadar walked with the rest, his shuffling progress well suited to theirs. He replied to additional questions and passed out pith for those without any.

Drowning out all of that was the thud of her heart, making clear that life had changed.

Chapter 25

Yu'ung and Kazeb scampered up the overwatch hill to track the crowd. Yu'ung listened to their thumping steps, the buzz of voices, Shanadar's calm responses, and the occasional laugh. Small groups broke away to go their own direction until the large group disintegrated into a few final families, eventually passing beyond her extreme sight.

Shanadar returned to the People's camp where Yu'ung and Kazeb waited. "What did you give them?"

He fixed his milky eye on Yu'ung, intimidating to any but her. "An excuse to trust us. That, with the seeds of doubt we planted for Mook, should be enough. Still, we must be cautious. He will take any opportunity to prove me wrong."

Kazeb shook his head. "Whatever Mook planned, you defused."

A shout from the shore, "Kazeb! We are ready!"

Kazeb acknowledged with a wave. "I'm going to help the youngers," and dashed to the raft.

Yu'ung rushed after him with a frustrated chuff. "Why does attaching twine to the end of a shaft with a barbed tip catch prey?"

Kazeb called to her, "It's designed for water."

She scowled. *That explains nothing.* She caught up and asked, "How does it work?"

"We impale fish and drag them onto the raft with the cordage. White meat hides are easy to puncture. The barbs keep it in the flesh."

Jvelk tugged on the fiber to check the firmness.

Grub jumped aboard the raft, speaking over his shoulder. "A good Lead has a multitude of methods to harvest meat. One won't always be the best, so he chooses the right fit for the circumstance. The People will rely on him—on Jvelk—for that."

Jvelk held the harpoon as he would a spear, but Grub corrected him. "Your grip is fine, but penetrating water takes more power than air."

B'o stared at the slender lance, chewing the last of a meaty leg. "So what should he do?"

"Come with us. You'll see."

B'o scrambled onto the raft. "What if the fish dives?"

"We dive."

B'o's eyes narrowed. "I can't breathe in water!"

Fierce chortled. "Draw in as much air as possible before you dive. Use one part to descend, one to catch your prey, and the last to return."

Yu'ung had often swum submerged when tracking strangers or prey by breathing through a hollow reed, its end poking above the surface as though just another stalk of grass. The biggest challenge was to not give away her presence in cold water by shivering.

Of course, today, they would submerge too deeply for that method.

Fierce poked Jvelk and then Laak. "Don't take me too seriously. You will acquire the skill long before you're in danger of dying. It's not as difficult as it sounds. Those in my home are equally talented in water and on land because lakes are common and herds not always. Sometimes, we capture so much white meat and shelled critters that we transport them in our mouths to leave our hands free to catch more."

Wik sputtered. "You carry *shells* between your teeth?"

"Of course. The most prolific among us are proud of their chipped teeth and red eyes." At Wik's confused look, he added, "Something in the deepest water streaks eyes red."

Fierce ran his hand down the slender shaft, thinner even than throwing spears. "I told Aynoh about harpoons while we migrated. I would have demonstrated, but there were no lakes, at least, none with life that survived Mountain's anger."

Kazeb hopped onto the raft. Yu'ung surprised herself by jumping on, too. "I saw a swarm from the overwatch. I can guide you to it," she announced, though that was just one reason. Another was to better appreciate Kazeb's goals. Then, there were others.

He grinned wider as though he saw through her subterfuge. "If you stay, I'll make sure you master this."

More boarded. Laak and others remained behind in case the threat of Mook returned. The craft shoved off, paddled with the tide to the clear water where underwater life was easy to spot. Fierce harpooned one, his partner another. Jvelk mimicked them. It didn't take long for no more to swim by the raft.

Fierce murmured, "We have become a predator to avoid. We'll have to dive. Jvelk—with me. Fill your lungs, empty them, fill them again, and submerge!"

Instruction completed, they dove. Everyone paired off, experienced with a novice.

"You're with me," Grub barked to Yu'ung, and dove.

She didn't question him, jumped in behind. The water soothed her skin. She copied his every movement and easily penetrated the warm upper layer to the cool one beneath and finally, touched bottom. She gripped the abundant seaweed until she re-established her balance and then mimicked how Grub searched for prey. It didn't take long for her lungs to tighten. She reflexively started to suck in, but stopped.

Remember. I can't breathe underwater.

A slender, serpentine body slid by. Grub stilled himself, and Yu'ung did the same.

Again, she almost sucked in, didn't, and forced a swallow.

One shot and I'll surface.

She flung, missed. Grub didn't.

He motioned, *Time to go*, his cord taut with the impaled weight.

Yu'ung kicked, scrunched her lips to keep the water out, paddled harder, and thrust vigorously, with minimal results. Grub moved ahead effortlessly, glanced back, seemed to think she was fine, and proceeded. She anticipated ascension to be the reverse of descension and couldn't have been more wrong. Fear washed through her as the chill leeched up her limbs. Soon, kicks were no more than flutters with little power or movement.

A shape twisted in front of her. *Kazeb.* His fingers wrapped around her arm. He made sure she paid attention to his face and then released the air held in his mouth. A few bubbles, a few additional.

He breathes out in small amounts.

She tried it, letting tiny air sacs float up. It gave her an immediate sense of relief. He exhaled again, and again as he rose to the surface, kicks lazy and unrushed. His presence boosted her confidence as they swam upward. Occasionally, he placed a hand against his mouth, a reminder to seal her lips. When they finally surfaced, she slipped onto the platform without help, hiding her shaking hands under the bulk of her trunk.

Kazeb blocked everyone's view of her. "You did admirably for a first time."

Tears blurred her sight. She started to lose herself in his luminous brown eyes, so turned away.

Did Aynoh feel the same?

Everyone who dived was onboard except Fierce and Jvelk.

Yu'ung peered into the depths. "Are they all right?"

Grub guffawed. "Fierce loves to dive. Jvelk wants to be Lead so emulates the best. He will do good when we leave."

Yu'ung blocked out everything visual and reveled in the sounds of this new world. Waves lapped the raft. Voices buzzed. The last of the water hunters surfaced. Fierce tossed a huge mound onto the deck.

Jvelk gasped in a mouthful of air and squealed, "There were more, but I exhausted my air."

Fierce barked, "I'll get them! I just came back to make sure Jvelk was all right."

"Wait for me!" Grub called.

Bodies sleek, harpoons held in their mouths, hands free to swim, Grub and Fierce breathed in as deeply as possible and dove, then wiggled to the bottom. The water was so clear, Yu'ung had no trouble tracing their progress. A fish longer than Fierce watched them with unblinking eyes. It was used to being an apex predator this far below the surface, it made no effort to escape. First Fierce, then Grub skewered it and headed up. Everyone helped drag the massive sea animal aboard.

Kazeb barked, "That's enough meat or we sink."

That night, they feasted—the Chosen, the People, Kazeb, and Flint who stayed with Jhat. Some fish were splayed out over the hearth, others steamed inside their shells until the carapaces were scorched black. Wik tossed a tortoise into the collection as well as an armful of small critters she and her entourage had scavenged. Ruk contributed berries.

Everyone fed, Jvelk approached Yu'ung. He held his nose and shook his head as Blaze and Ocha did to clear their ears.

"What's wrong, Jvelk?"

"My ears are clogged worse than I've ever felt."

Yu'ung poked around, then called for Aynoh who described Jvelk's problem to Fierce.

"Here's how Seer treats it."

They watched as he turned particular roots into a mulch and poked the salve into the ears as deeply as possible.

"Ears and nose heal together, Seer says."

As Yu'ung worked on the treatment, Grub wandered over with a similar complaint.

"I've had this problem before and it has cleared quickly, but tonight, it's worse than ever," and he slapped the sides of his skull while yawning.

Yu'ung stuffed the soft, thready mulch in both males' ears while Aynoh mimed, "Don't swim until the inflammation is gone. If the pain or redness persists or returns, you can't dive again."

Fierce added, "Stuff your ears with seaweed or leaves to keep the water out."

Wik clutched Grub's arm. "He'll do what's necessary," she said and dragged him away.

As Yu'ung and Aynoh relaxed, happy to have the emergencies over, Braanroorv lumbered toward them.

"I think I have the same problem. Seer treated me in the past, but never told me to avoid diving. This is worse than ever."

He shook his head violently.

Aynoh sat up straighter. "His cures may not require that last step."

Yu'ung sensed her mother's excitement to have another knowledgeable healer to compare ideas with, if it came to be.

Fierce chuckled. "Seer says he heals most illnesses and injuries by driving out the evil that enters the body through breaks in the skin, or when the wounds turn red and swollen with white and green pus. This doesn't fit either."

Aynoh stared into Braanroorv's ear. "I have an idea how to treat this. Seer can revise it when you reach him. It's different than what we discussed so far."

Braanroorv smashed his cupped hands on the sides of his head. "I don't know what you said."

Aynoh turned to Fierce. "Tell him the Primitives I lived with had a treatment for this with a particular mold I haven't seen here, though I haven't looked for it either. I must warn you, I never had a need to try it on our kind, or the Chosen."

Fierce detailed Aynoh's suggested therapy and concerns as clearly as possible.

Braanroorv responded, "If you asked me to consider something that may or may not work—yes. I must be able to hear."

Aynoh told Fierce what she needed, and he turned to Kazeb. "Where would we find this mold?"

Kazeb wasted no time answering, leaped to his feet and left with Fierce in tow. They reappeared not much later with branches of green-gray mold. Spores exploded as Aynoh pounded honey into it, then flattened the poultice, heated it, cooled it, and stuffed the sludge into Braanroorv's ears.

She mimed for Braanroorv while speaking, "Keep the mulch in all night. I'll repeat the process every day until you recover. You—"

"I guess diving is out," he interrupted.

Aynoh placed a hand on his cheek to get his attention. "Forever."

Braanroorv bobbed acknowledgement. "I can stand sentry. These," he said patting his broken ears, "do not affect my sight," and trotted into the dark.

Kazeb called Flint. "We must go." Eyes a bottomless brown, he added, "You have good People, Yu'ung. You are, too," and left.

She shouted to him, "Come tomorrow."

Why did I say that?

Aynoh rescued her. "We need more of that fungus."

Flint shouted, "I'll come with him. Tell Jhat—in case she needs more ... help." and sprinted off.

Chapter 26

Yu'ung tied her damp hair behind her neck with a strap and wiped the sweat from her brow. Kazeb kept their pace fast, understanding the urgency, but short of a sprint. The rigid surface jarred each step, soothing to one accustomed to it.

"I've foraged the close-in fruit so we have to go farther." He churned up a steep grade, feet digging into the ground, arms chugging, Yu'ung right behind. "We're almost there."

They scrambled over the top and down to a flat plateau with blotches of scrubby shrubs, boulders, and a sprinkle of seedlings. She spotted patches of the fruit nestled against an overhang, some shriveled, others molded, but many branches with fresh plump berries.

"I haven't had these since I left the mountains, Kazeb."

"Eat what you want. I'll harvest the others."

Mouth full, she plucked a blue-flowered plant, complete with roots. After swallowing, she said, "I've never seen this."

"Watch what I can do with it."

He pressed it between his palms and extended it to Yu'ung, the plant now sticky.

"It's like glue, Kazeb."

"In emergencies, we slather it on, let it dry. It will stick pieces together, but not as permanently as sap or cooked bark."

He rubbed his hands with grit to neutralize the gumminess and finished collecting the berries. Done, they made their way back. Yu'ung felt rejuvenated by the sweet fruit, the break, and the trip's success.

When they reached level ground, Kazeb said, "Ask your questions."

Yu'ung learned a lot from the reactions of others when she raised difficult topics. She started with the most upsetting.

"Turk resents Fierce. Can we change his mind?"

"It will take time," his voice anxious but hopeful. "Here's how leading was explained to me when Turk and I first became Alphas. Directing a tribe is like sanding a spear. Over-sanding weakens a spear. Under-sanding makes it useless for its purpose. An Alpha must smooth out disagreements, eliminate the splinters that impede progress, not so much that he quashes initiative and not so little that he fails to exert authority.

Yu'ung breathed out. "The Alpha is the sand that makes the tribe work smoothly. That makes sense."

"Turk understands that, too. He knows the difference between over- and under-sanding." He pulled his earlobe, then his lip. "I want the People and the Clan to live amicably. Mook ... his goal, I am more convinced than ever, is the opposite. My brother—given time—will align with us. He fought at my side to build a new home for the Clan. He won't forget that."

"You told him Mook and Druyl tried to kill you."

A line formed between Kazeb's brows. "Mook denies it, acts committed to the Clan's future in my presence while reinforcing Turk's accusations against the Chosen in my absence. I think he wants to fracture my relationship with Turk so he can step up as Alpha."

He fell silent so she gestured below to the narrow plain edged by a fringe of trees, a long pond, and a cracked dry riverbed that might flow with water in the cold air time.

"You said we would travel through an area where we are most likely to hunt small groups of meat animals. Is this it?"

He nodded. "Come," and led her around a copse to a field scattered with prints of deer, boar, and hare, overlaid with those who stalk them–Hyaena, Leopard, and Bear.

His finger traced fresh Clan footprints. "These are Clan families afraid to rejoin, but who remain close in case circumstances change. The upcoming hunt provides an opportunity. Tribes have by now exhausted their supplies of fat, long bones, tusks, and tendons. You working with both us and the Chosen should persuade everyone that the Chosen are friends."

He rubbed his forehead. "Mating becomes ever more important, too. Tribes can't mate with their own so rely on other groups. Without children, we expire. You have many willing females."

"And you?"

He picked at grass stalks, words soft, "And me, but I am ready for more than that."

Yu'ung's mating experience was nominal, pairmating non-existent, so she missed his meaning, focused instead on what danger his fractured tribe represented to hers.

"These Clan families didn't leave because they sided with Mook."

"No, but I'll be honest, we are more likely to reunite if Fierce and his band leave."

The muscles around her mouth tightened. His best outcome was the People's worst.

She forced a smile. "We appreciate the carcasses you shared. Our wraps are worn through, almost beyond mending." The pounding in her chest matched the thud in her ears.

He flushed. "I must check the herds."

"I, too, have another task," she responded, but he'd already sprinted away.

She had no idea what her "task" was.

Shanadar sat on his ledge, legs crossed. Yu'ung and Kazeb appeared in the distance, laden with moldy berries for the ear therapies. His burns itched and cracked, bled when he scratched them too vigorously, but his eye concerned him the most. The orb didn't work as it should. Yu'ung had remedies for the burns, but offered nothing to heal the eye. Shanadar assumed it would be what it would be. He now relied more on the other.

He intercepted Yu'ung after Kazeb left. "It's time."

"Shanadar! How do you arrive without being seen?"

He scrunched his brow, his relaxed pose in sharp contrast to her tension. "All creatures have blind spots, all nature shadows. The Canis taught me to blend into them."

"That sounds complicated."

"It requires practice. I had plenty of time on my journey."

"Xad didn't come to get more ointment."

"He's been busy."

But she'd already left. Shanadar withdrew Wise Stone from his shoulder sack, massaged it with his thumb, and soon, his lips formed soundless words as he crossed his arms and his feet patted in rhythm with the grasshopper's chirp and the squirrel's call. A distant thump grew louder….

Yu'ung skidded to a stop by his side. She snapped open the waxy leaf and lathered a gooey mucus on his tight dry spots. The fire calmed.

She handed him the leaves. "Use these when the burns become vexing."

Shanadar stuffed them into his pouch, wounds already forgotten. "How are Grub and Jvelk and Braanroorv, their ears?"

"Better, though Braanroorv heals slower. His were worse."

As Shanadar rose to leave, she asked, "When can we see what you do?"

He breathed out. “You can now. We’ll need as many torches as you can carry.”

“So our destination is far and dark.”

“It’s my sanctuary.”

“Which is beyond your cave?”

“And deep below the surface,” he said, his tone tinged with impatience.

She filled cones with sticky sap while Shanadar cut stalks and incised the tops. Fierce and Grub acknowledged them from a distance, but didn’t pause their labor. Beyond, children played a game where, rather than outrunning opponents, they evaded them, an approach suited to youngsters whose minds ran faster than their feet.

Satchels full to overflowing, Shanadar picked his way through the talus slopes, sidestepping jumbled mounds of cascaded gravel to a worn upward path. There, he began to climb, quickly and without pause, bracing himself at times, hanging by a hand and foot at others, never worried despite the almost-blind eye. She followed, copying his actions, and found it surprisingly easy.

In less time than she expected, they entered Shanadar’s vaulted cave. The hearth welcomed them. Recent rainwater pooled on the rough floor. The damp air sculpted the rock walls where it dribbled down from the ceiling. A nest of grass lay against what would be the wall best warmed by the fire.

“Ocha has a den?”

“And Blaze, but I have yet to find a passage to these heights for him.”

“Xad lives with you.”

Shanadar gave an exasperated huff. “You aren’t here to ask me questions. You inquired about my sanctuary. It is deep in Big Rock well beyond the easy tunnels.”

They inserted the cones into the split shafts until each had a supply of torches.

Yu’ung shoved her hair inside her shirt and asked, “Is there trace of others in these tunnels?”

Shanadar puckered his brow. "No," and he entered the tunnel.

A flock of birds exploded around him, their voices high-pitched with fear. Shanadar flapped gentle fingers through the flutter of wings. A few settled onto his arms and shoulders, flitted away as he murmured to them. Only then did he make his way into the dark realms.

Yu'ung dragged a hand along the clammy walls as her feet shuffled through the dust and dirt. She shivered as a critter scurried over her toes, unable to see more than the torch's dancing form in front. The farther they went, the more pungent the stale scent of mold and decay. Shanadar seemed to forget her presence, muttered to himself in words she couldn't make out.

The ceiling gradually lowered, forcing them to stoop, crawl, and finally creep through the grime and dead carapaces. Presented with options, Shanadar never equivocated over which tunnel, but she couldn't see any identifying signs. They scrabbled up an incline tight enough she had to collapse her chest to fit. Once, she tumbled down a chute, so snug she banged her shoulders and hips against the ragged rock walls. She hit bottom and splashed the ground with light. A vine hung that stopped just short of the bottom where she stood.

I should have climbed down.

She slapped at her pouch, relieved the spare cinder hadn't fallen out.

They sloshed through water at times, the sound thrumming with the steady drip from the roof, the stagnant air mustier the deeper they crawled. She let her torch expire, thinking his was enough, then his flickered out. The dark became absolute without even shades of black to indicate their bodies to each other. Her breathing shallowed and throat tightened.

"Shanadar! Did you run out of torches?"

"Why do you ask? The only direction is forward."

She scrambled to light one of hers when his words floated back, "Don't worry. We're almost there."

She smelled no fear which didn't surprise her. To him, darkness held no greater risk than light. The tunnel pinched inward, then curved at a sharp angle. Yu'ung squirmed to negotiate the bend, twisted around, and slipped into another corridor.

She forced herself to breathe in uniform pulls. A cool chill enveloped her, reminding her of Xhosa. The darkness ahead took on a different texture and Yu'ung slid to a stop.

"Shanadar?"

Nothing.

She tried again. "Shanadar!"

"I'm ahead." His words were muted.

A rushing sound became overwhelming, like dry water. Her elbows met air and she fell into shadows.

"Welcome to my sanctuary."

Chapter 27

Shanadar's calm, smooth voice reassured her. A torch illuminated the cavern and Yu'ung spun a slow circle. Stalagmites and stalactites grew everywhere, many loftier and broader than trees. Someone had positioned pieces of similar thickness and height in a circle, enclosing an area large enough for a gathering the size of the People.

"Did you create the ring, Shanadar?"

"Of course not. I am still learning, not yet ready to do."

Dark, sooty spots marred the area around the columns. "Who built the fires?"

Yu'ung waited for Shanadar to explain, but he didn't. Beside the huge circle was a smaller partial one, littered with charred bones. Scattered through the cavern lay piles of pillars as though construction stopped before completion. Colored designs decorated the walls, similar to the People's. These, with exceptions, appeared new.

Carved by newcomers to relay their story.

Shanadar splashed torchlight over an unblemished surface to the side. "Do you notice the picture?"

She frowned, saw no message, shapes, designs, or colors.

What does he see?

She said nothing and he moved on. Tunnels broke off the cavern, their blackness oppressive enough to swallow all sense of distance or direction. At the edge of her vision, shadows swayed, shifting as if someone inhaled and exhaled.

Of a sudden, the circle lit, illuminated through an opening that stretched upward to the outside. Above, she saw Moon, smiling down, the visage shockingly similar to Shanadar's Wise Stone.

Or is that Sun? How long have we been here? And how did anyone bore a hole?

"I don't see it."

"Spirits like Seer and Xhosa live here."

He crouched. She did the same, knees on grit and pebbles, toes curled.

"Close your eyes, Yu'ung. Place your hands on your thighs."

She did. A hollow sound reverberated around her. Steps approached. She snapped her eyes open. They were alone.

"Keep your eyes sealed," Shanadar whispered.

Squeaks, water drips, the sharp tang of feces, the gentle whoosh of air, a whistle, faint cracking as though behemoths shifted in their sleep, followed by an eerie, heavy quiet.

"Did you hear her?"

Yu'ung opened her eyes. Shanadar was standing so she stood also, scanned, saw nothing, and gave up.

"Shanadar. Why are the stalagmites in a circle?"

"To communicate with each other."

"Communicate what?"

"That I don't know. Yet. Xad and I are still gathering them, detaching the tips and bases so they stand level. I assume when we finish the ring our forebears started, Xhosa will tell me its purpose. Come," and he approached a collection of stalactites, their size and location distinctly unnatural.

He pinged them, one after another, and created tones so beautiful she shivered.

"How..." but she couldn't find words for what to say next.

Shanadar paced into the circle at the cavern's center, stood motionless and soundless beneath the tunnel in the ceiling.

"What does it tell you, Shanadar?"

"How the past and future mix."

A familiar fragrance floated through the air.

Old One!

He died far away, on the quest for a new home. A huff, then another.

Ocha! How did you get here? And where are we?

As though he heard her, Shanadar answered, "Here is where I receive wisdom from those who know."

She shivered in her layers of wraps.

"Bring the tribes, Yu'ung. We will light the sanctuary as done for past conclaves," and he indicated dark spots atop the stalagmites and next to them, the obvious residue of small hearths.

"Conclaves?" What was a *conclave*?

"Yes," was his only response.

"Why?"

Shanadar grinned, a smile that matched Xhosa's across the gulf of time, and then faded. "I won't know until we do it."

He spun a circle, eyes closed, senses open. "One truth I've learned already is you are home."

They fell silent.

Shanadar rubbed a callused thumb over Wise Stone. The slashed mouth smiled. Shanadar's lips flattened and he hummed, either ignoring Yu'ung's presence or forgetting it.

She waited. When he did nothing else, she wandered away to decipher what marks she could on the walls, and store the rest in memory until they found a home in some future event. The handprints baffled her, the widely spread fingers pressed hard enough against the wall to leave their shape and size. She'd never seen handprints in messages of her kind. Did someone try to penetrate the rock surface, touch what lay behind? Or were they marking their territory with color as predators do with urine? Or was it to frighten away enemies, protect those who lived here? Did they have anything to do with the towers being built or the chute to the outside?

And why were they mostly hued in ochre?

She moved on to the rest of the messages, etched more traditionally, but still unusual. Why did parts of the wall have depressions as well as color? The embedded ochre and black dust brought life to the rough indents. One made raw instinct rumble within her. This felt immediate, gut-level. It cleansed her thoughts. Another etching, farther down the wall, looked like a bird's print.

Shanadar murmured, "Clap your hands."

When she did, facing the clawed lines connected to a circle, it sounded like stampeding ostriches.

She moved on to a shape on a different wall, this one a zigzag form that might be a wandering river. Clapping her hands here made no reverberation. Did she expect a burbling stream, or were the previous sounds a coincidence? Or planned somehow by the original builders as echoes, like when she called from a mountain and heard her voice respond? She plodded back to the handprints, clapped, and here, too, nothing. Why just the bird prints?

She lost herself in the why.

Shanadar crouched, ate an herb that grew on the opposite shore to where they were now. Yu'ung chittered, but he had no time to listen. He clapped. A pillar chirped. Yu'ung asked about the clapping—why it reverberated at times and not others.

"It … just … does…."

He hummed, his mouth open. A different pillar sang, this one a caution. Yu'ung's head snapped toward it. Shanadar swayed side to side, feet light on the dusty surface, slapped his hands together, and was rewarded with a higher-toned chirrup. The crystals spoke their own language. Each time he visited, they responded quicker and longer. Sometimes, echoes overflowed the chamber and resonated within his body. The rhythm exhilarated him. Power flowed through his brain.

"What do they say, Shanadar?"

"They speak of the ground, the air, the rocks, the water. The Spirits."

He jerked. Invisible energy flooded the hollowness. "Go, Yu'ung! You must save the boy."

"Which boy?"

"*The* boy! Return here before the hunt, when Moon's full face will peer through to us. Bring enough torches to light each platform in the circle."

"How do I get out, Shanadar?"

"Retrace your route," and then he blotted her out, hearing nothing else beyond his noisy thoughts.

Hunger tightened his gut. He walked into another alcove where the Eagle cape awaited him. He donned it. The spidery feathers tingled to his touch. Yu'ung spoke nonsensical words. A bright flash, then feet pounded, hides scraped, and shuffles faded with the torch's light.

Music.

The song of today.

His hands patted around for the clay gourd Xhosa assured him would be there. It contained crushed seeds, bark, leaves, and honey, swirled together in warm water.

Drink it.

The mixture washed down his throat and settled in his belly. Eyes closed, he walked a dim corridor without standing, shadows so thick he couldn't see. The earth entered him, beat inside his torso, primal in nature, heavy. The thuds became part of him. His heart fluttered, and he welcomed those ancient ones.

Xhosa.

He approached a moss-covered tree and thumped the hollow trunk. The sound resonated through him.

I await your questions.

But they wouldn't leave his mouth. She tugged him into the gnarled root bundle, handed him a dry white flower, stalk gone to seed, and chewed another with him. He collapsed, butt on his legs, tumbled as though off a precipice, and jolted at the top of a twisted passage. He descended, but not far. The stench stopped him. A grave holding a small, desiccated skeleton. Blackened fires surrounded animal horns and a rhinoceros skull. Why place the bodies here? And why mourn them? Death was good. Did Xhosa want him to mimic these actions?

Endless notions yanked him in every direction, and he froze.

Chapter 28

Her exit went more easily than the entrance. Where she vacillated over a tunnel choice, a smell—often Shanadar's—made the decision easy. The occasional times a direction seemed unclear, Xad had left markers.

The biggest surprise was a spotted hyaena resting by Shanadar's hearth fire. One eye latched momentarily onto Yu'ung and then twitched shut. It was cautious, but not defensive, as though accustomed to her kind. Still, she trembled in its presence.

"When we're better friends, will you show me—or show Ocha—how you got here? Blaze would like to spend time with Xad and Shanadar."

She exited, drank in fresh pure air without the stale mustiness of the deep rocky warrens, and scrutinized the plateau. Shanadar promised this would be home. Everything inside her body and mind said he was right. Despite her longish absence, nothing seemed out of place except directly below. There, at Big Rock's base, Kazeb walked a tight line through the rubble, gaze bouncing from one end of the behemoth to the other.

Something bothers him.

When his gaze found her, it locked on and then his face lit with relief.

Why would he worry about me?

B'o deemed her a hunter, Aynoh the People's Alpha, but Kazeb knew her only from Fierce's sailing craft. She doubted that invoked trust—not yet—so why did she feel it for him?

Is this what Aynoh feels for Fierce? Faith that he will do what's right based on instinct rather than experience?

That was unusual for Yu'ung.

Kazeb sprinted toward Big Rock, then clambered up the flank.

Something happened. And then—*the child!*

Shanadar's command to save the child rang in her memory.

She matched Kazeb's fearless abandon and plummeted down the rock face, her phalanges gripping tiny ledges, propelling her onward at a pace no one would deem safe, but one she was accustomed to.

Does he have news of a child?

They scrambled onto the bird plateau at the same time. Sweat dripped over his prognathic sun-bleached brows. He swiped it away, ignoring the damp wrap basted to his body. Sweat prickled his armpits.

"What happened, Kazeb?"

"You disappeared, again. I—probably everyone—worried."

She pulled in a deep breath through clenched teeth and let it out slowly. "Shanadar wanted me to visit his sanctuary."

Before she could ask about the child, Kazeb's eyes sparked with anger, hands trembling, "And you couldn't take time to tell anyone?"

"Fierce saw us."

He pointed up to Sun's movement across the sky. "A long while ago," and scrunched his heavy brow.

She waited, enjoying his anger.

He waved a hand over his head, eyes nowhere. "Shanadar. He's the one who wears feathers in his hair, pulls it into a Canis tail." He tugged his hair back to demonstrate.

"And saved my life. I am always safe with him." She leaned forward. "You watched me at the fig tree, too."

"I wanted to be sure you found your way out. The tunnels down there are more confusing than they appear."

He scratched his neck where hair met skin. She could see the lice nested, which he hadn't taken time to groom. As a result, they feasted on his sweat and dead skin and made everything itchy.

He continued, "And no one saw you go down there. If you disappeared, they wouldn't know where to start the search." He folded one arm over his trunk, scrubbed an eye with his fist.

"So you waited outside."

"Of course I did! I know how confusing it is. The first time I explored, it was unlike any other cave. The whistling calls, the passages that went nowhere, the illuminated stone walls—"

"I found those, though I don't know how."

"I felt time called me, guiding me along worn paths created by countless feet, but always the goal was beyond my reach. It was disorienting. Then, the sounds, a mellow heartbeat of life like nothing I've ever heard. They guided me out. I don't think I would have found my way without them."

Yu'ung brushed her hands down her sides. "I was lost until Ocha came and took me to the exit." She didn't bother to mention Ocha's spirit essence and link to Xhosa. Maybe later.

"I kept going back, drawn to the tunnels, but I never heard the voices again. Each time, I discovered new oddities. Once, I came to a section of wall that I could see through but not pass through. Shapes—Uprights—on the other side carried columns. Lights flickered, from many flames. Handprints were splotched on the wall I peered through."

"Ochre?"

He nodded.

A physical weight lifted with his words.

"You describe what I saw today, Kazeb. Shanadar's sanctuary has a circle of rearranged stalagmites and old fire pits, impressions of hands on the walls as though someone tried to enter or leave and they're all red. Shanadar says the columns tell him secrets. He heard voices while I was with him and I heard some through him. How is that possible?"

"I don't know." He paced, head down, hands clenched and straightened. "I'm glad Ocha was with you, at the fig tree. If I'd known you had such a friend, I wouldn't have spied on you then, but this time, still would have!"

Yu'ung murmured without meaning to, "I'm glad you did," then she shook herself and pressed her palms to her cheeks, hard. "Something is happening in Shanadar's sanctuary and I think it has to do with Fierce's Seer. Shanadar said today, we left Big Rock. I believed him. We were nowhere I'd seen here or anywhere."

Kazeb's eyes glazed. "Maybe he's right."

Spoken like someone who knows of Xhosa, or of the Spirits.

She refrained from asking, but her belief in Kazeb deepened.

She swallowed. "Did you find the herd?"

He bobbed a yes.

"Shanadar wants to tell us something before the hunt. I think he plans to guide us as Seer does for the Chosen hunts. He also warned me 'Save the child' though wouldn't clarify who that was or from what."

They scanned everyone they could see below, the foragers, the food preparers, and the few Clan youngsters whose families spent most days with the People.

No one is struggling.

Yu'ung muttered, "Could it be someone who carries a child?" and skidded down the trail, spraying pebbles behind in a rush to reach the group.

She shouted to Ese as B'o's pairmate lumbered to a flat stone about to begin work pounding roots, "Where is Aynoh?"

Ese shaded her brow, beaming at Yu'ung. "Good to see you. She is with Ruk and his new friend, from your group, Kazeb."

Kazeb's brows rose. "What did this one look like?"

Ese shrugged. "Like any child."

Kazeb and Yu'ung raced along Aynoh's backtrail. The smell of damp dirt was fresh. A woof resounded from somewhere in front.

She and Kazeb sprinted into the clearing, found Blaze with Aynoh and Ruk. Blaze's ears perked, lips trembled, and then he leapt, first on Yu'ung, then Kazeb. They pushed him away, but still he wagged his entire body, his happiness at seeing his pack boundless.

Aynoh approached, the question in her eyes.

Yu'ung said, "We were worried," and briefly explained what Shanadar had told her.

Aynoh tipped her head. "We are all fine. Ruk's new playmate, he's not here right now."

Fierce trotted up holding a pair of long bones, cracked one open, twirled a twig inside to scoop out the marrow, and handed it to Aynoh. She licked the twig clean.

Could someone else carry a baby that I don't know about?

"Does Wik feel all right, Aynoh? And Ese?"

If anyone knew, it would be Aynoh, the tribe's healer.

"Yes. Why wouldn't they?"

"Since all children in both tribes seem healthy, I wondered if Shanadar meant unborn children." She turned to Fierce, embarrassed. "Where'd you find legs without the rest of the body?"

"Leopard chased down a gazelle last night, left the carcass in a tree. When I saw the legs remained, I took them. If anyone else carried a child, I would have given them the other."

Yu'ung wanted to grow into a leader like Fierce, aware of everything and not overbearing. Blaze rubbed against her, soothing her by his presence, and she tamped down the worry.

Fierce said, "You were with Shanadar."

"Yes. He cautioned me about a child in trouble and warned me about something else that makes no sense."

Fierce ticked off on his fingers, "Ruk is the People's only child. Can you explain the other?"

Yu'ung wanted to, but now, it seemed a blurred jumble of sounds and scents. She picked her way over to the pond, sucked water in to soothe her dust-laden throat, prickling from the long run. She plucked at the damp grass, found no answers there, and returned to the group, shoulders slumped.

"No. Not yet."

Aynoh fingered her hair into a cord. "All the People's children are accounted for." She turned to Kazeb.

He ran a hand over his forehead, swished away a sheen of sweat. "I will spread the word among our tribes to be careful and see if I can find Ruk's new friend. It's probably from a tribe arriving for the hunt."

Yu'ung crossed and uncrossed her arms. "Shanadar wants everyone at the sanctuary before the hunt."

Fierce chuckled. "As Seer always does," then, "I hear an unspoken 'but'."

She barked a laugh. "The passage is a challenge."

Fierce relaxed. "Which he doesn't care about. If I didn't know better, I would think they were communicating."

Kazeb said, "This Shanadar and your Seer, Fierce, they keep life interesting," and sprinted off.

Aynoh motioned toward the horizon. Sun's lower portion was already hidden. "Let's eat. Is Kazeb coming back, Yu'ung?" The presumption that she knew.

Because I am in charge, I see everything as Fierce does? Or because I have become the conduit for Kazeb's activities?

Unexpectedly, she didn't mind the latter. *Are Kazeb and I where Aynoh and Fierce started?*

She knew this answer because she and Kazeb had discussed adding males to the People's homebase when the Chosen departed.

"He told me Turk will remain in the Clan camp to redirect those who wished to come here and Kazeb would stay with us to help those settling in and around Big Rock."

Chapter 29

As always, establishing a new site required more work than rest. Aynoh, Ese, and one of the new arrivals chattered as they worked. Others foraged. The children collected stranded fish from the tidepools and Laak and Jvelk sharpened tools. A few simply observed. Kazeb's comfort with both the People and the Chosen eased the tension. Clan questions went to Kazeb, other decisions to Yu'ung and Fierce.

Kazeb and Yu'ung headed for an overwatch he recommended, to relax and catch up.

"This one is unlike the others. From here, I track Sun's arrival and departure in relation to the loftiest peak in the mountain range. Sun leaves the sky to the weak side in warm air time, to the strong side in cold air time. You can tell how close one is by Sun's position on the horizon."

"Always?"

His eyes sparkled. "The natural world provides clues about its plans, like thready clouds around Sun mean rain, but never absolutes."

They talked quietly, keeping their voices low while scanning the surroundings. They found no sign of whoever spied on them, but established many commonalities. After long enough, Yu'ung headed back to her tribe to see if any had heard where Ruk's unknown friend was. She intended to start with her mother, but slowed as she approached. Fierce was talking to Aynoh, sweat prickling his forehead, hands gesturing something that made no sense. Normally, when they had serious discussions, Yu'ung left them to it, but something was wrong.

She interrupted. "Mother?"

Fierce coughed. "Aynoh and I must talk. By ourselves—"

But Aynoh turned away. "I'm too late."

Fierce peered around. Satisfied no one could hear their conversation, he said, "Maybe Yu'ung can help. I don't know what to do."

She wriggled until her back was to Fierce and pressed her mother. "Too late for what?"

When Aynoh said nothing, he did. "My band wants to leave immediately. They are satisfied that the People are safe.

Aynoh snapped, "But I'm not. Satisfied."

Yu'ung forced her shoulders to relax. "I'm not either. What about Turk and Mook?"

Fierce answered quickly, "Kazeb assures me Turk will come around," but wouldn't meet her eye.

Yu'ung tilted until Fierce had to look into her face. "And Mook?"

Fierce ground his teeth and sweat prickled his skin. Yu'ung waited, giving him time.

"I don't think so. Nor does my band, but they believe one person isn't reason enough to delay our return, not with Kazeb now prepared to defend with the People, and Laak and Jvelk trained. We weren't sent here to guard other Uprights and they miss the life they left behind."

Aynoh blanched, but Yu'ung understood. The People lived in small gatherings. Each member, every day, did what needed doing. No one was told or ordered. Not so with the Chosen. Their home assemblages were large. According to Fierce, all did what Leaders and Leads told them. If they noticed, say, hides that needed to be scraped before rotting, they asked a Lead who then resolved how to accomplish the task. By the time the decision was made, the People would have finished. In the Chosen band, the slowness of decisions resulted in stress and chaos among well-meaning members who tried to do what needed to be done.

"You're the Leader, Fierce. Don't they follow your orders whether they agree or not?"

He crossed his arms. "Let me answer that with my own question. I admit, I see the wisdom of your system, that everyone does what needs doing, but what happens when someone is lazy, works slowly, or not at all, like Shanadar claims his old tribe accused him of."

"Laziness isn't tolerated. There are too many chores and too few tribe members. Eventually, each must find a suitable job or a different tribe. No one is permitted to live off the work of others. Even those injured, like Old One, always make themselves valuable."

"No Qads, then," from Fierce. Qad was Grub's brother, preferred avoiding work to performing it. He'd become a problem, especially for Aynoh, on the migration from the People's mountain homeland.

Yu'ung thinned her lips. "The People wouldn't tolerate him. I can't think of a time we had one. Maybe because we're small enough, everyone knows everyone, we groom daily, talk to each other often, the pressure to contribute is overwhelming."

Yu'ung's pale skin flushed. *That's why Aynoh blanched. She does not want to be told what to do, live where she can't perform tasks she knows to be necessary until approved by others. It brings back memories of Dhar, her first pairmate, who almost destroyed both of us.*

Yu'ung pinned Fierce with her gray gaze. "But you are Leader and have the power to make or change decisions. Insist they stay."

He forced a smile. "Yes, but in this case, I agree with them."

Yu'ung swallowed hard. "What?"

"If members of my band wish to leave, they should make that decision, not me." He twisted away, but left his hand on Aynoh's. "That's a colossal change in my thinking from when I left my homeland with my band. Then, my words were inviolate. After many of Moon's cycles, none of the band members any longer required supervision. They became like you, observant and self-directed. It worked better than I could ever have expected. I want them to value those lessons, take them back to our homeland, and teach them to others."

Aynoh fingered her red hair. "But still, they leave. You leave because you are their Leader."

He placed a hand on hers. "You missed my most important point. I, like them, make my own decision. For me, that is to stay here, with you."

Aynoh trembled and her eyes dampened, but when she spoke, her voice was strong. "You don't have to do that, Fierce. You are my pairmate. If you go, I go."

Yu'ung shot to her feet. "You are the People's Elder, our wisdom. Those exceed demands of a pairmate, Aynoh!"

"I have taught Ese to be an Elder. Jhat is learning healing and will continue with your help, and you are wise enough for anything the People face. I am no longer needed here, but I am necessary to my pairmate."

Yu'ung scrambled for a response. "The trip is too treacherous, Aynoh, for one who carries a baby."

"People always travel with babies."

"And Aynoh won't travel alone. Eknilk and Braanroorv will let Seer know what we have accomplished, that I will come when I can."

Aynoh leaned into Fierce until their chests touched. "Go with your warriors. The baby and I will find our way to you when it arrives. I will be safe, wearing your necklace."

Shock made Yu'ung's skin clammy. "A female and an infant—no. Predators will see opportunity."

Fierce's eyes softened. "Yu'ung is right. The area from the shoreless sea to our homebase swarms with hostiles. They fear the consequences of causing us trouble, but you, alone, even with the necklace … I won't test that."

He barked a laugh. "And one person can't sail across the channel. The currents suck you into the thin strait that divides shoreless sea and Endless Sea, where the water swirls in all directions with a vengeance. The Elders say its purpose is to sink any who impede their dominance. I am not so sure they're wrong. The winds are as unpredictable as the currents. If they don't crush you on the rugged shores or pummel you to the sea floor, they will spit you into Endless Sea, a vast lake without borders, without islands. No matter how far you sail, you never finish."

He shrugged. "At least, no one ever came back to tell us otherwise."

"Even in your boats?"

He nodded. "I've already talked with Eknilk, Bhidid, and Braanroorv. They will take one craft, Grub and me the next when you and Wik can travel."

Chapter 30

Yu'ung scanned the area. Ese was treating someone's gash. Aynoh was reapplying Braanroorv's mulch. She didn't bother with Grub's. Laak and Jvelk were challenging each other's skills. Since Jvelk's ears were clean, she assumed he had recovered. Everyone else was preparing for the upcoming hunt, with the Clan, or the upcoming meal. Farther down the shore were more caves—shimmering black holes in the rock face—and additional pasture, giving new arrivals a choice of where to establish homebases. She trotted up to Fierce. It was time to ask.

"Do you trust Kazeb?"

Fierce's dark features softened. "Yes."

"Should I?"

"Without reservation. Kazeb's lack of bitterness and hate after what his Clan went through and the influence of one as close to him as his brother—that is the mark of a Leader and a friend. To me, he is both."

Both stopped talking when Kazeb joined them. He couldn't miss the flush on Yu'ung's face. "Did I miss something?"

Yu'ung blurted out, "No. I was asking Fierce's advice on … homebases. The People have always lived in caves, but the Clan prefers open air. He … they …."

Fierce took over. "Your open-air sites, Kazeb, are much like the Chosen's, save for the lack of hides around the perimeter. I suspect you adapted because you don't have enough large animals here to provide the hides."

"And there are few predators or enemies to protect against, unlike the opposite side of the mountain range where we originally lived."

"On hunting trips, we use fire as a barrier or place one side of the camp against a rock wall."

Kazeb shrugged. "Turk and I disagreed on an approach here on Big Rock, but neither of us is set on one tactic."

Yu'ung said, "When Fierce's band leaves, our cave will have room for a select group."

She locked onto his eyes, didn't look away, hoped he understood. He did.

"Flint would like that, too. What about Turk?"

Yu'ung's eyes narrowed and Fierce grimaced. "If you trust him. Mook—no. Mook doesn't care who he hurts if it benefits him. That hasn't changed since I first met him."

Kazeb grinned. "I'll talk to Flint," and he trotted toward his camp.

Grub hurried up to Fierce, glancing over his shoulder at a group returning carrying spears and shoulder sacks.

"We found Clan sign, but no other Uprights. No one sees any danger to the People from others on the Big Rock. Are they wrong?"

Fierce shifted. "When we first arrived here, there weren't a lot of tribes, but something has changed since then." He shuffled to the side to make room for Aynoh. "As a child, I could always tell when danger was near. The hair on my neck rose or my stomach churned. Sometimes, I just felt a presence. I won't lie to you. I feel it now, not from the brothers and I don't believe from Kazeb's Clan members. Just the one we have been talking about."

Yu'ung looked through the mix of Clan and People, the camaraderie, the industry. "I walk through with Ocha whenever I can, to check her instincts. She reacts only to one."

Fierce's face hardened in concentration and then he strode out of the group toward the largest gathering.

"Which reminds me, time to teach the youngsters more about caution." He clapped his hands. "Let's play a game."

The children and subadults raced over. "This game hones tracking skills. My kind plays it with almost-adults, but your kind, People and Clan, achieve more despite youth. I expect we can include children and subadults."

Everyone straightened at the praise, and their young faces flickered with excitement.

"Here's how we play. I am prey. You are predators. Hide from me in root bundles, rotten logs, thick grass, or where I have to squint into the sun to see you, as though awaiting an opening to strike."

Voices rumbled as everyone thrilled to the challenge.

Fierce closed his eyes. "Scatter! I'll open my eyes in a handful of breaths. If I spot you, I point and you lose. If you touch me, I lose. Be prepared to fail because I don't."

He rapidly found all except one. The scent lingered in Fierce's memory from the game's start, but he had no image of the child. He rotated a full circle, but the odor was nowhere.

"Who is missing?"

"Ant," Ruk said immediately. "We were together when you announced the game."

Kazeb stuttered, "That's impossible. Ant died."

Ruk giggled. "He's good at hiding!"

Fierce growled, "Ruk. Do you know where his nest is?"

Ruk led them to a small overhang littered with knapping debris, foot covers, and fish scales.

Fierce muttered, "But no Ant. Are you sure he decided to play?"

"He was excited."

"That means he is still playing, and cleverly. Ruk, stay here in case he returns."

Black clouds pushed the white away overhead and the blue sky grayed.

Fierce raised his voice in hopes the child could hear. "We must locate him before the storm hits."

Yu'ung tugged her shirt tighter, remembering the tattered wrap worn by Ant. "Let's hurry."

The first flashes of fire split the sky, followed closely by the roll of thunder. A light rain went from drizzle to downpour in less than a few breaths. Ocha moaned and tucked her tail.

"Ocha lost the trail."

The storm ended as quickly as it started. Yu'ung stooped over sticky mud someone had swiped their fingers through.

"He screened his scent, but then left a muddy print trail like a novice would. Why do that?"

Fierce scowled. "He dangles his prowess in plain sight. He's too young to be this clever."

"Or old enough."

With the death of his tribe, he had to survive on his wits. I wonder if he pretends to make mistakes so we underestimate him.

Soon, the clouds disappeared and heat blanketed the land. Ant diverted to a shoal bed where his prints could no longer be tracked.

Fierce huffed annoyance as he scratched an armpit. "He doesn't win until he taps me and that won't happen."

They continued. Yu'ung picked up the occasional freshly broken twig, a branch bent by one passing in haste, and saliva dripped on leaves from panting. Yu'ung had no doubt Ant laid these clues with purpose, but he didn't count on this heat.

She said, mostly to Fierce, "He's going to need a pond to cool himself. We'll catch him there."

Fierce grinned for the first time on the hunt. "I smell one just ahead. Let's rehydrate and then re-acquire his trail."

At the pond, Yu'ung drenched herself in the cool water. She recovered from the heat enough to consider continuing when a giggle made her jerk around. A smiling face in a tattered hide stood in front of a chortling Fierce. Ant had won!

Based on Ant's shrewd tactics, Braanroorv agreed to train him as a scout. To become a Lead, he must compare what he saw *now* to memories of what it was *earlier*. The challenge became to teach this eager youngster everything before time ran out and the Chosen left.

Braanroorv studied the youngster. "You're Ruk's size. How do you know so much?"

Ant grinned. "Because I must."

Ruk ambled up to Ant's side. "I'm his partner."

Braanroorv scowled, "Are you talented enough?"

Ruk and Ant answered together. "Yes."

Ant tried to conceal his smile. Youth worked against him.

Yu'ung crossed her arms. "Ruk. Find your partner a nest in the cave, where the scouts sleep."

Ant's brow puckered. "Predators assume I will be there. They rely on it. Why not be where they don't expect?"

Fierce hid his laugh. "The child is indeed a natural. Listen to his instincts."

Braanroorv growled and marched off, Ant and Ruk on his backtrail. Fierce, Kazeb, and B'o trotted in the opposite direction to spy on Mook, Turk if necessary. The People could only trust the Clan if there was no confusion about who was prey or predator.

Yu'ung swiped sweat from her brow and scanned the coastline. Nothing had changed since the last time she checked save a few more flecks of gray foam on the shoreless sea.

Spying takes longer than I remember. Did they find trouble?

Yu'ung had started on an Ibex when they left, intending to turn the pelt into a wrap, but now it lay in her lap, untouched. Her eyes glazed, thoughts far from her work.

Wik stifled giggles as Ese asked, "Where's Kazeb, Yu'ung? Surely you know."

Again, as though he checks in with me.

"He left with Fierce, to locate the herd."

She punched holes in the pelt with an awl, hooked the pieces together with cordage, and ignored the murmured comments from others. Fierce and B'o returned, fox and wildcat slung around their necks.

B'o tossed the carcasses into the communal pile. "Pelts for small bodies."

And meat for stew.

Fierce squatted by Yu'ung. "I saw Turk and Mook. Something has changed."

"For the good?"

"Maybe...." He glanced around. "Is Kazeb not back yet?"

Yu'ung shivered, worried by the apprehension in his question. "Not yet."

Fierce looked into the distance, not at all worried. "He's setting up the hunt, talking to some of the Clan tribes."

"Tell me what to expect."

"It's a tiered approach that Kazeb will lead. Hunters skilled with the far-throwing spear will attack from on top of a cliff if there is one, or if not, a rise. Those who get past our spears, Kazeb's Clans will take down with thrusting spears. We kill those they miss. At the hunt's completion, meat is shared depending upon need. Kazeb and Turk, as Alphas, are in charge of distribution.

"Though we—the Chosen—are leaving, we wish to do so on the best terms possible. This hunt allows us to convince the scattered assemblages that the past is over."

As Fierce explained, he scanned the woods, the fields, the deepening shadows. Yu'ung did the same, searching as far as her extreme sight allowed.

Fierce murmured, as though in passing, or maybe hoping he wouldn't be heard, "We must leave the Big Rock before the air gets too cold and the water too rough to cross the channel."

Fierce stood to his full height. "B'o, Laak—let's practice spear skills."

Yu'ung dropped the hide, thrilled to have something more exciting to do than punch holes. "I'm coming, too." Jvelk pounded up. "I'll soon be Lead."

Wik, Ese, Jhat, and Flint surged to his side.

Fierce studied Flint. "Why are you with them?"

"The People need skilled warriors when you leave."

"Your tribe won't mind?"

He flushed. "Anyone associated with Mook is not where I belong anymore."

"Luckily, we have spare spears from the One attack." He called Bhidid over. "Your assistance is required."

Flint stilled for a breath and then shuddered. "From the mixed Chosen-Clan tribe who attacked you down the shoreless sea. Jhat told me about it."

Bhidid scratched his chin the way Chosen did. Yu'ung tried it once, but the motion annoyed more than comforted.

He grinned. "Training on spears is my favorite task."

Despite the sincerity of his tone, Bhidid said this about any job he undertook.

The rest of the day, Fierce, B'o, and Bhidid drilled those in attendance with a fervor. Even in dusk's low light, they didn't stop, repeating a mantra: *Living doesn't always occur in bright sunlight.*

Just as the group quit for the day, Kazeb sprinted in, panting heavily. Sweat glistened on his skin, and his torso heaved. Fierce waited while he caught his breath.

He finally rattled out, "We leave tomorrow's tomorrow. I've notified all who will join us."

Yu'ung said, "Then we go to Shanadar's sanctuary tomorrow."

Fierce hissed agreement. "As Seer did. Gathering with him always brought us good fortune."

"Shanadar said Seer gives him advice, but how?"

Fierce scratched. "I'm not sure. He doesn't allow anyone near during those events."

"Well, I appreciate his help. We haven't chased a herd since we lived in the mountains."

Fierce slapped his thighs. "So, it's decided. We finish preparations tomorrow, gather with Shanadar, and hunt on tomorrow's tomorrow."

Chapter 31

They spent the next day sharpening tips, smoothing shafts, knapping cutters, and preparing travel food. Sun neared the horizon as they traipsed up the ridge to Shanadar's cave. Those unable to efficiently climb remained behind to protect the homebase.

A sizzling fire tended by Xad welcomed them. The youngster scrutinized the gathering, but his eyes stopped on no one. His hands, with their delicate fingers, shook so he clenched them in front of his body. What he meant to be a smile melted to a frightened grimace. He'd grown taller since the last time Yu'ung saw him, his wraps more tattered. His feet were uncovered, she suspected to better grip the sometimes slippery passages she had experienced already. Shanadar's colors lined his cheeks, forehead, and shoulders, missing one stripe. He also wore his hair pulled back with a small feather inserted in the knot. A cord of teeth, talons, shells, and feathers hung from his neck, the same sequence as Shanadar's necklace, though without the Eagle plumage.

If Shanadar leaves to seek out Seer, will Xad also go?

She would ask another time.

Xad distributed lit torches and proceeded wordlessly into the tunnels. The explosion of birds, their squawk of displeasure and annoyed flutter of wings, comforted her. Yu'ung, Kazeb, Fierce, and Aynoh led with Ant, Laak, and Jvelk at the rear, the rest of the tribe arrayed in between. Sun's light soon faded from this labyrinth of dark, craggy passages, hiding unknown, risky gambles. Xad's pace was rapid despite the murkiness, with minimal disruption to the gravel underfoot. A somber hush surrounded them, broken by the faint plink of dripping, the distant skitter of rats or some other creature, and her own ragged breaths. Cool air clung to Yu'ung's exposed skin, the floor slick under her bare feet.

"This feels like the fig tree tunnels," said Kazeb, his voice low and calm, maybe with a touch of surprise.

Yu'ung realized with a start he was right.

Fierce asked, "Anything we should be prepared for, Yu'ung?"

"Nothing you can't handle," though she didn't mention the confining tunnel, the low ceiling, the precipitous drop, or the treacherous twists. Why do that? The group must proceed regardless of the challenges.

Kazeb murmured, "I heard that."

Does he hear my mind? As Fierce does Aynoh's? Or did I whisper?

Kazeb snorted, but said nothing.

The roof sank and she stooped. It dropped more and she crawled through crunchy insect carapaces, mouth tight after the first spider slipped between her lips. Grub behind her huffed as he squeezed his girth through.

If Wik's distended stomach fits, he will also.

The People were comforted by discomfort. Fierce's band seemed the same, but he claimed that wasn't true with others in his home.

Every time they came to a juncture, Xad effortlessly picked a tunnel. She tried to discern why—spiders' beds, the feel of the rocks, the size of the aperture—in case she again must make her way alone, but he gave her no time to study them. No surprise he vanished ahead without a sound, no whoosh and no thump.

Yu'ung announced, "You're coming to a drop. Use the vine to the side to lower yourself. Tell those behind you," and she slid down.

At the bottom, they sloshed through water. The stale air stuffier the farther they went, reminiscent of places all avoided. When the tunnel's walls pinched inward and then bent at a sharp angle, she heaved a sigh.

The end is close.

As was the end of the trip for Wik. Her girth was finally too great for the increasingly cramped tunnel. Grub stayed behind with her, as did Aynoh. Her stomach was smaller, but still cumbersome. The rest proceeded. Crawly critters attacked again, not spiders this time. These had stretched bodies with too many legs. They seemed intent not on biting but getting away from her, so she let them pass. A deep resonant reverberation somewhere ahead created an otherworldly hum. One of the subadults behind whispered that it resembled Moose's call to its mate. Everyone crawled in rhythm with the beats. A cool chill enveloped Yu'ung and the darkness took on a different texture.

"We're almost to Shanadar's sanctuary, but there's another drop ahead. Be prepared."

A rushing sound hit her and she found herself hanging in open air for the briefest of moments, then she dropped to a rough surface.

We're here.

As soon as she hit ground, she scrambled out of the way so others could take her position. A mellow gong vibrated through the massive space, bounced off the lofty walls and caromed through the slender stalagmites, infusing the air with mystery. When that stopped, Shanadar's hypnotic flute called them to gather in the center.

A voice intoned, "Light the fires atop the stalagmites."

All did as requested. The circle of flames twinkled like stars, pulsed with energy. Shadows created eerie shapes that danced and waved on the rock faces. The towers glittered. A boulder hung from the ceiling, anchored to the roof by a fragile spire. Xad swung a huge tree limb and its call filled the cavern, announcing the appearance of a spotlight that filled the space in the stalagmite circle. In the center stood Xhosa. She looked as she did so often in Yu'ung's dreams, with the addition of an ochre stripe splayed over her cheeks. Murmurs silenced. No one knew what to make of Xhosa. To Yu'ung, her presence was as comforting as a warm wind in a chill storm. A louder bong, a tree limb against the boulder, startled everyone, drew all eyes to Xad. By the time they refocused on the circle, moonlight remained but Xhosa had vanished.

Everyone murmured to each other, pointing to different pieces of the cavern, asking questions no one could answer. The geometric designs on the walls again drew Yu'ung. The symbols lit by Moon's radiance spoke clearly the story of those who lived here long ago, unraveling their mysteries. The towers sang, with greater purpose than the last time.

A figure slipped from the stygian interior of a tunnel, a Bird-Male with huge black wings.

"Who—what is that?"

Yu'ung stared, frozen. Energy radiated, a quiet authority.

Kazeb murmured reverently, "Shanadar has become an Eagle."

Yu'ung wouldn't have been sure it was him except for the clouded eye.

So many questions, but the one that popped out was, "How did he convince Eagle to forsake its body?"

Shanadar spread his wings, arms absorbed by the feathers, head tucked beneath Eagle's beak. The mighty tail hovered just above the ground. The Shanadar-Bird entered the stalagmite circle, aglow in Moon's beams. He stood motionless, the lone sound mellow beats against a hollow trunk.

Shanadar raised his arms. "I, with Xhosa and Seer, will ensure tomorrow's a success. Tell me you want that!"

Voices called out, "I do!" "I believe!" "You are powerful!"

They hung on his easy words, felt their weight. Yu'ung tingled with excitement. Shanadar, in Eagle's feathered form, spoke to them of ancestors, promising that anything was possible. Soon, though he continued to speak, he was no longer aware of them. No one seeing him would deny that Shanadar had found his purpose. And then Moon passed beyond the vent. The fires atop the stalagmites sputtered out and immersed everyone in darkness. Shanadar and Xad melted away.

Not again.

Worried mumbles.

I must stop this.

She waved a torch, calling everyone's attention. "Follow me out."

Words that should have been strong trembled with worry.

"Yu'ung." A small voice and a tug.

"Ant?"

"I can show the exit."

"How? This is your first time."

"Braanroorv told me." He picked up on her doubt. "He said to be a Lead Scout, I must know how to find my way in known and unknown locations. I will start now."

"Then lead, Ant!"

And he did, flawlessly, his torch bobbing at the front of the column.

The passage back was easier than the last time. In the main cavern slept the same spotted hyaena as though a sentinel to Shanadar's homebase. One sleepy eye latched onto Yu'ung. He snuffled in friendship. For the rest, his muzzle trembled.

The tired crowd traipsed into the People's cave, but Yu'ung climbed an overwatch hill. She pressed against the warm soil, marveled at the sky's slow revolution, that this was the same Moon seen in Shanadar's sanctuary. She greeted the radiant orb and its star pack, the one called Xho that never moved, named for Xhosa. The stars matched those in her former homebase, a reassuring message. Fierce lay at her side.

"Fierce. Was this passage like Seer's?"

He considered how to answer. "Seer has a sanctuary, but no one is allowed there, so I don't know."

She tugged on her lip. "Shanadar has changed, not for good or bad, just grown into whatever his destiny holds."

When she didn't continue, Fierce left to talk with Aynoh. Yu'ung fell asleep. During the night, a warm shape pressed against her. At first, she assumed it was Ocha, and then knew it wasn't.

Chapter 32

The Chosen, with most of the Clan, left as Sun shed its first rays. Kazeb led, Yu'ung with him, the rest arrayed behind. Flint, his partner Gik, and a reluctant Ant protected those remaining at the camp.

"From Mook," Ant clarified, mature beyond any predult. "Because no one else will attack us."

Flint tugged at his lip. "Mook has no qualms about killing youngsters and subadults. He's even shared stories about it. That's what you, Gik, and I will stop—"

"Attack us to distract the adults." From Ant again, his brain working through the strategy.

"Yes."

"That's not likely. What would he gain?"

Flint stomped away. "It's Fierce and Yu'ung's decision. You can make a different one when you are Leader."

Stalking prey with Canis was an experience Yu'ung assured Kazeb would change his mode of hunting.

Small Clan families merged with Kazeb and the People, a few at a time, more as they neared the herd. They appeared from every hill, plateau, and shady clump, out of the flatland that abutted the promontory, the shallow valleys with spotty elongated woods, the thirsty foothills by the snow-capped range, and shoreless sea's sandy shores. They covered the distance quickly, feet protected from prickly spikes by callused soles, no fear on their faces despite Fierce's presence. Yu'ung felt she had discovered the heart of this peninsula she so wanted to call home.

"Kazeb. Do you feel toward the earth as I do?"

He grinned. "The birds, the leaves in their earthy hues, the Canis with their unlimited shades and shapes, Cat and its stripes and spots and swaths of colors—all make it extraordinary."

She nodded. Her wealth of burnished hair swayed with her.

"And the Uprights who live here, your Clan. Now, my People."

She was comfortable with this male she'd met less than a Moon ago. He wore his memories like a protective wrap, mindless of the tatters from tragedy, the holes left by experiences, hide thinned by life, unattractive to some but a clarion call to Yu'ung that spoke of his undimmed spirit.

"We migrated often for food. Here, the supply is boundless. Why did it take so long for you to find it?"

"We always avoided the range."

"Where I came from, mountains were everywhere, broken by plunging valleys and a few flat fields. In cold air, we covered ourselves in layers of pelts. In hot air, we dripped with heat and escaped up their slopes. The higher we climbed, the cooler, until they drove us away."

"Our range never spews smoke or fire. Why did yours?"

"In past eruptions, molten rock darkened the sky, made every surface too hot to walk on, but in the end, the fires cleansed the soil, gifting the People with hard stones and a wealth of delectable plants. We would huddle in our caves waiting for the calm, but this time was different. The Mountain destroyed our food, poisoned the water, and cloaked Sun and Moon in billowing dark clouds. To inhale burned our mouths and throats. We choked on ash and cinder. We survived because Shanadar and Fierce brought us here."

They remained silent until Kazeb said, "You'll enjoy the hunt."

"I've missed the chaos, the pounding hearts, the rasp of labored lungs, the odor of dust mixed with blood, of sweat and urine, the exhilaration of pitting myself against prey. An animal on its knees always reserves a final trick, where instinct screams for it to defend one last time. We lost youngsters who failed to learn that lesson."

"As did we."

Fierce caught up to them. A storm brewed in his eyes. "Ant says Turk is in front."

Yu'ung startled. "Ant is supposed to be at the homebase."

He shrugged. "He said Braanroorv was there and could hear as well as ever, and Flint will run everyone into the tunnels at any sign of trouble, especially Mook."

Kazeb's jaw twitched. "Where did he see Turk?"

"Here, brother," and Turk stepped out from behind a boulder.

Yu'ung studied him. His hair blew in a mist around his face, brown-black instead of Kazeb's red, skin unmarred by color. Turk's chest was a slab of muscle, legs strong enough for any chore, wraps thin but repaired. It engulfed him in an aura of command. Unexpected respect swelled within her for him, a male unbent by the tragedy that destroyed many of his Clan. She related to that, once in the rock slide, again from Mountain's rage.

Kazeb relaxed at his brother's arrival as though a piece fell into place. "I expect this to be a good day. We all need new wraps," and chortled as he pointed to a particularly large hole in Turk's.

Yu'ung started to laugh also, but Blaze drew her attention as he growled a low warning to the boulder that had hidden Turk.

Turk gave an apologetic smile. "Mook wishes to participate."

If Mook intended to upset the gathering, he couldn't have been more wrong. Yu'ung wriggled with pleasure.

What better opportunity to keep watch over a potential enemy?

Broken nose poorly healed, chipped teeth, swollen knuckles, a scar that cut the width of one cheek and nearly cost him his vision. His hair was slick with mud, lance shoddy. Yu'ung would dismiss him if not for his eyes. Where Kazeb analyzed, Turk scrutinized. Mook didn't bother to evaluate. He painted his world in shades of cynicism, hate, and distrust. Mook studied her as she studied him. Her conclusion: Mook would never fight fair.

Fierce's hand tightened on his spear as he edged to the front. Blaze growled a cautionary alarm, warning of a predator on the stalk.

A crow cawed.

Voice neutral, Kazeb said, "Mook. You prefer scout duties."

"I finished," the words accompanied by a sneer. "Besides, Turk is my partner. I go where he goes."

Turk narrowed his eyes, but didn't correct the obvious lie.

Another crow cawed, followed by a thump. The voice was authentic, but birds didn't thump. Ant had moved to a new location. Yu'ung was as relieved as angry.

If it's serious, Ant won't just caw.

Yu'ung's gaze flicked to Mook. "I am–"

"Yu'ung," Mook interrupted her. "The fearless gray-eyed, red-haired female with unmatched skills, healer Kriina's daughter. Liis can't say enough about you."

Bitterness tinged his words.

"Liis?"

"It was his name before Kazeb."

Blaze cast a menacing glare at Mook.

Fierce crowded Mook. "We'll speak later."

Kazeb slapped his thighs. "Turk. Lead us."

They proceeded, Yu'ung prepared for the trap to spring. Relief flooded her when Ant trotted over.

"I sense the tension, too, Alpha Yu'ung. I am watching."

She grinned at him. "Go. If you find trouble, come for me."

He raced off as Turk shouted, "The herd is over the next hill."

Kazeb responded, "You, Yu'ung, Fierce, Blaze, and I will organize the attack."

"Blaze?"

"Of course."

Mook tried to elbow his way among the leaders, but Kazeb roughly pushed him away. "This is for those in charge."

"I am here at your brother's invitation."

Turk's face darkened. "That isn't true. We made no such agreement."

Blaze pressed heavily against Mook's side.

Yu'ung motioned with her hand. "Blaze will escort you away."

Snout lowered, fangs exposed, he closed his jaws around Mook's spear and dragged. The male could release his spear, but Blaze would simply adjust his hold. Mook figured that out and left. When Mook's footsteps were far enough away, Kazeb started.

"There is a valley surrounded by escarpments with no way out. We funnel the herd into it."

Yu'ung nodded. "Position those with far-throwing spears on the precipice. That is where I will be."

"And I," Jvelk and Laak chimed in.

Kazeb added, "I will be with Blaze and most of the Clan on the ground, with our thrusting spears."

B'o joined in, "And me."

Blaze padded to Yu'ung's side and sat on his haunches, a speck of blood on a fang, and leaned into Yu'ung's leg.

He is ready.

Discussion completed, it didn't take long for the lows of the herd to drown out their movement through the grass to agreed-upon locations.

It couldn't silence a scream.

Chapter 33

She arrived as Snake slithered away, already hidden in the undulating grass. Rather than berating the stupidity of the first-time hunter, she settled for a single scalding question.

"Did you not notice the outcrop where Snake was shielding from the heat?"

He lay on his side, panting, grasping his ankle. "I wasn't … looking there…."

Yu'ung folded to her knees to check the punctures and growled, "Describe Snake."

He stammered a description as she sucked on his wound and then poked a poultice into the punctures.

"That doesn't tell me if it will kill you." She clenched her jaw to squelch the balance of the tirade. Truth, his answer made no difference. He would live long enough to learn his lesson or not. Right now, Mammoth voices thundered and instead of harvesting meat for the People, she was treating a senseless youth who didn't watch where he was going.

Yu'ung slapped her thighs. "That's all I can do. If this reddens or swells, tell me," *if you can find me.*

"What would it mean?" His face was smooth with youth and inexperience.

"Probably that you will die. If you live but can't walk, find someone to help you."

Ant cawed, hidden in a stand of trees, and motioned ahead. She no longer had time to climb the cliff so would join those attacking from below, with thrusting spears. She sent a bird call to let them know she was down here rather than above, and then wished she hadn't.

Why are some with far-throwing spears down here? None are Chosen or People.

They didn't seem to realize she'd seen them, pressed against the rock face, out of sight from the hunters above. One pointed at her and then all eyes swiveled her way.

They aren't tracking Mammoth.

Yu'ung thinned her lips as furred ears perked above the grass tips, on a line with the would-be enemies. The massive Mammoth herd pounded forward, pulling everyone's attention down the field, away from Yu'ung. The Clan males who risked their lives for kill shots deserved to be backed up by their fellow hunters, but those who should protect them were stalking Yu'ung.

She barked a Canis call to Blaze, received his response, and sprinted on a path that would cross in front of the rogue hunters. She ignored them, knowing they would think her oblivious to their presence. One cocked his weapon, thrilled she made his job simpler, until the shaft was ripped away by a powerful, sharp-toothed jaw, and with it, a chunk of his hand. His shriek alerted Mammoth to danger and they veered away. Some hunters gave chase, others maintained a target on Yu'ung. By now, Yu'ung had drawn them away from the cliff into easy sight of those above. In no time, the Chosen above and Blaze below neutralized them.

The Canis howled his joy at what he loved most—defending his pack. The stampede thundered toward an intersection. One choice led to freedom, but Blaze had urinated there, ensuring the frenzied animals charged into a blind canyon. The rock wall stopped them. Foam speckled their mouths as their lungs gulped in desperately needed air and then bleated their terror. One exhausted pachyderm after another fell to the deadly lances from above, with lethal purpose. All knew meat not tainted by pain tasted better. Cows and calves were avoided, necessary to generate future meat. Those who escaped ran into the sharp tips of thrusting spears. No more were killed than could be carried.

Yu'ung's heart pounded, chest heaved. She came for these moments. A trapped animal did the unpredictable. Even brought to its knees, knowing death inevitable, it would try one final time to bury its horns or claws or hoof in the enemy. The instinct to live was strong.

Sometimes, it worked.

Everything stunk of blood, feces, urine, and work. Yu'ung tended to the injured, a few with broken limbs, most with gashes and deep bruises. The snake-bit Clan member lumbered through his tasks, accepting suffering as an ever-present part of his days. Even one Clan member who required a travois made no complaint.

Hunters cut the carcasses into pieces, tossed the offal, innards, and waste far from the meat to keep scavengers away. Yu'ung's unyielding gaze never left Mook even as she hacked thick slabs of mammoth meat. Fierce strode to her side. Blood painted him crimson and labor made his skin glisten.

"Be ready," and he hurried past the cheerful blood-spattered crowd, babbling as they chopped the mammoth into portable pieces, about who killed what and how many. Mook stood by Turk, rubbing shoulders as though that would buffer him against what was coming.

It didn't.

Voice gruff, Fierce asked, "What happened?"

Mook grinned, but Turk looked confused. "What do you mean?"

"Your supporters attacked Yu'ung."

Mook shouldered past a pale Turk. "Because your *pack* massacred my hunters for no reason?"

Fierce fixed Mook with a poisonous glare. A chill passed through Yu'ung as she stepped meaningfully to his side. Out of nowhere, Kazeb appeared, forming a wall with Yu'ung.

Fierce spoke low and controlled, "They died, Mook, attacking Yu'ung, the People's leader—"

Kazeb interrupted. "They would have killed her if Blaze hadn't stopped them."

A voice Yu'ung recognized piped in, "I saw that, too. The Canis leapt on one spear-wielding attacker about to kill Alpha Yu'ung, then others—our kind, not Tall Ones—stepped up to target her."

Another pitched in, "I've never seen anything like that. She didn't do anything!"

More grunted affirmation. "That's what I saw."

"As did I."

"They targeted Yu'ung for no reason. She is providing meat for all of us!"

Fierce's attention stuck to Mook as others shouted out what they had seen.

When everyone had spoken their piece, Fierce said, "Who told them to carry far-throwing spears, Turk? We can't ask them because they're all dead."

Turk slicked sweat from his forehead. "They must have been rogue, angry at past events."

Mook smirked. "You are still blamed for the deaths, Fierce. Be careful who you associate with. Those you call friends—and tribe mates—are also forewarned."

Yu'ung bristled and stepped up to Mook, close enough to smell the stench of a rotting tooth in his mouth.

"Are you sure, Mook, you want to threaten me?"

Kazeb swallowed whatever his intended response, satisfied Yu'ung could defend herself. Fierce remained in position, prepared.

Blaze snarled and growled, but Fierce's hand on his head kept him in place.

"Not yet."

Fierce spoke to Blaze, but never moved his attention from Mook. All recognized Mook for what he was. Yu'ung's sideways glance at Turk made clear his trust in this longtime friend had cracked.

Time to make sure Mook understands.

Yu'ung said, "You lie, Mook. We won't forgive that. Even if we would, our packmates won't."

A crow cawed.

Fierce forced a smile devoid of friendship. Even if Mook's supporters were erased today, Clan and People couldn't live together amicably if Mook were part of it.

Shanadar watched from his ledge as the entourage passed below him, bodies bent by the weight of carcasses. One by one, small groups broke away with their portions. Many stayed in the area while others discussed the possibility. Turk headed for his homebase with Kazeb while Mook proceeded down the shoreline.

Shanadar felt old. A surprise reflection in the pond as he rehydrated on his way to Eagle's nest showed a purposeful individual in place of the youthful journeyer, the one brimming with curiosity for the world and unable to focus on anything. Fierce claimed this matched Seer, which pleased Shanadar. He'd established the connection with Seer in his sanctuary and set out to mold himself in the Elder's image.

Yu'ung felt Shanadar's calm presence above, acknowledged him with a wan smile. She'd have given him more, but fatigue washed her body.

As everyone feasted on the fresh meat, celebrating the largess of organ sacks and marrow for the sick, she asked Fierce, "Did Seer celebrate when his visions proved true?"

"Rarely, maybe because they always did."

"We'll send meat, fat, tendons, and at least one hide up to Shanadar."

Outside, Flint ran to them. "An older male of our kind came soon after you left."

"A Clan member?"

"Maybe. He vaguely resembled someone. Gip and I tracked him when he left, but not far because we feared he might have intended to pull us away. When we returned, Ant was gone, mumbling something to the females about oversight in case the intruder wasn't alone."

Fierce shouted to Ant. The youngster sprinted to him, but at the sight of Fierce's glare, he wilted.

"You told no one you left?"

Ant's fear-soaked gape bounced from Flint to Yu'ung, Kazeb, and Fierce. "I–I–"

"No one ever put themselves in danger to protect you?"

"N-no.... Not—"

"Did your family, before the People?"

"Oh! Well, yes.... But not since...." His voice trailed to silence, and then, "I made a mistake. I won't again."

Yu'ung snatched the would-be Lead Scout to prevent him from bolting. "Did you recognize him?"

Ant padded one foot to another. "No."

He shook himself free and sprinted to the oversight.

He's not telling the truth, but why?

The males ate, yawned, and, exhausted from the day, slept. Yu'ung picked at a molar with a splinter. That did no good so she stabbed with a boar bristle. The relaxed post-chase time with its abundance of goodwill almost put her to sleep. She shook herself awake, headed to talk to Fierce and Kazeb.

Kazeb said, "Turk asks if a family can stay outside tonight, he with them."

"Is he—or they—responsible for the attempt on my life?"

"He is appalled by that. For the first time, he faults Mook."

Fierce spread his hands. "Turk is welcome as are any you recommend. Mook is not."

Ruk vaulted the bramble barrier, nimbly missing Blaze and Ocha. "I'm late for oversight with Ant."

Yu'ung was too tired to laugh. "Anyone who sneaks in will be surprised."

The next day, after the brothers departed, Mook sauntered into the encampment.

"Turk and I are to meet here."

Everyone ignored him. He mistook indifference for acceptance, leaned forward to snag a chunk of meat, and received a crack on his hand from Ese. When she wouldn't fight, he left.

Sun was high by the time the brothers finished their work. Turk returned to his camp, Kazeb to the People's where Yu'ung worked.

"Turk confronted Mook this morning about the attack on you. He avoided the question. Turk stalked off, told me Mook isn't who he thought. He now believes Mook relies on him for legitimacy because Mook has none of his own. Because of the hunt, families who left want to return. Turk thinks—as do I—Mook won't want to allow that because it destroys his story of evil Fierce and good Mook who stands up for the Clan."

Kazeb stepped closer to Yu'ung and glanced around. The camp was empty as far as she could see, everyone busy with tasks, many helping the new Clan get settled. Large bulbous clouds sat lazily over the mountains.

"I looked into Mook's eyes in that cave when he refused to help me. This is a male comfortable causing death. It didn't bother him at all, and what he did then wasn't his first time. I have no doubt he'd do it again."

"Do what? You and Turk were alone then. Now you have a tribe behind you."

"We had one then. It didn't even slow him down."

Reuniting the Clan was important to Kazeb. Was he saying he must return to his Clan, help Turk to keep them safe? He would have to leave the People to make that happen.

He touched her arm. "No. There's a better solution."

She rubbed a hand under her eyes, as relief washed through her. "Am I that transparent?"

"Only to me. I want us to pairmate."

She stiffened. "The same argument I used with Aynoh, why she should remain, applies to me."

"I agree. I've talked to Turk. I'll join the People. Turk will become the Clan's sole Alpha."

She gulped. "You would do that?"

"It will make both stronger. Why wouldn't I?"

Her mind spun, then she smiled.

"Yu'ung!" Aynoh, anxious. "Come! Wik's baby wishes to meet you!"

The first mixed child burst out with robust wails. A Chosen chin poked out below a red mouth, and the People's pronounced brows. The full-bodied screams brought grins to the adults. Wik secured the infant between her breasts where it quieted and began to feed. There it would travel most of the daylight until able to walk. Then, the child's name would be revealed to the parents.

Grub originally agreed to stay on the Big Rock, but with the early arrival of Wik's child, Grub would lead the band to the homebase. With the air cooler every day and the sea choppier, the time had come to leave. It took most of the day to check the boat for leaks and load it with supplies. Each traveler stocked his satchel with plants, stones, weapons, and the usual necessities for a journey. The voyage would take from dark to dark, the hike to the homebase a full cycle of Moon. Grub would address all questions about Fierce's absence, though Shanadar assured them Seer expected no additional details.

Grub in command at the bow, standing firm, the craft was launched into the frothy waves. With dexterous paddle work, they passed beyond the tide and through the roiling waters. Yu'ung shimmied to the overwatch ledge where she watched the long log boat make its way across the channel and fade even from her extreme sight. Fierce described how to tell where it moored. She would visualize a line between the tips of the crescent Moon. Where it disappeared was where Wik and the rest of the Chosen would dock.

Chapter 34

Yu'ung slept on the overwatch and then spent the next day watching the terrain. Fierce expected trouble when Mook's request to be part of the boat trip across the channel was refused. He seemed to accept the decision, but afterwards, asked surreptitious questions of anyone who might know whether the vessel could be navigated by one individual, did it require seasoned sailors like the Chosen, and when Fierce, Aynoh, Yu'ung, and Kazeb would go. He inferred willingness to step up as Alpha in the void, to help Turk and replace him if he chose to join his brother resettling in Fierce's homebase. He said he had already put in process a call to gather others from his former tribes who wished for a new homebase. He promised they would be a robust and valuable addition to the Clan.

I don't believe it.

Without the Chosen warriors, this would be Mook's best time to create havoc. Kazeb scouted the perimeter for trouble. Yu'ung occasionally saw him along the shore, dropping into and out of valleys, usually alone, at times with Flint or Turk.

Yu'ung washed a tuber down with water kept on the ledge and studied the cove where the twin to the launched craft was beached. A family trudged toward their former homebase. It was a small, dispirited gang in wraps too-often mended, the happiest among them the children. Kazeb approached them, spoke a few words, and helped them toward the re-established homebase.

Above her, Shanadar raised his arms to Sun, toes curled over the high edge, no concern that the porous rock would crumble beneath him.

Because his fate is not falling to his death.

Later, Yu'ung, Aynoh, and Ese cleaned flesh from a deer hide. Shanadar eased into a squat to her side. His bald pate, murky vacant eye, stark reminders he survived what killed most.

She commented on his new digging stick, this one decorated with shells and feathers.

"I need it to reach Eagle's nest. It is far from here, on a bluff I haven't explored. She left plumage for me. I don't want to disappoint her."

"I can come."

"Then who will guard against Mook?"

A memory nibbled at her brain. "Kazeb and Fierce said the same." She provided no details. His look said he expected none. "Are you also worried?"

"Worry is the wrong word, but I am aware. Concerned even. Last night, Xhosa warned me of a threat headed toward us. From where, by whom is unclear but of a magnitude too serious to be ignored. She filled the sanctuary with violent drumming that shook the walls and forced me out to the ledge overlooking the promontory. Owl should have hooted, but a heavy, dark silence hung over the night. Finally, Coyote lifted its cry to the moon, not calling its pack. Cautioning them."

The memory scratched harder. Yu'ung tried to seize ahold, but it dashed away.

Shanadar turned to her, his one working eye grabbing hers. "That means the danger is both inside the rock and outside."

She squirmed. "It's Mook, isn't it. He lives outside but passes through using tunnels no one else is aware of. He spies on us from within. That must be what Xhosa warns."

Shanadar shook his head. "I am not clear, Yu'ung, but I think it's something else, something worse. It's not just Xhosa warning me. The ground itself speaks to me. I'm barely learning its language and many of its declarations don't yet make sense."

She sprang to her feet and said, "I can stop Mook, then we deal with whatever else comes our way. We will handle this together as we have everything. Ant!"

"I'm here." His voice came from over her shoulder.

"Come," and Yu'ung entered the tunnels at the rear of the cavern.

Ant asked, "What do we seek?"

"An alternate entrance."

Eyes bright, he trotted after her. "The one Mook and Spotted Hyaena use. Mook blames you for his failure."

She snorted. "I won't allow him to damage the People the way he did the Clan."

"I blame him, too."

Something in his tone made Yu'ung feel like he knew more than he said, but she didn't take time to ask. Later.

She continued, "Nor will I let him hurt Kazeb again. Ant. Learn this lesson and live it: Waste no pity or energy on those who don't contribute."

"In this case, to the People."

Ocha was waiting, fangs and lips bloody in the torchlight from a recent meal, rat, judging by the hairless tail hanging from her mouth. With Ocha, Yu'ung led the way, adding marks to delineate where they'd been, what had been cleared. Yu'ung periodically checked the backtrail not for trouble—that she would hear—but to recognize the return journey. She didn't want a repeat of her problems in the fig tree caves.

Multiple passageways led to myriad caverns. She marked the ones the group checked. Dust and debris layered the entrance to others, patterned with paw prints. A few had Upright trace, but old. In one, the domed arch was so high, the torch melted into darkness. These didn't enter and she left them for later.

Many of the floors were slick. Yu'ung used the wall for balance, but Ant fell several times, unsteady in the dark, moving more quickly than he should. The last fall, he yelped, she thought in pain, but when she stooped, he pointed to the wall's base.

"A fresh circle with an X inside, different than Xad's." He left cross-hatches to guide his passage.

She puckered a brow. "I'll ask Kazeb if they are Mook's."

Now that they knew what to look for and where, they uncovered similar scorings. There were more subterranean lakes than Yu'ung expected, some salt-free but not all, and so tranquil that the surface mirrored the roofs above. Pale fish slithered through and tiny crustaceans gathered in thick piles on the shores. They ignored the pair's approach, the noises either familiar or too alien to frighten them.

How does anything live without Sun's light or warmth?

Ocha announced scents with a growl or whine. Most quickly dissipated, but one didn't, and they followed it to the back entrance.

"This is how he roams invisibly, Ant!" But it showed no indication of repeated travel, only occasional animal passage, some matching what was probably Hyaena.

It was always Blaze's choice where to spend his day. Today, after a discussion with Ocha, he chose to collect Eagle feathers with Shanadar. They left the camp, skirted the expanding Clan site where Blaze picked up a trace that made him prance with excitement. Shanadar only wondered briefly who it was before he inhaled the aroma.

"That's Kazeb. Do you want to stay with him?"

He flapped his ears and sneezed, a strong *No.*

"Do you know something I don't?" But Shanadar didn't wait for an answer.

A short distance later, Shanadar inhaled the stench he associated with Mook. Angry voices murmured, one a growl which sounded like Turk, one placating like Mook trying to get his way. Shanadar glanced at Blaze's raised hackles.

"You are not happy with either of these."

Turk's voice became louder, Mook's dismissive, and then a snarl as a set of feet stomped away.

One muttered, "I can do without either of them. I have options now."

There was nothing to be done, so Shanadar focused on his task.

"Xhosa left feathers for me. I'll retrieve those when Eagle leaves."

As usual, Shanadar lost track of time, missed the shortening and then lengthening of the shadows, the day birds' departures, and the arrival of the night critters. Sun was gone except for a few final rays by the time Eagle's nest came into view, high above, nothing Shanadar wanted to climb in the dark.

The next day took longer than Shanadar anticipated. Eagle had built her nest on the back side of a wasp's hive, expecting the territorial creatures to frighten intruders away. Few would brave wasps to reach the chicks. Nor would Shanadar who gave them a wide birth. When Mother finally left and Shanadar could poke his head up over the nest's edge, he found an aerie of tiny, fluffy eaglets. They squawked and squealed, loud enough for Eagle to hear unless she was well away. Shanadar dipped out of sight, gave them time to calm, heard the flap of adult Eagle wings, and again rose.

This time, he faced Mother. Shanadar considered throwing missiles to drive the bird away, but couldn't do that when her lone crime was a selfless commitment to family. As he tried to figure out another way, a howl warned her that peril didn't just prowl in the tree. She swooped down toward Blaze which gave Shanadar a chance to snatch discarded tail feathers. That made the eaglets squawk again and Mother shot back up with a war cry.

Shanadar froze in position, quills between his fingers, and tamped down his fear.

"Eagle. I wish you no distress. I respect you, admire your strength, revere your supremacy." Then, he told of his desire to honor her by wearing her plumage.

Eagle folded her wings, allowing Shanadar to insert one tuft in the strap that secured his hair, another in his pouch, and then descended.

To his surprise, an elderly pair squatted at the base of the tree, sharing a hare with Blaze. They greeted Shanadar as though they knew him, but how could they?

"We are Krekk and Jad, formerly of Liis' tribe. Blaze thought you might be able to help us."

Yu'ung had been sure Mook secreted himself within Big Rock to spy on the People, but as far as she could figure, there were no long-term residents. Whoever passed through the back entrance did so long before Mook's arrival. His devious plot remained a secret.

Shanadar must encourage Spotted Hyaena's visits as a guard against unwanted visitors, like Mook. I must talk to him.

Ant parted from her to see if Ruk needed help on overwatch. Yu'ung shuffled to the pond, mind spinning as she tried to unravel the mix of clues that made no sense. She drank her fill and then drenched herself in cooling water. When she looked up, Shanadar and Blaze approached with a shabby couple, their muscles ropey from too much walking, skin bronze from too much time in Sun's heat.

Yu'ung said, "You located Eagle," and poked her lips toward the fresh feather in his tail.

"And were you successful?"

"Ant and I located the back entrance, probably how Hyaena makes its way to your cavern, but we could find no trace of recent Upright prints."

A squeal cut off Shanadar's response and Ant sprinted to them.

Shanadar said, "This is Krekk and Jad. I think they just found their missing child."

Ant threw himself at the elders. "Mook said you died!"

They gently separated from their child's embrace. "Mook told us the same about you, suggested we leave for our own safety. We did, and might have remained away if Blaze hadn't found us."

They turned toward Yu'ung, voices strong in contradiction to their elder status. "When we heard about your return, we came to tell you what we have learned about Mook since he destroyed our Clan. We made a deadly mistake allowing him into our tribe." Then then relayed Mook's actions back when the brothers were new to their responsibilities.

They concluded with, "He wants to be Alpha of a tribe, it matters not which."

"Yu'ung!"

Ese.

Yu'ung sprang to her feet. "Ant will show you everything you need to know about the People. We will talk later."

Normally, outsiders weren't welcome, but Ant's reaction, Shanadar and Blaze's acceptance, persuaded her that this was an exception.

The dying sunlight painted the sprawling landscape by the time Yu'ung hurried into the cave, on edge from what Ese told her, but becoming accustomed to uninvited strangers. She found Ant's parents deep in conversation with Kazeb. He acknowledged Yu'ung, seeming to already know Ese's news. He looked angry, or fed up, Yu'ung couldn't decide which.

He clenched his fists. "Tell Yu'ung what you just told me."

Krekk turned calmly to the People's Alpha. "We, as part of Kazeb and Turk's Clan, lived amicably with Fierce's Tall Ones for a Moon's passage until Mook's arrival. He was the first to blame Fierce for the sicknesses after the Chosen left. We defended Fierce because there was no evidence that what Mook said was true, but then Ant disappeared, and we broke. Mook said he died, and we did, too."

Yu'ung started to promise Mook would never destroy another as he did Kazeb's Clan when Fierce shouted, "We're about to be visited by a sizeable armed crowd."

She waved Krekk and Jad to a safe area and, with Kazeb, confronted the gaggle. Disheveled, their hands clutched poorly maintained spears and chipped cudgels. Rage painted their gaunt faces.

She whispered to Kazeb, "Are these Clan?"

"No."

Does Mook think he can overtake us with transients?

She stepped forward, flanked by Ocha and Blaze, Kazeb, Fierce, and B'o a step behind. All the Uprights carried lances in both hands. The Canis were well-equipped with fangs, claws, and snarls.

Voice stiff, lips tight, she asked, "Who are you and why are you here?"

One shambled to the front, feet bare, teeth broken in his putrid mouth. "Mook told us all are welcome. We are his former tribe mates."

Blaze growled, hackles up.

"Friends are welcome. You aren't."

Mook elbowed his way through the motley crowd, grinning like a rabid wolf with a wagging tail. He exuded an energy that belied the weakness of this motley collection.

"These are friends. Turk … trusts … them."

Kazeb marched up to her side, bobbed his head side to side, and said, "I don't see him."

"He comes."

Yu'ung spoke, voice thick with conviction, "No one approaches our homebase without approval, no matter who vouches. Mook! Take this rabble to your homebase."

Laak and Jvelk took up overwatch positions, Ese and Jhat at the cave's mouth, missiles in hand.

Turk elbowed through the crowd, panting, a sheen of sweat across his body. Mook smirked, mouth open. His tongue darted out the way of a snake about to strike.

He said, "Turk offered the assistance of your healer—"

Turk snarled, "I did no such thing!"

Mook brushed him aside. "Some are ill, with the same poison the Tall Ones spread the last time they stopped here. Surely you can help."

Fierce growled. "Where I live, all are told the story of newcomers who ingratiated themselves into a new tribe. Within days, everyone fell ill, but none of the strangers. Luckily, the Leader and his Leads were gone when the illness spread. They determined with the assistance of the healer that the tribe members had been poisoned. After talking with Kazeb, I can tell you it was the same toxin used on the Clan—"

"We didn't kill anyone!"

Fierce spat out the rest of his story. "The Leaders fought back, forced those who brought the illness into the Endless Sea. Mook, you're pale, sweating. Did you know that person who brought the trouble to my friends? Is that where you learned this evil?"

Mook wheezed, coughed out, "Not me—no. He was almost dead when I found him washed up on the shore. He told me what happened, that he'd intended to cure the disease, be acclaimed a savior, but made a mistake—"

"You realized his mistake wasn't trying to be a hero. It was leaving them alive—"

"No, nothing like that—"

"Exactly like that, but when you tried it on the Clan, you killed everyone which left you no tribe to lead. Mook, you're suddenly very quiet. Why don't you answer?"

It snapped into place, what Shanadar alluded to, what instinct told her.

Kazeb took over. "Do these in front of me know how evil you are?"

Mook threw his head back and guffawed. "If I wanted to take over, I'd have unleashed the poison after Kazeb left. He was always difficult to influence, too smart, not like his brother."

Turk reddened, hands balled into fists, arms and shoulders trembling.

Fierce said through clenched teeth, "But when the illness started, Kazeb stayed to help his people."

Kazeb murmured, "We are ready this time."

Mook leered. "You're wrong. We have just begun."

He spun on his heel and left, the motley swarm following behind, stomping their feet, brandishing rough wood spikes at no one.

They settled far enough away that Yu'ung couldn't claim they were on the People's territory, but within distance to watch and be watched. Sun's final rays vanished as Yu'ung, Fierce, Kazeb, B'o, Blaze, and Ocha gathered.

Yu'ung said, "I am unsure of the when, but not the what. They mean to take our homebase."

Fierce's voice was cold. "I tried to leave that behind, but in truth, I am good at this. It will be a fight they don't want and can't win."

Chapter 35

The next day, everyone stayed together, save for brief forays to the pond. Mook's group made no secret of studying the People as though awaiting an opportunity. What that would be, Yu'ung had no idea, but she was determined to keep the tribe vigilant.

It seemed to work until Jhat raced up. "Yu'ung! Aynoh's baby! It won't come out!"

Yu'ung dropped the spear she was smoothing and raced over to the far side of the camp where her mother had chosen to birth her next child. She squatted, grunted, and pushed, face bright red, and still, the baby refused to exit its cozy womb. Yu'ung swabbed Aynoh with water brought by females, dribbled some between her lips while Jhat massaged the distended stomach. One final howl and a huge infant squeezed out. Everyone cheered at the new life.

Aynoh shook with exhaustion as the baby suckled. Jhat offered her a gourd which she declined, so Jhat sipped it, a sweaty sheen making her skin glisten. She breathed a contented sigh. When Aynoh fell asleep, the infant tight against her breast, Yu'ung asked Jhat about pairmating.

"It was Bhidid, but now seems to be Flint."

Jhat hugged herself. "I don't want to be separated from the People, Yu'ung. You are Alpha. Aynoh may leave with Fierce. The tribe needs a healer. I want to be one."

Yu'ung felt the stress drain from her body. Keeping Jhat here meant a lot.

"Aynoh says you have been sick in the mornings," she said with a smile because upset stomachs at the start of a day often preceded a child's arrival.

Jhat's response was a pant and Yu'ung turned to her. Sweat still bathed her skin despite the cooling breeze.

"Jhat? Are you ill?"

Jhat wiped her skin with a wrap. "I just need to rest," she said, and left.

Yu'ung thought little of it until she heard Jhat's retches. Then, steps pounded toward her.

"Yu'ung! It's Jhat!" Flint's panicked voice.

When Yu'ung reached her, Jhat's pallid complexion was tinged green, her limbs trembled, and her legs had cramped tight against her bloated stomach. Yu'ung needed none of Aynoh's specialized skills to diagnose what she saw.

"Ese. The water you brought for Aynoh—"

Ese hurried over. "From the pond."

"Did a dead animal poison the water?"

Ese paled and tears spilled. "No, of course not. I wouldn't—." Then she stopped, rigid. "One time, someone left a gourd, I assumed to save me a trip, or they were called away while delivering it."

Yu'ung snapped around. Several empty gourds lay around the birthing nest. "One of these, Ese?"

Ese picked one up. "This one, with the notch."

Yu'ung sniffed and sneezed. *Jhat drank poisoned water meant for Aynoh. The only hope was that the culprit put a nonlethal amount in the water, intended to warn, not kill, or Jhat would fight the toxin.*

The day after the next, Jhat died a painful death that Kazeb claimed to be identical to those the Clan went through. Flint and Yu'ung, with help from Fierce and Kazeb, carried what had been Jhat away. Ruk stayed with Ant on overwatch. Though young, he understood loss of family better than most.

Flint's eyes were red from fatigue, hair sticky with detritus, hands gouged, nails torn as though he fought a boulder.

Shanadar, in his eagle feather cape, led them to a small wall where he etched in triangles and dots, "We honor Jhat and the child."

She carried a child?

No one knew.

Fierce dropped Jhat's form into a hole well away from habitation. Because the cavity was smaller than her, they drew her knees up and folded her arms over them. If the baby had arrived and died without an identity, the People would bury it on its side, wrapped around a deer bone or another powerful animal, but this child hadn't yet shown in Jhat's body.

Flint arranged a bead-and-claw necklace on Jhat's chest that matched the one he wore. "This was to celebrate our pairmate."

He tucked an ostrich shell into the corner of the cavity brimful of sweet water, its aperture plugged with moss.

"This will suffice until she finds a waterhole wherever she is going."

Shanadar played his flute while the body was covered with dirt, leaving no mark of its presence for hungry scavengers. Tears sprang to Yu'ung's eyes as they trudged away. No one would cherish her the way Flint did Jhat.

Mook waited at the base. His weak eye glowed a watery green, the good one swollen black, his cheek shades of purple, blue, and yellow. No one wanted to hear him whine his sorrow. Flint howled while Fierce glared.

Yu'ung marched forward, but Flint beat her to it.

"You! I relied on you!" And he flung his lance.

Flint was so distraught that his usual expert aim sailed harmlessly over Mook's head. A malicious smile crept over the one Flint not long ago had trusted as Leader. Flint charged and might have made it except Fierce grabbed him.

Flint wailed, "Why kill Jhat?"

"Her death was a mistake," Mook said. "I'll do better next time," and he left.

The water was for Aynoh. He didn't even try to hide it.

Fierce launched himself forward, but Flint's broken sobs stopped him.

Yu'ung took his arm. "Let Mook leave. Flint needs us more."

Flint had to be forced to eat, reminded his weakness played into Mook's goals. Yu'ung looked across the clearing at B'o, her most trusted among the People. She didn't have to talk to him to know his thoughts.

How are we to defend against invisible weapons?

Ant plopped beside Yu'ung. "While I cut cat-tails at the stream, grungy unknowns confronted me. One blamed Flint for the confrontation, called Mook Leader."

Anger rolled through her body and she shot to her feet. "Where is this interloper?"

Fierce answered, "I took care of him."

"How?"

"He found me."

Yu'ung spent much time talking with Krekk about his experiences with Mook. He shared what had happened to the Clan after the Chosen left, while the brothers were distracted trying to save lives. Mook acted like the most helpful of tribe members, but his presence made everyone uncomfortable. Krekk left, hoping to move on from the loss of his child, but couldn't escape the unease that followed him about Mook and his part in the tragedy, more a gut reaction to the oddity of a newcomer arriving and the tribe disintegrating than based on facts, so he set out to see if there were clues from Mook's past to support Krekk's instinctive reaction. If the male was guilty of more than being in the wrong place, Krekk would hold him accountable.

Rather than settle, Krekk and his pairmate visited the tribes Mook had tried to join prior to the Clan and there were many. They talked with the Elders, why a young male wasn't welcomed, and developed a picture of an individual so desperate for power regardless of the cost to those around him that he couldn't hide it. Some tribes simply kicked him out, but others exiled him, calling him dangerous to any he spent time with.

When Krekk heard that Mook remained in the Clan and the Chosen had returned, Krekk realized it fell to him to right the wrongs of the past as best he could.

Yu'ung picked her teeth with a porcupine quill, fiddled with the contents of her travel sack packed earlier in preparation, removed her foot covering, and massaged her toes—actions designed to make her invisible because everyone did them. Finally, sure no one was watching, she slipped out of the clearing and down a path she hoped led to Mook. A good distance from the tribe, she paused mid-stride at the sight of broken branches and prints.

Bear tracks!

Huge claws pressed into the ground, the faint scent of its last meal hanging in the air. There, far ahead, the bruin ambled up the hill, without a cub, but no one was safe within sensory range of an adult bear. Yu'ung crouched, waited for Bear to trundle away, using the time to eat the leftover stew she brought. Finally, Bear lumbered out of sight.

Yu'ung stood and the world spun. She stumbled with a loud grunt. Bear stood upright, furred ears poking above the hilltop. The massive fanged skull swung in her direction. Beady eyes scanned its habitat, where it was the apex predator. The powerful olfactory muzzle inhaled in search of who dared enter its territory.

Yu'ung staggered, tripped, sprawled, lumbered to her feet, and shuffled toward a forest. The scuff of dead leaves and the snap of dry branches allowed Bear to locate the poorly hidden trail. It bellowed and thundered down the hill. She raised her lance, tried to cock it, but dropped it instead, hands too clumsy to hold on. She fumbled to retrieve it, fell to her knees as Bear swatted her with a mighty paw, and threw her backward. She slammed into a rotten log, too stunned to crawl away as the monster raked sharp claws across. She rose, but her legs buckled and she fell over the log into a gap between it and another. With energy she didn't know she had, she crawled as far as she could go, hoping Bear couldn't. It roared in frustration. Its immense dome swayed, its weak vision searching for the lost prey. She unconsciously picked a good hiding spot. The wood's putrid rot shrouded her aroma.

For now.

She clamped thick fingers on the gash. Shock waves pulsed through her body and she couldn't stop shaking. She layered moss and leaves one-handed over the gushing tear.

If I can't stop this bleeding, I'll run out of blood.

She couldn't feel her digits and her brain was fuzzy. Yellow fangs gleamed as the bruin scrutinized the rotten log, drooled in anticipation of the prey that could only elude it so long. Yu'ung no longer cared. She'd done everything possible. The pain evaporated. The separation between herself and reality grew, between now and a future that seemed farther away with each blink. She became an observer of events, the responsibility to the People a mishmash of whys and whats.

A shape hobbled her way. *I've missed you, Old One.*

This isn't your time.

A howl stopped the behemoth as she tried to determine what Old One meant.

If you're here, I'm dead.

Not yet. You are not finished.

The bruin stretched a clawed paw beneath the log, flailed around to reach her.

She whispered, *You're almost here.*

It howled and then collapsed. Yu'ung tried to rise, but darkness enveloped her.

She woke with a sudden inhale, the ache sharp. *Is Bear eating me?*

"Either I sew the gash or you lose what little blood remains in your body."

She swallowed the pain and croaked, "Clean first." She coughed to clear her dust-clogged throat, but it did no good.

Fierce mellowed. "I did. Aynoh will treat it."

Sweat bathed Yu'ung, her hair dank, body clammy. "Why … a travois?"

"I wouldn't need to if you hadn't angered the sow."

"Sow? I missed the cubs ... stopped to eat … the dizziness … She blindsided me." Fresh fire seared through her stomach.

"They weren't with her." He tied the logs with the last vine. The platform was now a shoulder's width. "But close enough she considered your scrambling and scratching a problem she couldn't ignore."

He sniffed at a pile of vomit. "The odor matches the gourd Jhat drank from, but how could it? No one used the gourd after that. We threw it down a fissure. Did you eat anything the rest didn't?"

Fierce had to press forward to hear her soft words. "I ate the stew, nothing else … put the leftovers in my pouch … left."

"Everyone ate the stew. Tell me how you prepared for this scouting."

He listened as she mumbled in agonized and halting detail. She forced herself to focus, concentrate on his questions, because she knew her life and others could depend upon it.

He asked, "Why did you travel by yourself? Kazeb or I—or B'o—would have come with you?"

"Not … a hunt…." She paused for a breath. "Mook was coming for Aynoh, again. I had to stop him. There was no time."

She jerked, but before she could say anything, her head spun and she vomited again. Fierce crouched, gaze easy, as though he'd done this too many times.

"You thought of something?"

"He poisoned my … pouch."

Fierce sniffed the discarded organ.

"Poison. He knew you would take this. I'll throw it in the fissure with the gourd."

She tried to fight the darkness, scrabbled to her elbows, pushed upward, but passed out.

She woke to a rhythmic bounce and Fierce's heavy pants. Every jostle sent ripples burning through her body. Sometime later, a voice yelled her name. A cool finger caressed her.

Yu'ung opened her eye, a slit. Her hip and torso on fire, she managed only a nudge at a time, paused to assess each fresh fiery result, rejected it forcefully, until Shanadar hummed. His song reset her mind. His smile faltered, but remained. She appreciated the effort.

"Your gashes are red but without toxin."

His visage blurred as she shivered.

"Aynoh treated you with a root."

Yu'ung grunted. "I know that one…. It works well…. No wonder I feel dizzy…."

Her body burned, her thoughts delirious. The world spun. The infection from Bear…. In a lucid moment, Aynoh told her to fight the poison with all her body's resources…. win…. She must not quit.

Sun splashed the cavern. Individuals came and went. Aynoh swabbed her with cool water. Voices chattered….

When did Kazeb get here? Huddled with Fierce.

"Not Turk, Fierce. Mook failed with Aynoh, so he decided to ruin me by taking my future pairmate." Kazeb's voice cracked. "It would."

Shanadar situated himself to the side in a pelt painted with a circle, triangle, dots, and a shape that could be Ump.

Where did he get that?

She murmured, "Why do I live if the poison killed Jhat?"

Shanadar shrugged. "It's a good question. Fierce dragged you here on a travois. You were delirious when you got here, so Kazeb submerged you in the pond, up to your nose, and stayed with you the entire time. It calmed you."

"How is Aynoh's baby?"

"Good."

She flattened her palms and lowered her arms, but couldn't raise herself before the wooziness again took over.

Shanadar pointed at Kazeb with his lips. "He has not left since Fierce brought you in. He yelled at you to fight, that you had more to accomplish. We thought you heard him, but you passed out. Again."

"You touched me, with your hand, Kazeb. Then you said, 'I stay with you, always.' I tried to speak, blink, tell you to wait for me, that I would recover, but I don't think words came out."

Chapter 36

Old One told Yu'ung that with mortal danger came clarity. Yu'ung planned to find out.

She glanced around the cave. Empty. Deep breaths hurt her ribcage so she kept them shallow. She pushed to her hands and knees and stalled. Aynoh had left mulch by her nest which she swabbed on her gouges and gashes as her head swam. Her stomach tightened and she threw up. That hurt her ribs. She held that position until her eyes focused and ears picked up voices.

Outside. They sound serious.

She crawled over to the wall, dragged herself with the rough juts until she was upright. Everything blurred and then came back into focus. She inhaled and exhaled, keeping it shallow until she felt steady. Then, she wobbled over to a slab of fish and a gourd of water left by the hearth, nibbled and sipped. Enough energy returned, she made her way outside. Fierce was talking with Aynoh, Kazeb, and Ant's father.

"I won't leave until Mook is no longer a problem."

He glanced at Yu'ung's shuffling approach, as did the rest, but the People were accustomed to injury. Once she managed to stand, it was assumed she would begin self-care. She would.

Kazeb said, "We are discussing Mook."

Krekk said, "I found out he always preyed on the weak. He wouldn't quit until stopped by the tribe," and his eyes sparkled.

Yu'ung turned gray eyes on the newcomer. "You have an idea."

"I do," and he focused on Fierce. "It requires your boat."

Krekk shambled into Mook's camp. The false Leader gawped at the Elder. A flash of recognition became distrust. Even hidden in the brush, Yu'ung could see the question. Why did an unarmed Elder come alone? Yu'ung had voiced a similar question. If Mook attacked Krekk, she couldn't defend him, not with her injuries, but Kazeb reminded her that even a poorly aimed shaft would startle Mook enough to give Fierce time.

Krekk called it unnecessary, but didn't explain why.

"Mook! I've found you!"

Krekk strolled amiably forward, laughed with apparent joy at the appearance of a friend.

Mook's forehead furrowed.

He anticipated a different reception.

"You left us when we needed you most, Leader."

"You did too, Krekk. Why have you returned?" He scratched his louse-infested body hair and yawned.

At Mook's piercing stare, Krekk prevaricated, "I never left, just waited at a distance. Besides, where would I go? Who takes in a lone Elder? I hoped the illness would die away and I could return. I see you are healthy and those who brought trouble last time are back for retribution. We need you, Leader Mook, to rectify the wrongs."

Mook glanced at his scruffy assemblage. His body shook. "I am—"

"I've spent time with them," Krekk continued as though Mook hadn't spoken. "They considered me a doddering Elder. I listened to Fierce's fury over Jhat's death and the Alpha's near-death. He wants to force you over the range to Shanadar's former territory, where no one welcomes strangers. Shanadar says you and your kind will die. Failing that, Fierce will kill you himself."

Mook laughed. "Let him try! If they expel us, we will leave a gift and move on as we've done before."

Krekk dragged a toe through the dirt. "Yes, yes. There is a better way. As I said, I wandered through the site and listened. They hid nothing from an unarmed, shambling Elder. Fierce's vast home, overrun with herds, is controlled by no one. You can conquer as you have done in the past, or settle where it is uninhabited. The Chosen are the only ones who don't hate or fear Fierce and his band. If you tell the other tribes you beat him, you will be hailed as heroes."

Mook guffawed. "Why believe us?"

Krekk dipped his head to the inlet. "Because you'll be in Fierce's vessel, with his weapons."

Mook pivoted to the inlet where the craft moored, eyes crazed with excitement.

"The boat…. It's always guarded."

Krekk grinned. "Most are gone. Yu'ung is sick. She ate toxic food, collapsed, and then Bear savaged her. No one knows if she will live. The scouts, their attention is in the wrong direction." He picked up a tiny critter as it crawled over his shirt and popped it into his mouth. "No one checks the craft, at least, they haven't for … a while. That will change soon when Fierce's pairmate, Aynoh, can travel. You have a short time to decide to do … whatever…."

Mook turned to his followers. They stared at him, waiting. "Anyone able to sail a Chosen boat?"

All looked away. Mook confessed, "Me, either."

Krekk waved a hand through the air. "Did you watch the first one leave? Maneuvering that vessel is as easy as paddling a bulky raft. A female of our kind went with them and did it with no problem."

Mook padded in place. "Easy, hunh."

"Their home is not far over the horizon. Arrive in Fierce's vessel, loaded with his weaponry—"

"He stows weapons in it?"

Krekk nodded. "I told you. He prepares to leave. Everything you need is on the vessel. After you arrive, beach the craft anywhere.

Those you run into will see *his* plunder in *his* craft, sailed by *you.* They will hail you as the one who killed the mighty Fierce. No one will say otherwise. You won't want for food or shelter, and with your own contingent, no one will challenge you. He won't be able to prove you wrong until he's built another, and that—on his own—will take a long time."

Mook scratched his neck as he tried to decide if Krekk spoke the truth or laid a trap.

Krekk sweetened the temptation. "He would have left already except you attacked Yu'ung. He promised to stay until she was well enough to lead."

Mook grinned. "We are ready for a new home." He looked about to say something else but Krekk stopped him.

"I am too old. I will stay here. The People will welcome one more to their decimated tribe, even one as old as me."

Krekk started to leave, but barked over his shoulder, "Go today. They intend to come for you tomorrow. This is your chance. No one will miss the craft until you're too far away to stop."

He lumbered away, never looking at Mook, pace unchanged as he shuffled out of sight. Mook and his motley collection grinned, snatched travel sacks, and raced for the inlet.

Krekk did it!

Yu'ung scooted toward a different overwatch with a better view of the cove. Fierce, Kazeb, and Turk waited, prickly with excitement.

Fierce said, "The channel waters are choppy today, worse than usual. It's like they know an enemy will try to use them to escape, and want no part of it."

"Will Mook make it?" was all she cared about.

"No one who hasn't sailed our vessels can do it in normal seas." He chortled. "But we took no chances. While Krekk talked with Mook, Laak and Jvelk loosened the caulk. It won't take long before water will seep into my beautiful vessel. Mook's cohorts can't bail fast enough to avoid what comes next. If they manage to patch the leaks and reach my home, Mook's subterfuge will not confuse Grub. When he arrives on my craft, he and his interlopers will be destroyed."

Everyone assembled atop Big Rock to watch as the vessel slipped quietly from its mooring. The water was smooth with barely a ripple. Those paddling guffawed at the ease of their escape until they hit the channel. There, as Fierce expected, their fortunes changed. The placid waters from the shoreless sea mixed with the tumultuous Endless Sea and slammed into the escapees from all sides. The deck heaved as waves sloshed over the sides and the compromised caulking gave way.

Kazeb laughed aloud. "Not just the channel is furious! The seas and the land are enraged! I've never seen it this violent before!"

Dark storm clouds choked the sky. Light rain turned into biting torrents accompanied by wind gusts that would blow anyone away not anchored to a well-rooted shrub. Those not paddling the boat zealously scooped water, but the hull filled faster than they could empty it. The seas seemed determined to sink the vessel and crew.

Yu'ung shouted, "B'o—Angry Mountain caught up with us!"

Kazeb bellowed above the wind's roar, "We have to find shelter!"

Yu'ung spread her feet, gaze fixed on Mook's ship. "Not. Yet. We first confirm Mook no longer presents a threat."

Kazeb bellowed to be heard. "The coast is close enough that those who can swim will try to make their way there when the boat sinks."

Yu'ung asked, "Can they?'

Fierce muttered, "We would, but Mook was never known for physicality."

Yu'ung thinned her lips. "I want to go down there, prevent any who think they can straggle out of the water from doing so!"

Turk shouted, "We might not have time. See that dark swirl of clouds—the one scooping water from the sea? I've seen them out on Endless Sea. This one is on course for us!"

Yu'ung stared, fists clenched and unclenched. "It's just a big storm, right, Kazeb?"

"No. That spiral funnel will swamp what little is left of the boat, drown any survivors, and then make its way onto land where it'll attack us!"

As the words left his mouth, a huge wave threw the craft skyward like straw in the wind. It crashed into the sea upside down and splattered bodies, wood, and supplies into the stormy waters. Anything loose smashed together and broke into pieces.

"Can they survive that?" Yu'ung's voice dispassionate.

"No. Their bodies will wash ashore when the storm ends if the sea creatures don't eat them." Kazeb tugged her arm. "We have to go or the funnel will swamp us, too!"

Without groundcover, the pouring rain shuttled down the slope. The congested valleys became rivers of rushing water, drowning everything. She dodged to avoid the worst, pummeled by the gusting wind. A flurry of sharp, cold rain stung her face as she finally reached the side protected by the promontory's girth. Shanadar's hearth glowed, proof enough he was safe so she continued to the People's cave.

The ground had stopped shaking by the time all of them huddled around the hearth, warming themselves in the fire, drying their wraps. The storm's roar drowned out conversation. The entire night, trees crashed, rocks fractured, and the promontory cried at the assault. The surge overwhelmed the clearing in front and would force the People to the high ledges in their tunnels if it didn't slow.

A loud rumble jolted Yu'ung to her feet. Big Rock shook. A roar echoed through the subterranean tunnels as though the very foundation cracked. Memories of the cave-in blocked all other thoughts.

"Out!"

Everyone fled the cave and sheltered under thick canopies or damp hides until the last of the boulders bounced down from above and the world quieted save for the patter of rain. Yu'ung and Kazeb walked through the gathering, checking for injuries, offering help where necessary.

Yu'ung scanned the muddy, huddled gathering, mentally ticking off those who should be there.

Kazeb said, "Everyone's here."

Yu'ung jerked in a circle. "Not Shanadar." Her head snapped up. Rubble blocked his shelter.

She raced up the cliff. "Shanadar!"

No one answered. The storm had cut a chasm into the promontory's surface, separating where she stood from him. She sped up, launched herself into the air, brawny legs vaulting her across the emptiness.

I won't make it, so stretched farther than she ever had and seized the sodden ledge with her fingertips. There she clung, chest banged against the damp fissure, toes scrambling for purchase. Found it and levered herself up, over the lip. Just as she stood, the freshly exposed nub crumbled and with it, her balance. She flung her arms out front, grasped at air. One final perilous thrust, and she fell forward. Her nails tore at the fresh dirt. Fear clawed at her stomach as she forced herself onward.

Her previous finger- and toeholds had disintegrated in the storm, but she found new ones, sprinted past the plateau, relieved the birds clung to the wall, healthy enough to chitter. Shanadar's ledge came into view. Xad slumped on the crumbled edge, a gray mound, shoulders wilted, face streaked with tears.

"He is trapped in his sanctuary, Yu'ung. The tunnel collapsed. I can't get to him!"

She turned away, her voice as steady as the rock she stood on. "I'll get in."

"Ocha is with him."

Ocha!

Without another word, Yu'ung flew to the rear, sprinted recklessly through treacherous rubble-strewn passages, her lungs on fire and heart about to explode as it hammered between her ears, guided by Ocha's muted bark.

The back entrance had disintegrated, how far in, she couldn't tell, so she screamed, "Shanadar! Ocha!"

Inside, Shanadar's bone flute sang its haunting songs. Kazeb and Fierce panted up to her.

Tears coated her cheeks. "He's alive! Get everyone to dig!"

She slashed with her nails, flung rubble and debris aside, but always, more replaced it. Soon, endless hands dug and tore and tossed. Inside, Shanadar's flute called them.

Why doesn't he dig out?

A voice whispered that Shanadar accepted his fate. Xad would carry on.

Yu'ung screamed, "No! You will live, Shanadar! Hold on—we're almost to you!"

The thicker the rubble, the worse the devastation. She yelled at him to keep playing. She'd find him. He must have heard because his music continued, accompanied by Ocha's yips, yowls, and cries. Shanadar played hopeful tones, enigmatic and emotive like no bird she had ever heard. Blaze whined and stomped with his paws, unable to reach his packmates trapped inside, powerless to help the one who saved him so often.

Shanadar's melodies slowed. Yu'ung didn't, nor did she when they died.

He could live, but be unable to blow his flute.

Until Ocha limped out of the debris, tail tucked. She whimpered, licked Yu'ung, and left.

She stopped digging.

Epilogue

The distant copses were shiny with rain, leaves limp with the water's weight. Crushed soggy stems matted the fields, but the storm had ended. Sun shone. The rain-slick surfaces sparkled. A rainbow glowed over the mountain range the day Blaze dragged himself back into the camp. Mud caked his fur, prickly with twigs. His tail hung.

Moon waned, re-emerged, and faded again. Fierce could build another boat to carry himself and Aynoh to his homeland, but without help, it'd be an extended and tedious task. Yu'ung offered to assist.

He declined. "Later," but didn't hurry "later."

Rockslides blocked both accesses to Shanadar's sanctuary. It devastated Xad. He spent all his time searching for entree to the inner sanctum or passage to the alcove Shanadar favored. Hyaena stayed with him, as though knowing this Upright couldn't survive without him. Xad was convinced that if he could eat Shanadar's special fungus, he could talk to the male who saved his life, ask him what to do now, and beg to go wherever he now resided, but Shanadar's supplies were lost to the storm and Xad didn't know where to find replacements.

Earth's shaking didn't touch the fig tree or the pond at its base and the tunnels.

Yu'ung and Kazeb pairmated.

The child squirmed inside, but she kept her pace. After the losses, members had more work than ever. With the passage of time, the combined groups settled into their new reality, excited to be together.

Without conscious thought, Yu'ung listened to the sounds Kazeb made while knapping stone. Even without looking, she could tell what chore he performed, be it knapping or spear honing, or something else. The wind whistled through the tall grass and the fig tree. It blossomed now. Soon, she would harvest the fruit, but today's journey was for a different purpose.

She and Kazeb dropped down the fig tree roots, lit a torch, and set out for the message wall. She carried her etching and paint kit, intent on telling the stories of Shanadar, Ocha, and the People who called Big Rock home, caution new inhabitants about strangers who weren't what they seemed.

They took their time, finished when the story was told, and headed for an alcove Kazeb identified. There, they spread out a nest and waited. They emerged days later carrying a new member of the People.

Yu'ung never saw Ocha or Xhosa again.

Afterword

Neanderthals lived good and worthy lives on Gibraltar until the end of their existence. *Homo sapiens*—the Tall Ones, aka the Chosen—returned after thousands of years. Whether friends or enemies, history is unclear, but the return marked the Neanderthal's demise.

Despite their extinction, their genetics live on, 2-4% in each of us born outside Africa, and a full 30% throughout modern man. What they gave to man—the strength, the wisdom, the creative attitude to solve problems—can't be overstated.

Preview of Book 1 in *Savage Land*

Endangered Species

Chapter 1

75,000 years ago,
What we call Germany today

Jun was lost. Again. He gripped his thick-shafted spear in one hand, throwing stones in the other, and brushed aside the prickle of fear that flooded his body.

It wasn't being alone that worried him. This was his first time hunting with the clan. He'd wanted to do well.

Initially, Jun had kept pace with the hunters, his strides long and easy, eyes firmly locked on the back of the male in front of him, but—as too often happened—he became distracted by a bird's call and wandered off to find it, maybe talk to it. Someone shouted his name, far away and so muted, he barely heard it. He didn't respond, of course. Upright voices would frighten the bird if it hadn't already fled. He hunkered into the underbrush, reduced his breathing, and squatted there long … longer … but the bird fell silent.

I'll look for it next time I'm out here.

He stood. Feet spread, ears perked, he twisted around, and to his horror, didn't recognize where he was. Nor did he hear the sounds of his fellow hunters moving along Deer's trail.

I wandered farther than I intended.

He hurried away, through the leaves and dirt, hoping to find Deer's trace or his clan's prints, but found neither so he shouted. The sound echoed harshly through the trees.

No response.

They can't be far. By now, they must know I'm not with them.

He hugged his arms around his chest, suddenly cold, and tilted his head up. Sun had moved, a lot. Instead of worrying him, it comforted him.

I'll stay here until they return.

He crouched, picked at the forest's hearty overgrowth, ate a few worms, and waited. No one came. He called several times, but all he heard were insects, a snake slithering, and squirrels chattering.

I'll go where Deer is.

He knew where the herd headed because he'd followed it several times to where it ate the fresh young grasses, safe it thought from prying eyes. He trotted down what he hoped would end up their trail, searching for trace, listening for the rustle of hide-covered bodies passing through dense brush carrying carcasses. Finally, later than expected, he found Deer's path, but they didn't stop in their usual place. They must have known they were being stalked—the hunters were noisy—and trotted into a scree pile as though knowing that would conceal prints, which it did. Jun could either keep wandering until he re-located the clan's path or make his way back to the camp.

He checked Sun, but it was now hidden by clouds.

He crouched, comfortable in his waiting. No one would be surprised. He often returned late with tales of an excursion rather than armloads of meat to feed the clan. The group would have ejected him, forcing him to make his way alone, but his mother was the clan healer and wouldn't allow it. She was training him to take over when her stiff joints and failing eyesight meant she could no longer fulfill her duties. He had no interest in illnesses, but understood he must fulfill some duty or lose the tribe's protection. As a result, he assisted her if he couldn't avoid it and learned enough about herbs and mulches and poultices to be tolerated.

None of which helped him now.

I can't wait.

He scrambled up a hillock, found a landmark he knew, and headed toward it along a debris-laden forest floor, head up, eyes shut to concentrate on a panoply of delightful odors. He heard the hiss but as background noise to his meandering daydreams. By the time it stiffened his hackles and his eyes popped open, it was too late.

Snake!

Jun stabbed with his spear, to frighten not kill, but missed. Snake didn't. A blur of movement and pain seared through Jun's body. He collapsed with a thud and Snake slithered away. Jun attempted to stand and crumpled.

I'll crawl along the path. The hunters will see me on their way back. Sweat broke out across his forehead. *As will predators.*

He scuttled into the dirt-clotted root ball of a towering tree, sharing the cozy space with worms, slugs, and spiders.

I'll call out if I hear someone.

He tamped down the pain and dug through his shoulder sack. No surprise, he forgot to restock his treatments. He tried to blink the dust from his eyes and then rubbed, using the cleanest part of a grubby finger. He mulled over what to do as his ankle swelled bigger than his calf and heat flushed through his body. Everything around him spun and his eyes drooped. The more he strained to think, the more his head throbbed. He tucked his legs against his chest and imagined Snake's poison infecting his insides.

How do I stop it before it stops me?

He solved it by passing out.

The scrape of a foot awoke Jun. Every part of his body hurt, but he managed to crack one eye. An Upright female not his kind strode toward him, a spear in one hand and a blistering frown on her face. He should say something, but his mouth was too dry.

She acts like she knows me.

He tried to rise, but no part of his body cooperated so he stared at her, worried and somewhat disturbed by the dark fury she directed at him.

Why is she so angry? I've done nothing to her.

Seeing his swollen red ankle did nothing to soften her attitude. Disgust washed over her in waves and her fists clenched a rough-hewn lance so tightly, the whites of her knuckles gleamed.

There is something familiar about her ...

She had the small skull, long limbs, and narrow torso of a Primitive, lacking the musculature common to Jun's kind. And it hit him.

"Xhosa?"

She growled in response, a sound so like hatred, he would have pulled back if the tree trunk didn't stop him.

The female Xhosa visited his dreams often and they got along well. They discussed topics no one shared his interest in—where the herds went during their migrations, why Spider's thin silken strands were so strong, why Sun left if Moon arrived. Did one orb fear the other or had they arranged to share the sky in this way? These types of curious queries annoyed everyone in his tribe, but excited Xhosa.

"Why are you here? I only see you in dreams." He squiggled, attempted to stand, and collapsed. "Am I dreaming?"

"No, Shanadar. You have forced me to come in person. Night is approaching. It is not safe to be out here alone. Return to your homebase. I have plans for you and being eaten by Cat isn't one of them."

Her lips didn't move nor were her words the clan's, but he understood what she said. He wanted to ask why she cared if the night stalkers ate him, but what he said was something else entirely.

"Snake poisoned me."

Shock flashed through her eyes and she scowled. "I see. You won't be leaving on schedule."

His head spun, started to ask what schedule, but stopped himself. Whatever the answer was no longer mattered.

"Xhosa. Snake killed me. Well, there are treatments for Snake's venom, but I didn't bring them. Mother has them, but I can't get to her fast enough. And the hunters—I don't know what happened to them. They should have come by now ..."

His voice trailed off. Talking exhausted him. Still, he owed her one more explanation. "Whatever your plan, it can no longer include me."

She dismissed him with a flip of her fingers. "You're not going to die, Shanadar. Come. My kith can take care of you."

"Shanadar," he mumbled. "She keeps calling me Shanadar." She didn't explain why and he didn't ask. Or mind.

But he did ask about kith as Xhosa yanked him to his feet—foot, the injured one dangling uselessly above the ground—encircled her arm around his waist and draped his around her shoulder before replying.

"You call your group a clan. Ours is kith. The Tall Ones are a band, the Canis Pack."

Tall Ones? He tried to make sense of her answer, but the words got lost in his muddy thoughts.

I'll ask later.

They slid through the forest, well beyond his clan's area and Deer's favorite eating spots, past a tree tall enough to touch Sun. He'd never seen it before. Did it just grow? Soon, they reached a gathering of Primitives the size of Jun's clan crouched by an overhang. All had low foreheads, prominent brow ridges, and body shapes like a shorter version of the tall slender strangers who occasionally passed through the clan's territory—

That's who she called Tall Ones!

The kith members wore long wraps or capes like Xhosa's, unsewn, as though they simply cut a hole in a pelt big enough for their head to push through. No capes or wraps, and foot coverings were fur or bark strapped to feet.

But the dark, deep eyes, fixed on the new arrival, shone with intelligence. They blinked a greeting before resuming their work.

"They expected us?"

"No. They have adjusted to strangers trailing in here with me."

Jun's eyes popped open. "Other Uprights?"

She chuckled, the first smile he'd seen from her since she showed up. "Usually pawed and tailed."

He had no idea what to ask about that and didn't bother trying. Ignoring the growing ache in his leg took all his energy. *She has much to explain, but it will wait until I recover.*

Xhosa pushed him gently toward a boulder. "Crouch there."

He collapsed. His good leg was numb. Even if she hadn't told him to rest, he couldn't have gone farther. The relief to his pounding ankle was overwhelming. He stilled his entire body, his breathing shallow as another Primitive approached, holding supplies eerily similar to those Jun's mother carried. Then, before he could blink, she cut across Snake's puncture and squeezed. He started to scream, but stopped because he felt nothing. The poison dried up and Xhosa scrubbed the puncture. Once she deemed it clean, she applied moss to suck out new impurities, as his mother would. All Xhosa's ministrations were like his mother's except Xhosa's didn't hurt. Mother's always did.

Xhosa rotated back on her heels with a grunt of either satisfaction or hopelessness. Jun was too hot, tired, and sick to care.

She stood. "I will deposit you where I found you. You will awake groggy, feeling unwell, but you will be fine."

When I awake? What does she mean?

"I am—"

But Xhosa wasn't listening.

Questions You Ask

Neanderthals aren't unsophisticated cave dwellers.

The time-tested Neanderthal image of mentally challenged hominids who carried clubs over stooped shoulders is long debunked by evidence. Neanderthals cooked glue, made fire, sewed clothes, talked, played music on various "instruments", created art, and other skills possessed by modern man, applied in ways suited to the rigors of life in a world with a high value on physical strength.

A study in PLOS ONE explains the complex cognitive control necessary to knap the Neanderthal hand axe:

> *"For the first time, we've showed a relationship between the degree of prefrontal brain activity, the ability to make technological judgments, and success in actually making stone tools," says Stout. "The findings are relevant to ongoing debates regarding the origins of modern human cognition, and the role of technological and social complexity in brain evolution across species." Most hand axes produced by the modern hands and minds of the study subjects "… weren't up to the high standards of 500,000 years ago," Stout says.*

Describe the Neanderthal appearance.

Based on skeletal remains, Neanderthals stood about five-five on average with robust bones, a spread rib cage, a sloped forehead, an expansive nose, a brain moderately more spacious than ours housed in a skull smaller in front than back. Their hair was probably straightish and dark, with more than the projected quantity of redheads.

No surprise skin color doesn't preserve so scientists disagree whether Neanderthals were white, brown, or black. Their homes were in Eurasia with its less direct sun.

A note: cellular mtDNA offers species data 100,000 years in the past. The length of this timeline provides considerable information about our Neanderthal ancestors.

Why did *Homo sapiens* have curly hair unlike Neanderthals' straight hair?

There's a theory behind African Homo sapiens' *curly hair. The tightly curled locks created air gaps to minimize heat absorption and maximize loss from the skull. That was unnecessary in Eurasia, native Neanderthal homes.*

Could Neanderthals talk?

Most evidence indicates yes for three reasons: 1) a hyoid (a prerequisite to speech) positioned above ours fuels speculation their voices were pitched higher than modern man, 2) their ears were evolved to listen for voices, and 3) Neanderthal tasks often require collaboration, difficult without the ability to speak among yourselves. In Savage Land, *I've given Neanderthals voices enhanced with body language.*

An addendum: Thirty-two geometric signs have been found in caves throughout Europe for over a hundred thousand years. Research hints Neanderthals communicated via common-to-them geometric signs, comparable to Chinese or Japanese symbols. The translation is lost in time.

You say they squat rather than sit?

Nominal physical evidence includes tell-tale divots in the Neanderthal femur, tibia, and ankle bone caused by squatting a lot. This shouldn't surprise us. At least a fourth of modern man crouches in a deep squat at rest or work. Squatting is far more natural for the body and makes standing quicker should that be required. Chairs were invented less than 6,000 years ago, available only to the wealthy.

How did Neanderthals tell time?

Similar to today's primitive communities, Neanderthals possessed no concept of hours or minutes. Their metric was remaining daylight. Characters in this book indicate time in two ways: 1) future time indicated by a place in the sky where the sun would be, the inference, "Return when Sun reaches here in the sky." 2) present time by placement of fingers next to the sun. A finger represents around fifteen minutes, the time the sun takes to cross the sky a finger's distance. A hand is four fingers or an hour. Test it yourself. Place a finger alongside the sun. The sun requires approximately fifteen minutes to cross to your finger's far side.

How did Neanderthals navigate without a map, GPS, or compass?

A process called Natural Navigation describes the ability to maneuver through geographic terrain not with technical tools but a pensive brain. It relies on the eleven million data bits received every second by our senses to assess, extrapolate, and guide. They are often ignored by the "civilized" world, despite how critical they are to the survival of hunter-gatherers, survivalists, and nature lovers.

If you're interested in the topic, search "natural navigation" in your browser.

Can Neanderthals run down prey?

Yes! Scientists call the ability to run endlessly the "Endurance Running Hypothesis." Our ancestors ran slower *than herds but* harder. *They could run all day without a problem. The* Homo *genus (which includes Neanderthals) evolved a stable skull, loose hips, shock-absorbent joints, and springy feet, well suited to continuous running. Further alterations meant humans neither tired nor overheated as is the norm in the preponderance of mammals. Most mammals sprint short expanses before being forced to catch their breath and cool their bodies. Evolution corrected that flaw in man.*

Did Neanderthals count?

The short answer is: They didn't, at least, not as we do. Modern primitive tribes—as recently as the 1900s—had little need for exact counts. "One," "two," "some," or "many" sufficiently described a herd, fruit trees, or distance. They recognized a member's absence by the smaller group size and/or the absent scent. They relied on an exceptional memory able to compare current impressions with the stored mental image to decipher change. Compare this to when you listen to music and the musician misses a measure. You can't say how many measures are in the piece, but you recognize one was omitted.

60,000 years ago, in western France, a Neanderthal cut nine notches into a hyaena femur. Scientists speculate this was to count regardless of most evidence indicating Neanderthals were anumeric, which is logical. Numbers were of little importance in pre-agriculture societies.

Did Neanderthals store water in ostrich egg shells as in the story?

A human can stand on an ostrich's eggshell. Proof exists that even 105,000 years ago, man collected rainwater in these shells. Today's Kalahari San use them for a canteen. They puncture a small hole in the end, clean the inside, fill the shell with water, and reseal the gap with beeswax or reeds.

Did Neanderthals play music?

Shanadar's flute is modeled on the 60,000-year-old Divje Babe bone flute produced from a hollowed-out cave bear thigh bone, among the oldest instruments. It has three holes on one side and one on the opposite, and the ends are open. In an expert's hands, the ancient instrument plays pretty much any song our sophisticated modern ones can. If interested, click for a video (not available in print books). Be prepared to be amazed.

Besides the flute, Neanderthals seem to have had the power to turn natural elements such as rocks, hollow trunks, and stalagmites/stalactites into music. Here's a video (not available in print books) where you can listen to organ-like music created by stalactites in caves that Neanderthals deemed home.

Did Neanderthals use fire?

Fire played a key role in our genus's evolution. It provided heat, protection, the ability to cook raw food and make glue, activities that could only be performed in daylight before. The question becomes whether Neanderthals made *fire or* captured *it. No one disputes Neanderthal cleverness in creating fire, but without proof, scientists are reluctant to draw conclusions. Clues that did preserve include:*

- *Stone circles deep in Bruniquel Cave (in France) show the debris of fires that lit the dark spaces.*
- *Neanderthals cooked food.*
- *Neanderthals cooked pitch (a material nowhere in nature) and bark to create a glue to attach tips to wood shafts.*
- *Neanderthals hardened spear tips and digging sticks with fire, a method still used today.*

Did Neanderthals care for the sick?

The injuries to Old One, a character in Book 1 and 2, are modeled on a Siberian Neanderthal named Shanidar. Skeletal evidence indicates he suffered a serious blow to his left eye socket which might have blinded him or resulted in brain damage. His right humerus broke and healed in two places. His right forearm is missing. His right foot revealed fractures. Osteoarthritis in his leg joints made movement painful. Despite these infirmities, he survived past fifty. University of York researcher, Penny Spikins, says: "… he was looked after for about 10 to 15 years."

Another example: A Neanderthal with a bent spine, a broken-but-healed clavicle and femur, osteoarthritis, and lung disease lasted for fifty-plus years. He, too, was cared for. A final famous case is the Old Man of La Chapelle-aux-Saints who is missing many teeth and suffered severe periodontal ailment in addition to joint degeneration in his hips. These injuries required ongoing care.

Additionally, food remnants indicate Neanderthals self-medicated with chamomile—an anti-inflammatory–and yarrow—a natural astringent.

Were Neanderthal lives boring?

Well, they did spend a preponderance of time in a search for food, in meal preparation and the creation of their wraps, knapping tools, and migrating (activities deemed 'boring' by some), but the use of fire (for warmth, protection, and seeing in the dark), the invention of cooked glue and stitched clothes gave them free time to ask why events happened and draw conclusions based on reflective deliberation. Artifacts support the idea that Neanderthals discovered art and music, and may have credited creatures greater than themselves for life events. Such cerebral advances arguably kept everyday existence anything but boring.

Did Neanderthal genetics affect who we are?

Modern humans are 2-4% Neanderthal. Roughly 30% of the Neanderthal genome is preserved in ours, albeit throughout our population. As a result, many Neanderthal traits persevere today. Most of us descend from humans alive 50,000-80,000 years ago, before the time Homo sapiens *populated Europe. How do we know this? Our species possesses two kinds of DNA, one from both parents called simply "DNA", and one from the mother termed "mtDNA". MtDNA tracks our genetic heritage for 100,000 years for those able to read it.*

Which story elements are true to prehistory?

The Neanderthal's Altai Mountain home—before they were driven away by a massive volcanic eruption—was in what paleo-archeologists call Denisova Cave. The well-researched site indicates Neanderthals and Denisovans co-existed there.

Others include:

- *the Toba Eruption—about 75,000 years ago and reputed to be the worst to happen in man's existence on Earth*
- *the Neanderthal Gibraltar home*
- *the haunting gong in Shanadar's sanctuary—based on the Somcuba's Gong in South Africa*
- *Shanadar's Wise Stone—modeled on the Berekhat Ram*
- *Shanadar's bone flute—modeled on the Divje Babe bone flute*
- *Shanadar's sanctuary—modeled on Bruniquel Cave in France*
- *the subterranean journey to Shanadar's sanctuary—modeled on the Rising Star's winding tunnels to* Homo naledi

Many are detailed in these notes, their stories fleshed out in the trilogy.

Is Shanadar's Gibraltar sanctuary authentic?

Gibraltar is honeycombed with an extensive cave system. The tunnels to Shanadar's Gibraltar sanctuary (in Book 3) are based on two subterranean habitats occupied by prehistoric species who co-existed with Neanderthals. The first is the Rising Star system in South Africa, home to Homo naledi *(not Neanderthals) circa 300,000 years ago. The second is Bruniquel Cave in France, built by Neanderthals circa 175,000 years ago. Evidence exists that the interior was illuminated by fire and Neanderthals transported two tons of stalagmites three hundred meters, broke them into four hundred similarly sized pieces, and arranged them in a circle—for no obvious reason. A prominent theory revolves around spiritual/religious purposes. Regardless of the factual answer, it demonstrates Neanderthals mastered both maneuvering in the dark and symbolic thought.*

What about the gong Xad plays in Shanadar's sanctuary?

That is fashioned after Somcuba's Gong in the Sudwala Cave in Mpumalanga, South Africa. This is a porous flowstone structure formed from Precambrian dolomite, approximately 2.8 billion years ago. It is notable for producing distinctive hollow sounds when struck. The Swazi people continue to use it as an alarm.

Explain the stone Shanadar carries.

Shanadar's Wise Stone is modeled on the 250,000-year-old Berekhat Ram, a palm-sized volcanic scoria colored by charcoal. Grooves in the neck are caused by natural elements and deliberate modifications. The indentations accentuate the female shape. The artifact's age suggests it was fashioned in the time of Homo erectus *(Xhosa's species, predecessors to Neanderthals).*

Did a natural disaster destroy Neanderthals?

The supervolcano, Mt. Toba, erupted approximately 75,000 years ago in Indonesia, ranked by many scientists as the worst natural disaster experienced by our genus. The Toba super-eruption fired out approximately 720 cubic miles (3,000 cubic km) of rock and ash which spread across the world, blocked out the sun and created a so-called volcanic winter. "Volcanic winter," defined by World Atlas as—

> *"a dramatic drop in temperatures experienced globally, in the aftermath of a massive volcanic eruption.... As a result, typical winter conditions are amplified while the winter season becomes longer."*

It spanned six to ten years (depending upon whom you talk to). The eruption's plume exploded twenty-five miles upward and deposited a six-inch ash layer that extended as far as India. Climate models suggest the planet cooled 3.5–9 °C with a 25% reduction in precipitation. Volcanologists include Mt. Toba among the most destructive eruptions in human existence.

The Savage Land *trilogy fictionalizes how the historic Mt. Toba eruption devastated the Neanderthal People and inspired migration to Gibraltar and continental shores.*

Did the human population decline at the time of *Savage Land*?

Concurrent to Mt. Toba's eruption, our genus suffered a genetic bottleneck that could have triggered man's extinction. Our population dropped to an estimated 10,000 worldwide (possibly as low as 2,000), numbers unsustainable for our kind's continuation. At first, scientists blamed Mt. Toba's eruption. Today, many dispute the causal effect. Additionally, no one agrees on how or why we populated and now rule the planet as apex predators.

Were Neanderthals religious?

Opinions vary because proof is almost non-existent. Shamanism may have started around 100,000 years ago, which preceded Neanderthals in Savage Land. *The circular structure in Bruniquel Cave is speculated to represent curiosity about the hereafter, spiritual beings who control natural events and facilitate miracles. Additional evidence exists that they buried the dead, maybe with flowers.*

In these pages, I explore religion's roots without drawing conclusions.

Are the Canis (proto-wolves) spirits?

I leave this unclear. Throughout time, spirits have been nebulous creatures, Gods or gods.

Is prehistoric fiction boring?

If you enjoy adventure, death-defying odds, humans who routinely do the impossible, the answer is, "Not even a little." We first categorized the Man vs. Nature *trilogies as "prehistoric thrillers" because the characters and plots share traits from both of those genres. The individuals you meet in* Savage Land *are tasked to outsmart bigger and stronger enemies.*

I read the books out of order. Will the story make sense?

Each book in the trilogy includes details on prior events. As such, they can be consumed in any order you choose. You may enhance the experience by reading the books consecutively. Here's a synopsis of the three books:

Endangered Species *(Book 1)—how the worst volcanic eruption man ever lived through forced the People to abandon their homes.*

Badlands *(Book 2)—the People and the Chosen leave the Altai Mountains to migrate beyond what we call the Mediterranean Sea.*

Balance of Nature *(Book 3)— A tribe haunted by the past. Lies that threaten the future. A reason to find the truth.*

Bibliography

Allen, E.A. 1885. The Prehistoric World or Vanished Races. Central Publishing House.

Berger, Lee and Hawks, John. 2017. Almost Human: The Astonishing Story of Homo naledi and the Discovery That Changed Our Human Story. National Geographic.

Boismier, William, et al (editors). 2012. Neanderthals Among Mammoths: Excavations at Lynford Quarry, Norfolk. English Heritage.

Allen, E.A. 1885. The Prehistoric World or Vanished Races. Central Publishing House.

Brown Jr., Tom. 1983. Tom Brown's Field Guide: Wilderness Survival. Berkley Books.

Caird, Rod. 1994. Apeman: The Story of Human Evolution. MacMillan.

Carss, Bob. 2009. The SAS Guide to Tracking. Lyons Press: Guilford Conn.

Cavalli-Sforza, Luigi Luca and Cavalli-Sforza, Francesco. 1995. The Great Human Diasporas: The History of Diversity and Evolution. Perseus Press.

Charles River Editors. 2020. The Pleistocene Era: The History of the Ice Age and the Dawn of Modern Humans. Charles River Editors.

Conant, Levi Leonard. 1931. The Number Concept: Its Origin and Development. Toronto: Macmillan and Co.

Diamond, Jared. 1992. The Third Chimpanzee. Harper Perennial.

Everett, Daniel. 2008. Don't Sleep There are Snakes. Pantheon Books.

Gooley, Tristan. 2015. The Lost Art of Reading Nature's Signs. New York: The Experiment.

Gooley, Tristan 2023. How to Read a Tree. New York: The Experiment.

Mather, Tamsin. 2024. Adventures in Volcanoland: What Volcanoes Tell Us About the World and Ourselves. Hanover Square Press.

Mead, Margaret. 1977. Letters from the Field 1925-1975. Perennial.

Mithen, Steven. 2006. The Singing Neanderthals: The Origins of Music, Language, Mind, and Body. Harvard University Press.

Morris, Desmond. 1999. The Naked Ape. Dell Publishing.

Morris, Desmond. 1969. The Human Zoo. Kodansha International.

Paabo, Svante. 2014. Neanderthal Man: In Search of Lost Genomes. New York Basic Books.

Pattison, Kermit. 2009. Fossil Men: The Quest for the Oldest Skeleton and the Origins of Humankind. William Morrow.

Rezendes, Paul. 1999. Tracking and the Art of Seeing: How to Read Animal Tracks and Sign Quill: A HarperResource Book.

Saenger, H. G. 2023. Neanderthals: Unraveling the Secrets of our Ancient Relatives.

Slimak, Ludovic. 2024. The Naked Neanderthal. Pegasus Books.

Stringer, Chris, and McKie, Robin. 1996. African Exodus: The Origins of Modern Humanity. Henry Holt and Co. NY.

Tattersall, Ian. 1999. Becoming Human: Evolution and Human Uniqueness. Harvest Books.

Thomas, Elizabeth Marshall. 2008. The Old Way: A Story of the First People. Sarah Crichton Books.

Tudge Colin. 1996. The Time Before History. Touchstone Books.

Vogel, Shawna. 1995. Naked Earth: The New Geophysics. Dutton.

Vygotsky, Lev. 1930. The Connection Between Thought and the Development of Language in Primitive Society.

Walker, Alan and Shipman, Pat. 1996. The Wisdom of the Bones: In Search of Human Origins Vintage Books.

Wills, Christopher. 1993. Runaway Brain: The Evolution of Human Uniqueness. Basic Books.

Wragg Sykes, Rebecca. 2020. Kindred: Neanderthal Life, Love, Death and Art. Bloomsbury Sigma.

About the Author

Jacqui Murray lives in California with her husband and Casey, the world's greatest dog. She has written fiction and nonfiction for 30 years and is an adjunct professor in technology-in-education.

You can reach Jacqui Murray on her **blog**:
https://worddreams.wordpress.com

X:
https://twitter.com/WordDreams

LinkedIn:
https://www.linkedin.com/in/jacquimurray

Instagram
https://www.instagram.com/jacquimurraywriter/

Newsletter
https://jacqui-murray.aweb.page/p/46e8c9bf-eaed-4252-8aad-3688e233a4cc

Reader's Workshop Questions

Setting

- Why did Neanderthals occupy such a wide swath of geography—from Europe to Asia?
- Did Neanderthals have a preference for climate type—cold (like Siberia) or warm (like Gibraltar)?

Themes

- Discuss how Neanderthals respect animals. Why? Was it in part because they didn't know animals weren't smart and clever like our species is (or we think we are)?
- Why did Neanderthals survive for so long despite their constant migrations, small group size, and lack of the advanced innovations used by *Homo sapiens*?
- What inventions were part of Neanderthal heritage, such as cooking, sewing clothing, glue, medical treatments, and creation of fire (not just the use of fire)?
- Did it surprise you to learn that Neanderthals treated their kindred empathetically, as humans do? That they cared for those chronically ill?
- Neanderthals are believed to have left geometric symbols in caves throughout Europe that could indicate an effort at communication. What are your thoughts on that?
- We know Neanderthals were replaced by the more-advanced *Homo sapiens*. What characteristics and traits in this story help explain why?

Character Realism

- The Neanderthal are presented with many characteristics identifiable in today's hunter-gatherers. Your thoughts on that?

- Neanderthals were nomadic, unlike most hunter-gatherer tribes today. If you are familiar with nomadic civilizations, what similarities/differences do you see between them?
- The start of spiritualism in man is oft-discussed. Shamanism is believed to have begun around 100,000 years ago. What do you think of the spiritual behavior found in this story? How about what isn't found?
- There is mixed evidence of religion, art, and music in artifacts from Neanderthals and early *Homo sapiens*. Do you think they appreciated these?

Character Choices

- What moral/ethical choices did the characters in this book make regarding animals and their treatment?
- Discuss how Yu'ung's and Fierce's kind raised children. Do other of today's primitive tribes handle families this way?
- Discuss the Neanderthal attitude toward ownership of belongings?

Construction

- Discuss the different approaches to managing a tribe evidenced by Neanderthals and the Tall Ones (*Homo sapiens*). One followed authoritarian leadership, the other groupthink. What other animals display either? Do you see them in other geopolitical cultures around the world?
- Scientists disagree over how or whether Neanderthals could speak, or whether they relied primarily on body language, gestures, facial expressions, as well as the rare vocalization. What are your thoughts on this?
- Discuss how Neanderthals described quantities (such as "Sun traveled a hand" or "as many as fit under the tree by homebase").

- How did Neanderthals explain the moon disappearing and reappearing time and again? Do their observations make sense to you?

Reactions to the Book

- Did the book lead you to a new awareness of how man evolved into who we are today? Did it help you understand something in your life that you didn't before, maybe seemed a "gut feeling" or instinctual?
- Did the book fulfill your expectations?

Other Questions

- What do you think will happen to the characters? Would you like to see a sequel to this trilogy?
- Discuss books you've read with a similar theme or set in a prehistoric time.

www.ingramcontent.com/pod-product-compliance
Lightning Source LLC
LaVergne TN
LVHW020041110826
845155LV00029B/590